An Integral Approach to Development Economics

Transformation and Innovation Series

Series Editors:
Ronnie Lessem, University of Buckingham, UK
Alexander Schieffer, University of St. Gallen, Switzerland

This series on enterprise transformation and social innovation comprises a range of books informing practitioners, consultants, organization developers, development agents and academics how businesses and other organizations, as well as the discipline of economics itself, can and will have to be transformed. The series prepares the ground for viable twenty-first century enterprises and a sustainable macroeconomic system. A new kind of R & D, involving social, as well as technological innovation, needs to be supported by integrated and participative action research in the social sciences. Focusing on new, emerging kinds of public, social and sustainable entrepreneurship originating from all corners of the world and from different cultures, books in this series will help those operating at the interface between enterprise and society to mediate between the two and will help schools teaching management and economics to re-engage with their founding principles.

Current titles in this series

Integral Community:
Political Economy to Social Commons
Ronnie Lessem, Paul Chidara Muchineripi and Steve Kada
ISBN 978-1-4094-4679-8

Spiritual Capital:
A Moral Core for Social and Economic Justice
Samuel D. Rima
ISBN 978-1-4094-0484-2

Remaking Ourselves, Enterprise and Society:
An Indian Approach to Human Values in Management
G.P. Rao
ISBN 978-1-4094-4884-6

An Integral Approach to Development Economics

Islamic Finance in an African Context

BASHEER A. OSHODI

Routledge
Taylor & Francis Group

LONDON AND NEW YORK

First published 2014 by Routledge

2 Park Square, Milton Park, Abingdon, Oxon OX14 4RN
711 Third Avenue, New York, NY 10017, USA

Routledge is an imprint of the Taylor & Francis Group, an informa business

First issued in paperback 2016

Gower Applied Business Research
Our programme provides leaders, practitioners, scholars and researchers with thought provoking, cutting edge books that combine conceptual insights, interdisciplinary rigour and practical relevance in key areas of business and management.

British Library Cataloguing in Publication Data
A catalogue record for this book is available from the British Library.

The Library of Congress has cataloged the printed edition as follows:
Library of Congress data has been applied for.

ISBN 978-1-4724-1125-9 (hbk)
ISBN 978-1-138-24709-3 (pbk)

Contents

List of Figures

List of Tables

About the Author

Dr Basheer Oshodi has work experience in banking, management consultancy, real estate, Islamic finance and research. His overall experience in government, state-owned businesses and the organized private sector has greatly influenced his perception of his research interest and focus. He joined Stanbic IBTC Bank in 2009 as Manager of Islamic Banking Risk and Compliance, where he structured Islamic finance business and value propositions. He initiated the privately managed the Shariah Compliant Portfolio at Stanbic IBTC Asset Management Ltd, developing the overall value customer architecture for Islamic banking and finance in the bank, as well as the first liability products that are Shariah-compliant end-to-end in Nigeria with absolute account separation from conventional funds of the bank. He has developed other risk-asset products and *sukuk* (Islamic financial certificates) propositions based on several Islamic finance contracts which align with specific business requirements.

He is engaged with the team designing the first Shariah-compliant short-term liquidity management instrument for the country, comprising several Islamic financial contracts. In 2009, he became a member of the Nigerian Islamic Finance Working Group set up by EFInA (Enhancing Financial Innovation and Access) – a Department for International Development (DFID) programme that promotes financial inclusion. He also played a very active role in the working group to ensure that Islamic finance is subject to the regulatory infrastructure required to achieve the primary purpose of this financial model by working closely with financial regulators. He worked briefly with EFInA as Programme Manager of Non-Interest Finance and Research Manager, co-ordinating the activities of the working group until December 2012. The group sets regulatory and operational policy for the Islamic finance industry in Nigeria while helping with overall innovation, research, capacity building and advocacy in the financial industry. In January 2013, Sterling Bank appointed Oshodi as the Group Head of its Non-Interest Banking Window, where he currently drives the entire Islamic finance proposition. His primary strategy at Sterling Bank is to set forth a unique pattern of development for the Islamic finance industry, borrowing from the applied concept of TIPS – management of technology, innovation and people – and the systemic thinking approach. In the same vein, he seeks to apply pragmatic managerial leadership competency models in order to achieve self-, organizational, societal, national and global renewal. In summary, Oshodi is one of the pioneers of Islamic banking and finance in Nigeria, and the co-founder of the Centre for Islamic Socio-Economic Research (CISER). He is also a co-founder of the Centre for *Integral* Social and Economic Research (C*I*SER), where real transformational ideas are created and implemented via action research.

Oshodi obtained a BSc. in Estate Management and MSc in Management from the University of Lagos and the PGD Institute of Islamic Banking and Insurance in London, an MRes. (Masters in Research) in Business and Management from London Metropolitan Business School, started an MPhil. in Economics at the University of Buckingham, and was awarded a PhD in Management of Innovation and Technology at the DaVinci Institute in South Africa in conjunction with the TRANS4M Centre for Integral Development in Geneva. His research is focused on integral development, covering overall development economics grounded in indigenous socio-economic practice, emerging through the spirituality of Islamic economics and finance, navigating along the path of the African triple heritage of indigenous culture, Westernized Christianity and Islam, thereby effecting a new development economic model derived from burning issues around poverty and unemployment. He has published both research and journal articles. Some of his publications include: 'Reducing Poverty: The Prospects of Islamic Finance in Africa',[1] 'Islamic Economics and Finance within the Context of Development Economics in Nigeria',[2] 'Unfolding the Integral African World System Thought',[3] 'Good Governance and State-led Development in Nigeria: Comparative Analysis with India'[4] and 'Appraising the Good Enough Governance Agenda and State-led

1   Basheer A. Oshodi, 'Reducing Poverty: The Prospects of Islamic Finance in Africa', Social Science Research Network (SSRN), 9 May 2012: http://dx.doi.org/10.2139/ssrn.2055126 (accessed 19 August 2013).
2   Basheer A. Oshodi, 'Islamic Economics and Finance within the Context of Development Economics in Nigeria', SSRN, 9 May 2012: http://dx.doi.org/10.2139/ssrn.2055093 (accessed 19 August 2013).
3   Basheer A. Oshodi, 'Unfolding the Integral African World System Thought', SSRN, 4 October 2010: http://dx.doi.org/10.2139/ssrn.1688462 (accessed 19 August 2013).
4   Basheer A. Oshodi, 'Good Governance and State-led Development in Nigeria: Comparative Analysis with India', SSRN, 28 August 2008: http://dx.doi.org/10.2139/ssrn.1145648 (accessed 19 August 2013).

Development: Towards Achieving Private Sector Development in Sub-Saharan Africa'.[5] His non-research articles have been published on websites and in journals such as *Hedge Fund News*, *New Horizon* and *Global Islamic Finance News* as well as many other local publications.

Oshodi has recently been made a member of the Nigerian Securities & Exchange Commission (SEC) Alternative Capital Market Products Master Plan Committee.

---

5 Basheer A. Oshodi, 'Appraising the Good Enough Governance Agenda and State-led Development: Towards Achieving Private Sector Development in Sub-Saharan Africa', SSRN, 1 September 2008: http://dx.doi.org/10.2139/ssrn.1145664 (accessed 19 August 2013).

Foreword

An Integral Approach to Development Economics: Islamic Finance in an African Context reflects the general nature of the development of economic analysis. For Basheer Oshodi, it was necessary to firstly unfold his own personal experiences based on the environment in which he found himself – a typical African state, Nigeria. This book beautifully analyses issues around development economics from the perspective of historical trends starting with economic history which address social atmosphere, political situations, behavioural patterns and perceptions, research styles in various jurisdictions, cultural and indigenous elements, and also focuses on 'institutions'. Basheer is both a development economist and a banker underpinned by moral values. It is this dual characteristic that leads him to put so much weight on the history of economic development in Nigeria – his native home, where he dwells on realities within the current socio-economic setting of the country. This book shows that economic prescriptions for developing Africa can hardly be effective without taking note of the impact of good governance issues and the historical trends that to some extent paint a picture of the future, unless precautions are taken in good time. This book describes poverty and unemployment in an innovative and very realistic manner. Basheer has used real-life cases and experiences to illustrate poverty and the pain in African minds.

Why would Africa forget some of its greatest works in history, such as the socio-economic findings of Ibn Khaldun? Basheer observes that Ibn Khaldun, born in Tunis in 1332, could have informed the work of Adam Smith, David Ricardo, Karl Marx, John Maynard Keynes, Sir Henry Roy Forbes Harrod, Evsey Domar and William Easterly. The book further examines the pre-colonial political history of Nigeria, indigenous informal African financial systems and the economic pattern of development in Africa. He places much emphasis on moral economics, the constituencies of the moral economic core spreading to the Jewish moral economic theory, the Buddhist moral economic system, Aristotle's moral economic masterworks, the biblical moral economic elements and the Islamic economic system. Basheer's underlying interest is the question of what economic model would best develop Africa, or rather, what degree of neo-modern mix of economic thought would lead to good communal life in Africa. The book then explores modernization theories, dependency theories, world system thoughts and evolving economic theories.

For Basheer, the only practical and institutionalized moral economic structure is Islamic banking and finance as embedded in the enlarged Islamic economic system. Hence, moral economics is grounded in Islamic business ethics, Islamic banking contracts and Islamic banking value proposition within the realm not just of Shariah compliance, but of poverty reduction. The book concludes by developing economic theories that are home-grown – from Africa. After reading Basheer's book, I believe that it will provide valuable material and a reference point for those engaged in academia, banking and finance, development matters, governance and overall policy formulation. Basheer's ability to capture the complexities of Southern economies is indeed intriguing. I strongly recommend this book, which sets out an integrated approach to economic development.

Abubakar Suleiman

Chief Financial Officer, Sterling Bank Plc

Lagos, Nigeria

Preface:
Development Economics

Before the development of the economics of information (and also the development of game theoretic models of political economy), economist lacked a broad framework for understanding of the sources of the imperfections in markets. Economist who tried to design policies to fit developing country markets generally assumed rigidities in markets, but did not explain them by reference to a choice-based perspective.

Hoff and Stiglitz (2008)

How do we start to revisit the issues around economic development – not just economic growth as championed by the West, but rather socio-economic development in a typical African context? Why would the world still continue to assume that all humans are somewhat alike, or rather, that all humans can be made to behave in a similar fashion, that patterns of economic development can be alike, that the economic ideas that developed the West will also develop the South? How about the political structure? Many parts of the West abandoned the feudal hierarchy for democracy. What a good thing this is. It yielded development and advancement in state formation. This then becomes the solution for other distinct political settlements. I grew up first in Lagos Island, and listened to my father tell me the story of how the British sent Oba (King) Kosoko of Lagos and his army lord, Chief Oshodi Tapa, into exile and installed Oba Akintoye, whose son later ceded the island as a colony to the British. Soon after, organized Christianity emerged, which somewhat weakened traditional institutions and the already fragile Islam in that area of today's Nigeria. Broad Street was built, and British financial institutions occupied it. The locals who agreed to adopt English names worked for the colonial masters, attended Kings College and imbibed the newly 'civilized culture'. From Kings College to the University of London, many studied law and built on the English legal system when they returned home. Those who studied economics and business management stuck to neo-classical economic theories and disregarded the wisdom in indigenous ideas. Many left Islam for Christianity and paid less attention to their extended families. It is this storyline that led me to examine the works of Ali Mazrui's African triple heritage and its effects on socio-economic development. I, a Muslim, an African, a banker and researcher, tried to decolonize my heart and my perception as I let loose my thoughts. However, I have also been influenced by the forces of this triple heritage in my overall personal, emotional, spiritual, professional and academic affairs.

I have travelled quite widely, but have spent the bulk of my life in Nigeria, a country where the combined efforts of international economic experts, indigenous specialists in various fields of study, the consistent financial 'aid' from the 'developed' world and economic prescriptions have been somewhat fruitless, or less effective. The reforms led to extractive institutions and even more aggressive corruption plus more current cases of terrorism and kidnap. Africans have indeed learnt so much from the West – from how financial aid is to be utilized to security consultancy, from the measures of development indicators to governance, and from capitalism to research methods and methodologies.

Until recently, Nigeria achieved consistent economic growth, but its socio-economic development realities worsen. More specifically, poverty and unemployment are reflected in the overall environment and in the lives of majority of the citizens. This concern evoked the burning issues in this book – why poverty, and why unemployment in the midst of plenty? It also influenced and shaped issues centred around evolving economic development theories based on the African triple heritage, implementation of Islamic banking principles on the foundations of moral economic cores based on the African triple heritage, and the creation of integral financial institutions addressing these. Governance and economic growth indicators for a developing country like Nigeria, just like many other African countries, have been unable to tell the true story of economic development since they are based on microdata, hence this book has adopted a more people-centred inquiry approach which gives a clearer picture of honest circumstances.

This book is structured in terms of an Integral Research Framework following the Eastern path of Realization, dwelling on narrative method, hermeneutics methodology, critical theory and co-operative inquiry. The research method is the knowledge-creating tool wherein tacit knowledge advances towards the explicit in order to achieve the narrative of 'becoming', thus sweeping through the concept and nature of economic development in the Nigerian state. The research methodology is based on hermeneutics, which is a classical discipline aimed at the interpretation and understanding of texts that relates to modernization theories, dependency theories, world system theories and emerging twenty-first-century economic theories in the light of moral economics and Islamic economics. The critique is termed critical theory, which is associated with enforcing radical change and is different from the traditional theory spelling out the ingredients of moral economics associated with Islamic economics and finance and in connection with the African triple heritage. The book then adopts integration, and more specifically co-operative inquiry derived from the field of psychological research, seeking inquiry based on human behaviour and intelligence within the development of a revolving theory in Islamic finance since it captures the moral core theoretically. Based on the platform of the four types of knowing in a co-operative inquiry – experiential knowing, presentational knowing, propositional knowing and practical knowing – it sets forth a theory. It states that where most necessary effective regulations are in place, in line with the values of the goals of Islam – which primarily translates into achieving human well-being and a communal good life – Islamic finance will fulfil its primary purpose of maintaining socio-economic justice in society, hence resolving the challenges of poverty and unemployment if the moral core values embedded in the overall Islamic economic system are embedded in 'effective regulation' while borrowing, where necessary, from other ethical socio-economic and political models or theories grounded in African humanism. This is validated by the ongoing cyclical review of regulations over time. Furthermore, in a bid to translate research into action, three more economic development models emerge. The first model is the Integral African Development Theoretical Economic Model, which inter-relates development theories, the African triple heritage, Islamic banking and the *esusu* (rotational savings/labour) model. The second model is the Integral African Development Practical Economic Model Establishing Islamic Finance in Nigeria, which achieved the successful operation of Islamic banking in three Nigerian banks, influenced financial regulators, led to the setting up of the Centre for Islamic Socio-Economic Research (CISER), and laid the groundwork for new integral financial institutions. The third model is the Generic Integral Development Economics Model, which is trans-cultural, acknowledging the relevance of market co-ordination, state co-ordination, spiritual co-ordination and people co-ordination in order to achieve overall economic development in any jurisdiction. A new global institution, the Centre for *Integral* Social and Economic Research (C*I*SER), is positioned to lead this transformational process.

I have reflected my own personal experience of poverty and that of a few Nigerians in this study; I have provided images that demonstrate unimaginable poverty in Africa – even in oil-rich Nigeria; I have redefined poverty outside the common people living on less than US$1 or US$2 per day; I have thus dedicated this book to all those who have experienced one form of poverty or the other – not just among those in yesterday or today's Africa, but also those living in that one room in central London who cannot afford their next meal, those working for the royal family in Saudi Arabia who do not have rights, those who are being displaced from their land in the USA, in the Middle East and in Australia. Again, I look at China and India and their vast population. Many have forgotten that the poorest people live in these sub-continents – all they say is, 'They are tomorrow's greatest economies.' I dedicate this book to all these poor households which do not have access to basic medical care. I also dedicate this book to all those who are suffering from the poverty of political exclusion – they are oppressed and killed merely because they ask for simple rights. I will also not forget our past heroes – the free men and women taken away from the comfort of their villages in West Africa, dehumanized, humiliated, treated worse than animals and shipped to the Americas by the slave merchants. Finally, I dedicate this book to all seekers of justice – women across the world who are being marginalized and oppressed, children who are being traded and abused, and the voiceless.

How would I have been able to acquire this knowledge of socio-economic history, of economic development patterns, and further appreciate ingenious thoughts if not for Professor Ronnie Lessem, who discovered my strengths? I published a write-up immediately after I completed my MRes. at the London Metropolitan Business School where I worked on good governance matters and state-led development issues. Professor Lessem saw that little piece and invited me for a chat at the Business School at the University of Buckingham. He listened as I discussed my completed work, and said, 'You will be a good PhD candidate, Basheer.' He is a patient teacher, a gentle father and an eminent scholar. A year into my PhD, I shared material on Islamic finance with him, and he said, 'Basheer, we are going to include Islamic finance in your work, and that will be your niche specialization theoretically and practically.' This was after I had written more than 20,000 words on governance and economic matters. Thereafter, I gradually started to develop more theoretical competencies in this area and other indigenous ideas. He and Dr Alexander Schieffer supervised my PhD and encouraged me to write this book. Dr Schieffer was abundantly helpful and offered invaluable assistance and guidance at all times. He would reply to emails and share his thoughts within minutes. His graphic design skills are exceptional, and he also advised that theories are better illustrated in diagram form. My deepest gratitude also goes to Professor Bennie Anderson, CEO of the DaVinci Institute for Technology Management, South Africa. He exposed me to unique and innovative concepts required to implement my research models. Special thanks go to Dr Sam Rima, since I borrowed so much from his Spiritual Capital Theory. His understanding of Aristotle's work and Marx's *Capital* concept is amazing. Professor Mashood Baderin of the School of Oriental and African Studies (SOAS) at the University of London and a UN Independent Expert on Human Rights in the Sudan has also contributed so much in terms of fatherly advice, professional career guidance, my PhD thesis and this book.

In May 2012, at the fourth WANA (West Asia-North Africa) forum, I met a great man with unique charisma, a pluralist with sound leadership characteristics, a man who is not only visionary but who offers feasible solutions, the greatest speaker I know, yet the most friendly monarch – His Royal Highness Prince El Hassan bin Talal. He took much interest in my presentation at the forum and shared some ideas in the process of writing this book. I extend my utmost gratitude to him.

In less than three months working in my new organization, I have learnt so much from my boss, friend and mentor Abubakar Suleiman, the Chief Financial Officer at Sterling Bank – whom I refer to as my jewel of inestimable value. He is an economist, a seasoned banker, a distinguished gentleman and a sound strategist. He is very practical in his approach to problem-solving and has supported me in completing this book, mainly by sharing from his fund of experience in banking and finance. He also agreed to write the Foreword for me. I am indeed exceedingly grateful to him.

My appreciation also goes to all my co-researchers who challenge me intellectually, and to my friends, cousins and colleagues whose faith in me kept me focused. I am exceedingly grateful to my mum and brothers, Bayo, Dayo and AbdulRahman, whose support is consistent and exceptional. I owe extreme appreciation to Folake, my wife, my life, my heart, my breath, my everything, for having faith in me, for sharing inexorable love and affection.

I have set up two unique institutions that will live after us. One of them is the Centre for Islamic Socio-Economic Research, co-founded by the Honorable Hakeem Kosoko, Special Advisor to the Lagos State Government. His interest and support in all I embark on has been immeasurable. I also thank my co-transformers and co-founders of the Centre for *Integral* Social and Economic Research for what I will describe as perpetual commitment towards societal renewal. They include Akeem Oyewale, Folusho Titiloye, Abas Al-Hassan and the Honorable Ade Adegbenjo. Finally, I owe very special thanks to Martin West for agreeing to publish this book, and to every member of the Gower family for their guidance through the production process, their interest in developing economies, their passion for the African economic perception, and their overall kindness. I say a big thank you to the team, and offer my warmest regards.

Basheer A. Oshodi
Victoria Island, Lagos, Nigeria

List of Abbreviations

ACE	Advisory Committee of Experts
AfDB	African Development Bank
AIAE	African Institute for Applied Economics
AICE	African Institute for Cultural Economy
BECANS	Business Environment and Competitiveness Across Nigerian States
BTD	Business Training and Development
CBN	Central Bank of Nigeria
CISER	Centre for Islamic Socio-Economic Research
C*ISE*R	Centre for *Integral* Social and Economic Research
DFID	Department for International Development (UK)
DMO	Debt Management Office (Nigeria)
EFInA	Enhancing Financial Innovation and Access
EUREKA	Energizing, Understanding, Research, Education, Know-how and Application
FCO	Foreign and Commonwealth Office (UK)
FIRS	Federal Inland Revenue Service (Nigeria)
GCC	Gulf Cooperation Council
GDP	Gross Domestic Product
GENE	Grounding, Emerging, Navigating and Effecting
GIZ	Deutsche Gesellschaft für Internationale Zusammenarbeit
GNI	Gross National Income
HPI	Human Poverty Index
IDB	Islamic Development Bank
IFC	Islamic Finance Council
IFI	Islamic financial institution
LSM	Living Standard Measure
MASC	Movement for the Advancement of Spiritual Capital
NBS	Nigerian Bureau of Statistics
NICOM	National Insurance Commission (Nigeria)

NSE   Nigerian Stock Exchange
OECD   Organization for Economic Cooperation and Development
PenCom   National Pension Commission (Nigeria)
PPP   Purchasing Power Parity
SPV   special purpose vehicle
SSRN   Social Science Research Network
TIPS   Technology, Innovation, People, Systems
UNCTAD   United Nations Conference on Trade and Development

1

Introduction

The Story I Am

This book, titled *An Integral Approach to Development Economics: Islamic Finance in an African Context*, is built on the foundation of the Integral Research Framework. It is unique and integral in its approach to overall analysis of a typical African state, Nigeria, and its socio-political setting, which has shaped the country's economic prospects. This chapter will give a general overview of the entire research. It is further focused on my personal GENE (Grounding, Emerging, Navigating and Effecting). Chapter 2 draws out the elements of economic development. Chapter 3 focuses on the African socio-economic world, highlighting the continent's nature from its inception. Chapter 4 covers moral economics – the glowing light of my thesis. Chapter 5 examines the constituents of economic ideas. Chapter 6 details the characteristics of Islamic economics and finance. Finally, Chapter 7 translates the overall research theory into action. The ultimate aim of this book is to evolve an economic system that is cast in a newly integral guise, thereby effecting connection between theoretical models and the achievements of reality.

EUREKA

Social innovation, according to Lessem and Schieffer (2010b), has its source in six core ingredients known as EUREKA – Energizing, Understanding, Research, Education, Know-how and Application. Energizing happens when a particular issue of concern energizes the social innovator-to-be. Understanding happens when the researcher is immersed in nature and culture in order to evoke deep understanding of the real issues concerning social development. Research here represents the researcher's grasp of past and present activities that build the foundation for later innovation. In education, the researcher sets forth the path to add to the body of knowledge. Know-how is the glue or path that binds and links theory with practice, which further sets the stage for social innovation, while application brings social innovation to life, transforming self, organizations and society. The EUREKA framework then becomes a model that helps the scholar to purposefully build on his or her area of interest in a defined manner that will resist the pressure of analytic criticism while standing the test of time.

ENERGIZING

Increased economic growth and the good performance of Nigeria's development indicators, especially since the beginning of the new and stable democracy, have raised the novel question of whether a strong relationship exists between economic growth and economic development. Real issues of poverty have yet to be addressed via the constant economic growth recorded by the Nigerian government and international agencies. This reality calls for a review and reappraisal of economic models adopted by a developing country like Nigeria. From my perspective, within the Islamic Banking unit at Stanbic IBTC Bank – a member of Standard Bank Group, EFInA (Enhancing Financial Innovation and Access, the Department for International Development's financial inclusion project), Sterling Bank and recent developments in the world at large, there is need for an integral economic model that recognizes moral elements in economics, with particular reference in our case to the Islamic economic system. Such a model, economically speaking, specifically takes up where the Ali Mazrui's African triple heritage left off. This research is energized by my socio-economic and religio-political experience in Nigeria, as well as statistical records on Nigeria's growth pattern, which has not improved the lives of Nigerians. My storyline as a Muslim, in terms of self, others and social context, has led to experiences which have generally influenced my thoughts and burning desire, leading to some unanswered questions. A stable democracy over the past fourteen years has attracted huge foreign funds and investments in the Nigerian economy, leading the country to graduate from 'low-income' to 'lower-middle-income' based on World Bank's 2010 Gross National Income (GNI) indicator of US$1,006–3,975. Wealth-creation or capital-formation through foreign investments and aid are now constant activities in the economy, usually channelled via government agencies, non-governmental organizations (NGOs) and financial institutions.

However, this has not reduced the number of Nigerians without good drinking water, electricity, two good meals a day, adequate household income, effective primary healthcare, nor addressed the income and education inequality gap and the 50 million working-class still unemployed, according to the World Bank. More than half of the Nigerian population is Muslim, with the northern population constituting the Nigerian government and the military. However, Muslims are also the least educated, the most unemployed, and suffer the worst health challenges. Nigeria is one of the least developed states, whose unskilled labour force, which is mainly Muslim, also has a very small manufacturing industry.

Out of the 46 million financially excluded Nigerian adults, over 30 million are Muslims (EFInA 2008). On one hand, at least in theory, we have morally infused Islamic economics and finance, and on the other hand, we have rampant poverty and dereliction among practising Muslims.

UNDERSTANDING

Understanding these issues requires segregating elements of classical economics, political economics and development economics as they relate to cultural and behavioural economics, in order to derive the 'moral economic core' (Lessem and Schieffer 2010b), or moral economics. We must also borrow from an indigenous moral financial system, Christian neo-classical sources of moral economics and Islamic economic sources, whereby moral or spiritual capital is formed. The real foundation of the Islamic economic system may be linked to the pre-Christian era. However, it has also been fully captured in the primary sources of Shariah (Islamic law), the Quran and Hadiths (deeds and sayings of Prophet Mohammed). This understanding of Islamic economic sources must extend to the original nature of the African socio-economic world contained within African humanism (Serequeberhan 1999, Serequeberhan 2000), must include capital formation or an *esusu* (rotational savings/labour) model (which sustained the African economic structure before colonialism, and still does so in some contexts today) and must reshape the African world system in the light of new realities. Today, the African socio-economic world is split into three models: one is based on the Islamic socio-economic structure, the second is traditional, and the third is a Christian socio-economic model. Mazrui (1986) suggested an overall split in the African and Nigerian cultures – what he refers to as a 'triple heritage'.

RESEARCH

Contributing to the body of knowledge in a typical African setting like Nigeria requires an entirely new research style based on the Integral Framework

(Lessem and Schieffer 2010b) with an emphasis on the Eastern path of Renewal (Lessem and Schieffer 2010b; Oshodi 2012a). Co-operative inquiry, building on narrative method (origination), interpretive methodology (foundation) and also critical theory (emancipation) is the most transformative integral approach, where co-researchers share expertise and create knowledge in order to achieve a 'becoming' process (Heron 1971; Heron 1996). Relationships between the Integral Four Worlds (Lessem and Schieffer 2009) and TIPS (DaVinci Institute) is also derived here and further aligned to the integral moral economic architecture within the African environment with a particular orientation towards the Islamic socio-economic model for the betterment of all.

EDUCATION

Further educational themes are drawn upon through the analysis of development studies ranging from modernization theories to dependency theories, world system ideas and various versions of what are akin to integral economics (Lessem and Schieffer 2010a) or twenty-first-century economic theories. Integral economics is wide-ranging, and covers ideas from the redefinition of capital and labour to moral economic development, drawing from the four corners of the globe, as well as different moral centres, hence giving birth to integral development. Readings (Chapra 2008a; Chapra 2008c) show evidence that the principles and philosophies of the Islamic economic system are somewhat embedded, hidden or aligned with aspects of modernization theories, dependency theories, world system ideas and modern integral economics. These similarities, or subsets, need to be highlighted or revealed and then combined in the enlarged Islamic socio-economic world.

KNOW-HOW

A comprehensive analysis of the enlarged (Asian, Arabic, African) Islamic economic system is undertaken, starting with the theoretical framework that has been designed over a forty-year period to provide the guiding principles and philosophies of banking and finance. A recap of global Islamic banking, finance assessment and practice across the integral four worlds (South, East, North and West) are examined. Islamic economics and finance not only stress moral and ethical considerations, but also expose capitalistic attributes. At times, it is paradoxically aligned with socialistic principles. More importantly, its source lies in welfare state and humanistic perspectives. While in theory the humanistic perspectives might outweigh the pragmatic ones, in practice it tends to be the other way around. In this book, I seek to uncover and apply a stronger balance.

The structure of this book is designed on the platform of the TRANS4M Institute's Integral Framework (pragmatic, rational, humanistic, holistic) and DaVinci's TIPS (Technology, Innovation, People, Systems) in order to develop not only knowledge, but also know-how, in order to respond both to societal and to work-based practical challenges, ultimately through co-operative inquiry. This critical analysis exposes the effectiveness of Islamic finance and its ability to address socio-economic challenges in the Nigerian state. The big question then becomes how systemic, and indeed how integral, the Islamic economic system really is. To the extent that such a system becomes 'integral', it would need to embrace humanistic, holistic, rational and pragmatic principles and processes in much the same way as Islam incorporates the Jewish and Christian prophets as well as Mohammed (May the Peace and Blessings of God be with him).

APPLICATION

The application of the co-operative inquiry, building on prior narrative, interpretation, and emancipatory critique, arises in a manner that evolves a theory that consistently revalidates itself over time. Hence, this human exploration seeks to achieve an unfolding process by pooling together financial actors from among the regulators, policy and research organizations, and financial operators in the development of cyclical theory development, focusing on the positive impact of effective Islamic finance regulation, which ultimately aims to achieve a better life for the enlarged community.

Three similar theories emerge: the first drawing on development theories, the African triple heritage, Islamic banking and *esusu*. The second, a theory-to-action model, spells out research achievements through the setting up of Islamic finance in a local Nigerian bank, the influence on financial regulators through co-operative inquiry, creation of the Centre for Islamic Socio-Economic Research (CISER), and the integral financial institution. The final model is generic across jurisdiction, and releases the GENE that cements market co-ordination, state co-ordination, spiritual co-ordination, and people co-ordination.

This whole action research and innovation-based human inquiry, specifically co-operative inquiry (Reason 2002), serves to generally actualize socio-economic transformation, as well as specifically addressing practical elements in the Islamic moral economic system. These elements may be obscure for an individual reader or practitioner who simply applies methodologies from the West and North. The critical theory, which was developed from research, adds new facts to the body of knowledge, although there is room for further development. New national and international policies can be tapped from these new concepts and applications, specifically, evolving who we are, in terms of Mazrui's 'Africans', albeit primarily in an economic context.

This book is largely influenced by my personal life experience as a Nigerian living primarily in Nigeria with Western influences. The topic of this study developed gradually through the influence of my socio-cultural background from childhood through my educational experience, my work experience, the nature of the Nigerian state in my lifetime, the impact of colonialism, and external influences in development, predatory governance within the country, neo-liberal and Keynesian forces, and ethno-religious factors.

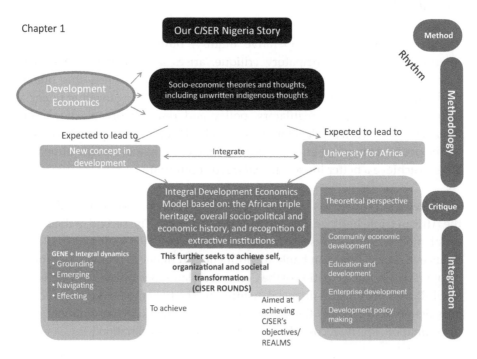

Figure 1.1   Overall framework
Source: Oshodi (2012b).

My Personal GENE

The passages above set out the overall framework of this book based on the EUREKA Model, briefly highlighting the contents therein, which spilled over into 'my personal GENE'. Generally, research may be viewed from different perspectives, which are usually a function of academic background and a backdrop of perceptions. Research in economics has been particularly influenced by quantitative investigation leading to a theory where the variables used are disconnected from social ontology. The emergence of development economics has now opened up a whole new approach to economic research which stresses the need to understand those who will be the subjects of research, those who will participate in research, the environment that influences their perception, their culture, their pains and emotions, and the reasons why they behave in the ways they do. In the light of this new approach to research and the crystallization of research questions, further derived from burning issues, Lessem and Schieffer evolved the integral Four World Model that embeds several other research concepts. One of these unique concepts is GENE – Grounding, Emerging, Navigating and Effecting – which is applied here with Randall's work on 'the stories we are' (Randall 1995), and the narrative element of the Eastern path of Renewal (Lessem and Schieffer 2010b).

GENE in Research

Part of the Integral Research Framework consists of GENE, which is basically associated with how a person, community or society releases his, her or its innermost GENEius. In research, the inner driver that releases the GENEius is aimed at social innovation (Lessem and Schieffer 2010b). More specifically, the Four World GENE constituting Integral Research is two-sided. First, each of the four paths in the Integral Research Framework has its share of the GENE. The Southern Relational path of the framework is strongest on Grounding, the Eastern path of Renewal is prominent in Emergence, the Northern path of Reason is associated with Navigation, and the Western path of Realization is more potent in its practical Effect. Secondly, each of the paths has its own fourfold path GENE. There is movement from within the layers all around the four paths. Layer one is the origination (grounding) of research, layer two is the foundation (emergence) which accommodates research methodology, layer three is the emancipation (navigation) on which critique rests, and layer four is innovation (transformation) – integration of research into action (Lessem and Schieffer 2010b).

This chapter is mainly concerned with my own personal GENE as it relates to my burning issues and the internal GENE that drove me to embark on writing this book, the factors that have motivated or influenced my thinking and perception, and what I seek to achieve at the end of this volume in terms of socio-economic transformation. GENE allows a social researcher to become a social innovator.

Grounding deals with research issues. This is where the researcher grounds himself or herself in the phenomenon of burning significance, in relation to the application of the uniqueness of self, by soaking in the waters of general social research within a particular nature and culture that he or she is engaged with. In this regard, the researcher begins to envision the kind of social innovation that is either in the stage of becoming, or in the stage of being evolved. This allows a connection with natural and cultural soils of self, organization and society (Lessem and Schieffer 2010b).

Emerging – the research question emerges as the result of a process of immersing oneself in their personal, spiritual, cultural, ethnic and professional context. These questions are either influenced by self, others and social context, or based on individual, organizational and societal origins. It draws on tradition, yet seeks modernity, creating a symbiotic relationship between the two. The researcher then interprets the research question in his or her imagination or definition connecting the past, present and future. This structures the overall storyline, developing concrete phenomena based on 'strongly fermented wine', or old thoughts that are being researched, while mixing it with 'new wine', creating new or emerging thoughts characterized by envisaged abstract and innovative ideas (Lessem and Schieffer 2010b).

Navigating through a literature search involves building on prior knowledge grounded in perception or experience, understanding the indigenous knowledge of the immediate society, and the researcher's society as it develops from historical engagement with self, others and social context. Then, the researcher builds on explicit wisdom of the key thinkers, ideologies or paradigms in the field of concern. In this regard, there is a focus on relevant conventional wisdom based on aspects of the social sciences as the main spur for social innovation. This further allows for the formulation of a hypothesis or the development of a scenario which combines with all that has come before, allowing navigation into prospective fieldwork. This then creates room for theory and conjecture to be tested, alongside fact and observation, in order to reach a viable conclusion (Lessem and Schieffer 2010b).

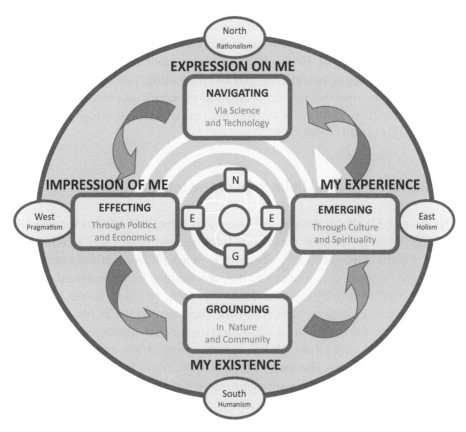

Figure 1.2   My creative GENE within the integral GENE
Source: Derived from Lessem et al. (2013).

Effecting in the research field brings about innovation. Lessem and Schieffer assert that this empirical 'doing' of research and innovation follows being immersed in it in the first place, forming the visible and accessible knowledge branches, or know-how arising out of the research. Being original in this progressively emerging interpretation of the research field allows the building of a conceptual foundation for the researcher's interpretation. This doing of research then builds on prior being, becoming and knowing. Consequently, empirically based co-creation is now purposely targeted at observation and experimentation (Lessem and Schieffer 2010a).

In essence, GENE displays the inner rhythm of knowledge and value generation, making research lead to innovation and generally connect with learning rhythm of humans. Integral Research's four paths and layers integrate perfectly with GENE in a non-linear manner, moving back and forth around the layers while connecting the roots of the research with the underlying soils. Next, the main stem of the 'research-and-innovation tree, the branches and ultimate fruits begin healing the planet, promoting peaceful co-evolution, building up an open society, and creating economic opportunity' (Lessem and Schieffer 2010b). This now leads to my personal GENE, which reflects the integral Four World GENE.

My GENE: A Practical Reflection of the Integral GENE

The research GENE, as defined in Lessem and Schieffer's Integral Framework, is merged with my real-life experience, thinking, and what I seek to achieve in terms of turning the world into a better place through research and innovation. This is then examined as it relates to how my burning issues morphed into the 'becoming' of my burning issues, and then the 'doing' or action desired to achieve socio-economic change or transformation. This is grounded in my indigenous self, others and the society in which I found myself. This grounding also reflects my exogenous journey through life, together with others around me, in my society, acknowledging the forces of the African triple heritage. My personal integral Four World GENE is emerging, since it is being interpreted by myself based on my understanding of socio-economic issues as incorporated in this body of research, seeking a renewal of society. Emerging further navigates swiftly into the wide ocean of knowledge and research in my world, picking the jewels of the ocean in order to allow me to develop my hypotheses, or create new theories after learning from the enlarged world – theories of economic development which reflect the African triple heritage in Nigeria. Why stop research at the junction of theory? Believing someone else, of another generation, will perhaps review the theory and implement it, I then take it upon myself, as defined in the GENE model, to effect what I started, not just by setting the stage for action to take place or putting in place a mechanism to effect it, but to actually implement it. Like a project manager, my new morally biased economic development theory is made to run, to happen, to effect, and to lead to social innovation.

THE RHYTHM OF MY CREATIVE SELF

My existence

I started with the aesthetics of living by narrating my existence, the outside story of what has happened in the past, and indeed the total sum of my life story. I incorporated everything, the emotional to the interpersonal, as well as the physical to the atomic (Randall 1995). Perception generally has to do with the interrelationship of a person's background, experience, culture, knowledge, beliefs and interpretation of the perceived. The socio-cultural and ethno-political setting I found myself in from birth has largely influenced my life, my thinking, my research and the legacies I wish to leave behind. I was born in 1974, at a time when Nigeria started to experience a windfall from crude oil. My father, a noble Lagos Muslim lawyer, was a top state government official during this period, and my mother was from a simple and reserved Anglican family who became a Muslim a few years after I was born. The word I heard most often from my mum each time we were in the large supermarket to buy household needs was 'austerity'. She tried to tell us that we could not have everything because things had become too expensive. This was in the early 1980s, when the pound sterling and the naira (NGN) had the same value. My father was a chief magistrate with a personal police officer guarding him and a fleet of cars at his disposal. He spent his time attending launching events and contributing happily to society. I watched as the Nigerian economy swung between periods of austerity into the Structural Adjustment Programme (SAP) and then into persistent poverty. I experienced several military take-overs, political killings, worker strikes, infrastructure decay, loss of primary health and educational standards, consistent loss of the value of the Naira, conversions of factories, industries and warehouses into churches, and today's new dawn of democracy. I never understood the meaning of poverty until I was at university and found that most students could barely afford one good meal a day, much less to buy books. Then federal universities became heavily subsidized and tuition fees and accommodation barely cost US$100 per session. My academic and work experiences further exposed me to people from several other socio-economic backgrounds, and I realized for the first time that poverty for most Nigerians is a normal way of life. That was the most important part of my experience, until I lost my father.

On Friday 22 February 2002, I returned from work in the evening and found my father unwell. It was the first time in my life when this strong man had been ill, and it was a mild stroke. Early on Saturday, we took him to the general hospital where we have all the specialist doctors. On Sunday evening, he was back to sound health, talking all day, joking, laughing and eating properly. What a good day, we thought! Early Monday morning, 25 February, while he was shaving, he had a second stroke and died. We buried him by 4.30 p.m. on the same day, according to Muslim rites. The first month was filled with visitors, and by the second month the realities of his death became clear.

No more guests. I was the only one from a relatively large polygamous family that had finished university and possessed a master's degree. It was time to pay my school fees and the running costs of a relatively large house. That was when, coupled with intra-family conflict and the reality of my emotions, true poverty set in. These are the realities of the Nigerian state. My mum and I worked to support the immediate and extended family. I was beginning to understand what the average Nigerian household felt like in a country where neither the government nor anyone else was there to support you – no affordable health service, no soft loan to pay school fees, no benefits, and no sustainable employment. I remember that the general hospital lacked proper amenities back then. It seems better now. There was no train system available, and the roads leading there were bad, so emergencies were challenging. The supply of electricity was an overall failure as well, being very sporadic in urban areas and much more so in rural ones. Another reality that set in is that while I concentrated on trying to support a large family, my own personal life had to be put on hold. I postponed getting married until loved ones grew up and moved on. All this is a reflection of the emotional side of my story, the story of who I am. All of this makes up my GENE, a GENE that is grounded in real-life experience, having emerged through experience, and the insights gained through those experiences.

My experience

My experience is characterized by the story of my life as accessible to me and interpreted by me, or the story of my creation (Jerome Bruner, in Randall 1995). I attended Corona Primary School – a unique and expensive private primary school in Lagos with kids of diplomats, foreign expatriates and top government officials – while my secondary school was a subsidized military school in Kaduna, northern Nigeria. I wanted to go to the military college for my tertiary education to become a military officer and take part in governance, since the military were the ones always in power. Unexpectedly, I was admitted to the University of Lagos to study Estate Management. At the university, I took many economics modules, exposing me to the nature, structure and problems of the Nigerian economy. I was exposed to econometrics, statistics and real estate finance – this module woke me up from my 'deep sleep'. From then on, my thoughts started to take another shape. I started to wonder how real estate, and the estate sector as a whole, could attract long-term funds in Nigeria, where banks charge very high interest rates, from mainly short-term transactions or loans since they use short- and medium-term depositors' funds most of the time. I went back to study for an MSc. in Management in

2001, which exposed me to strategic management concepts aimed at achieving organizational objectives. I completed my final dissertation on the feasibility of the interest-free banking model in Nigeria, in which I was able to develop five hypotheses and test them statistically. This is the only research method I was taught, and indeed the only research method most undergraduate and post-graduate courses from Nigerian universities are familiar with. Even those who study architecture and English use this method. In a bid to understand other unconventional economic models or in search of a 'moral' financial model, I completed a course in Islamic Finance at the Institute of Islamic Banking and Insurance in London. What an interesting model it is! However, could it solve the complicated socio-economic challenges in Nigeria? I did not think this system alone could solve the problems of inadequate capital and its cost, unemployment, poverty and the huge income inequalities in the Nigerian state, characterized by ethno-religious diversity.

I was then motivated to seek a Masters in Research (MRes), Business and Management at London Metropolitan University in order to examine the workings of private equity and venture capital companies, since this is the closest concept to Islamic finance. However, my supervisor was more concerned with the preconditions of investment in the fragile Nigerian state, which led me to concentrate more on issues of good governance and state-directed development, as these are assumed imperatives for real economic development. This helped me to grasp the bigger picture of the rudiments that expose the mechanism of economies. Therefore, a PhD became necessary – a PhD designed to effect social-economic transformation, tailored along the 'realistic' path of renewal. Professor Ronnie Lessem from the University of Buckingham read my research proposal and accepted me for an MPhil. in Economics, specifically in Social and Economic Transformation, in association with the TRANS4M Institute for Integral Innovation in Geneva. From there, I moved to the DaVinci Institute for Technology Management in Modderfontein, South Africa, a school started in the 1990s by Nelson Mandela. The DaVinci Institute is grounded in several areas: managing technology, innovation, people and systems, with a special focus on managerial leadership competencies; understanding of self, others and social contexts, and the application of problem-solving, creating thinking and decision-making tools. My research evolved in Islamic economic and finance, within the context of overall development economics alluding to the African socio-economic setting, stressing poverty and unemployment issues.

I started my work experience as a financial analyst trainee with Union Bank of Nigeria in 1999 and began to wonder how Nigerian business organizations could make a profit. These organizations had to pay more than 20 per cent interest on loan advancements (usually as short-term working capital) and a 30 per cent company tax on their gross profit to the federal government. Capital was available to an extent, but too expensive, and could not achieve sustainable economic development. I moved to a state-owned mortgage bank as a financial analyst. Although it enjoyed fund allocations from the state government, which supported operations, it was short on innovation and was not a learning organization. I also realized, generally, that state establishments were exposed to overall ineffectiveness due to organized corruption by top management, while the state government of the day used funds from those institutions to support political party programmes. In March 2003, I moved to Concept Partners, a management consultancy firm. While there, I developed effective strategic management and financial analyst skills while my interest in politics and love for change in governance grew. I stood for a constituency seat in the Lagos State House of Assembly in October 2003, but was asked to step down on the day of the primaries by the state governor as he had someone else in mind. Thereafter, I was offered the position of Relationship Lands Officer in the Lands Bureau, a division under the Lagos State Governor's Office. Nigerian public sector workers are used to gross corruption: project prices are happily inflated; rent-seeking behaviour is the norm; public officers would gladly convert government cheques, and the private sector willingly negotiated deals with all categories of government officials. For me, my natural self did not find comfort in the Nigerian public sector, so I decided to do two things. First, I set up an NGO called the Ade-Oshodi Foundation, intended to touch the lives of a tiny fraction of my immediate community in a small way. Second, I started a research programme in the UK, which contributed, to my Masters in Research (MRes) on the interplay of good governance indicators and development indicators, comparing Nigeria and India. While in the UK, I took a four-week holiday job at the Foreign and Commonwealth Office (FCO). While there, I learned that government services should come at zero cost to the people and that zero tolerance for corruption is a culture. I also worked as a business analyst with ScrollSolutions, developing competence in organizational restructuring. In February 2009, I moved back to Nigeria, where Stanbic IBTC Bank, a member of Standard Bank Group, offered me a middle management position as Head of Islamic Banking Risk and Compliance. This position piqued my interest in developing Islamic banking and finance in Nigeria with an extra interest in poverty reduction via this innovative economic model together with other development economic thinking. In August 2012, I moved to EFInA, a financial inclusion programme sponsored by the Department for International Development (DFID) and the Bill & Melinda Gates Foundation. There I was Manager of Non-Interest Finance, juggling this with the role of Research Manager. In January 2013, urgent market demands for experts in the Islamic finance market lead me to become the Group Head of Non-Interest Banking at Sterling Bank – an indigenous Nigerian bank.

My experience in the Nigerian state has deeply influenced my life. I have lived and worked in Nigeria for the bulk of my life. I was educated about Nigeria in school, and I feel Nigeria in my blood. What is unique about this country? Nigeria is a West African country bordering the Gulf of Guinea, between Benin and Cameroon. It is endowed with natural gas, petroleum, tin, iron ore, coal, limestone, zinc, lead, niobium and very good arable land. Muslim Fulani from north-central Africa conquered the northern part of the country in the eleventh century, while European slave traders took the southern coastal land in the eighteenth century. British colonialists created Nigeria in 1914, and granted it independence in 1960. Over 80 ethnic groups are present in Nigeria, with more than 200 languages or dialects. The country's greatest strength lies in the entrepreneurial zeal of its people, its high population and its enormous natural resources. Even with all this, the country has developed rather slowly since its independence, with little or no improvement in the socio-economic status of its people. The political terrain has been very rough, with a civil war during 1967–9 in which there were several ethno-religious crises. Due to relative political stability, the inflow of foreign capital and improvements in several other quantitative development indicators, the economy is assumed to have improved over the past 13 years.

The quality of life for the majority of the over 170 million Nigerian people has not improved, with most living below the poverty line of US$1 per day. More than half of the adult population earn less than the monthly minimum wage of US$112.50, while more than 99 per cent of the population earn less than US$1,250 per month (EFInA 2012); 47.3 per cent of adults earn less than US$83.2 per month or have no income, and only 4.5 per cent of adults earn more than US$448 per month (National Bureau of Statistics, EFInA 2012). The World Bank, IMF, United Nations and DFID say the country is growing rapidly because of the skyrocketing of the Gross Domestic Product (GDP) and GNI over the last decade. In reality, the majority of households cannot afford to pay for even one good meal a day or the US$2 it costs to treat malaria, much less think about fair living conditions. Several structural adjustment programmes and poverty reduction measures by international bodies have had little or no impact, with governance efforts yet to be felt. The country experiences various forms of poverty – national poverty that everyone suffers from factors such as infrastructural decay, some due to governance and financial failures, while most is the result of inappropriate application of economic models or the misuse of feasible economic systems. From the days of colonialism, the West has dominated the Nigerian economy and still shows an interest because of the enormous natural and human endowments of the country. The influence of Western-controlled international organizations and the manipulation of African leaders have not been able to create sufficient and sustainable employment for the Nigerian people. Many see economic inequality as having been predestined.

The big question now is whether any economic model brought into Nigeria from outside sub-Saharan Africa can have any real impact on its development. Perhaps these economic models have not been morally motivated, so they are unable to appeal to the minds of Africans. Perhaps alternative moral economic systems will be needed that would build an ethical socio-economic development pattern for sub-Saharan Africa. These factors, and my experience within the Nigerian state, motivate me to be engaged in this study.

Expression on me

Expression is the story of each individual version of my inside story that I convey to others (Kaufmann 1987, in Randall 1995). This story navigates rapidly into the layers of the Integral Four Worlds – my four worlds. I grew up being a very quiet person and never wanted to express myself. I was extremely quiet in primary and secondary school, and only began to talk more towards the tail end of my first degree. What was I talking about? It was about the evils of an interest-based economy. I read the Hadiths (sayings and deeds of the Prophet Mohammed SAW), Volume 3, 'The Book of Transaction', where *riba* (interest) within the context of the Hadiths was defined; I also read the relevant verses in the Quran, coupled with my module on real estate finance. I started with my colleagues when they talked about the social, political and economic situation in Nigeria. I would go into their midst and say that the solution was an interest-free economy. Fifteen years after school, all my friends remember is my arguments about an interest-free economy, on Islamic banking and on ethical ways of doing business. In my MSc. programme, I completed my thesis on 'Environmental and Organisational Appraisal on Non-Interest Banking in Nigeria', in which I measured perceptions quantitatively. I now frequently deliver lectures and presentations on Islamic banking to a wide and mixed audience.

More so, I am a member of the Nigerian Islamic Finance Working Group and work with a bank where I champion Islamic finance. The story of myself I tell to others is the story of a morally based economic system founded in Islamic economics with which people resonate. It seems that is the only story of me people know. One day, in mid-2011, I walked into a restaurant in Victoria Island, Lagos and saw a university classmate with his family. I was amazed to hear him say, 'I hope you have now set up an Islamic bank?' I must now have a new story to tell – a story that navigates through the rigour of 'knowledge searching', the story of an integral socio-economic and morally shaped model which is beyond Shariah compliance, leading down the path of poverty reduction while maintaining consciousness of the African triple heritage and its influences on economic development – a path of a whole new theory derived from theoretical perspectives and from co-operative inquiry. This new subject in 'the story I am' would find its path into others and society, creating a way for effecting social innovation.

Impression of me

Impression is the story of my life that is entertained about me by those who know me (Kaufman 1987 and Runyan 1984, in Randall 1995). The impression people generally have of me is largely of someone who can effect change. They see my passion, energy and desire to make socio-economic transformation take place. I am constantly recommended to advise people about their education, career paths, businesses, charity propositions, politics, policies, international development, research and religious issues. These impressions of me attract a wide mix of people interested in me and what I do. In this regard, I have been exposed to several activities of others, ranging from delivering papers on a number of subjects to taking part directly in charities and NGO movements. Many others remember and talk about my involvement in politics and government, and my ability to develop fair policies. I have been referred to in several academic and career decision-making discussions relating to future job opportunities. References from international organizations relating to research across the African triple heritage have been very consistent lately. People setting up business organizations of various sizes and in various fields also come to me for advice on developing value proposition and strategy. Overall, people who know me believe largely that I am able to make positive changes in their lives and in society. It is in this regard, coupled with my whole life experience, that my GENEius is being released. Being grounded in my existence, emerged through my experience, navigated through the expression of me, and effected in others' impressions of me leads to the combination of my burning issues.

Burning Issues

The story I am, enveloped in existence, experience, expression and impression, evolved through my GENE, is the platform my burning issues spring from. Thus, I ask myself:

- Why is there poverty, and what constitutes poverty in Nigeria? Can a morally structured economic development model solve this challenge?

- Why is there high unemployment in Nigeria? Can lowering the high cost of capital while tackling societal moral issues reduce it?

Based on the issues raised above, this book seeks to determine the effect of development and post-development economic models together with the Islamic economic system in relation to real poverty and unemployment issues in Nigeria.

Three main sub-issues are furthered derived from this main burning issue:

- to evolve an economic development theory based on the African triple heritage;

- to Implement Islamic banking principles on the foundations of a moral economic core based on the African triple heritage;

- to create a new integral financial institution specifically addressing these issues.

Conclusion

Until the 1980s, economic development theories over the last four centuries had been largely Eurocentric. In the same vein, research methodologies in economics seem more readily recognized when they are quantitative or based on microdata. The transplanting of these models, as I will seek to demonstrate in this book, is glaringly unfavourable to the South, and especially the African continent. It is in this regard that this book sets forth a different kind of proposition grounded in the 'story of self, others and immediate social context'. The book acknowledges the pressures posed by the external forces of Islam and Western Christianity together with the indigenous background. A very important aspect of this book is the moral core which illuminates the whole study. More specifically, moral elements influence the co-operative inquiry and the three sets of development economic models that emerged.

The development of my burning issues is based on the overall narration of self, the story of my life as I interpret it, my story as I convey it to others, and the impression those who know me have about me – each combining with my GENE in a cyclic manner. This evokes my personal GENEius and allows me to be involved in this research and innovation. Hence, my GENE is lodged in the Integral Four Worlds framework, which is further grounded in nature and community, emerging through culture and spirituality, navigating via science and technology, and effecting through politics and economics. This model permeates this book, following the Eastern path of Renewal and ascending each of the four layers, and in particular Nigeria's triple heritage. The story of my life is indeed the bedrock on which this book rests. This story of who I am within the context of the Nigerian state leads to the next chapter on economic development issues in Nigeria, which over time have been viewed quantitatively from the angle of economic growth. Here, the approach has been further evolved, acknowledging past research but placing a lot more weight on real economic development while examining the quality of life and perceptions of the indigenous people.

2

Economic Development in Nigeria

Introduction

Chapter 1 analysed the factors that shaped my burning issues, starting with the general research GENE and then applying it to my own personal GENE which drew out my GENEius, as it were, and hence this research as a whole. This chapter paints a picture of Nigeria's overall economic development within a socio-political setting since there is a combination of several interrelated variables that affect the country's economic prospects. Good governance indicators, two major development indicators and the BECANS (Business Environment and Competitiveness Across Nigerian States) benchmark in Nigeria trace the incidence of poverty and unemployment in the country, which is the reason why extraneous economic models applied in Nigeria never work. The application of the capitalist and communist schools may still face some implementation challenges if realistic factors concerning socio-political and economic facts are not extensively appraised. Whether borrowing from the West or the North or adopting state-led development through an Eastern approach, or through embracing the integral moral economic replica from the religious books, which come from the Middle East, or finally, perhaps through the new economic thoughts from Africans living in Africa or those that understand indigenous Africanism, the application must be appraised. This chapter analyses some relevant factors that affect the overall economic development through the perception of both the neo-liberal school and through the use of qualitative evidence which includes the researcher's experience in order to give a clear portrait of Nigeria's socio-political and economic situation while building a foundation from which the body of knowledge can be further developed.

The Narrative of the Current Economic Context

Keynes (1940), Tinbergen (1939), Acemoglu et al. (2001), Mookherjee (2005), Basu (2005), Ray (2007), Lessem and Schieffer (2009), Todaro and Smith (2009), Cypher and Dietz (2009) and Obasanjo (2007) all frown on the applicability of economic statistics in isolation in developing economics. Mookherjee (2005) and Banerjee (2005) assert that the theory is hardly regarded in today's economic development and that it has lost its position. Cypher and Dietz, when analysing the works of early development economics, observed that 'they formed a loose school of thought on the issues of economic development, emphasizing a less theoretical, and more historical and practical approach than the neo-classicists' (Cypher and Dietz 2009). In this light, the book further examines the real socio-economic situation from a people inquiry (Reason 2002) and practical position. The author has lived in Nigeria for over thirty-five years, and travels around the country often, so he has a sound understanding of the poverty trends which form part of this study.

NIGERIANS' PERCEPTIONS OF SOCIO-ECONOMIC ISSUES

In order to further verify perceptions of the Nigerian government, I engaged in in-depth interviews with five people from different geopolitical zones of the country who belong to various ethno-religious backgrounds. Ibrahim is a Muslim, 34 years of age, from north-east Nigeria, who thinks the business environment is very ineffective. As a small-scale businessperson, he goes to the neighbouring Benin Republic to import textile materials to resell in Nigeria. He says that although the transportation infrastructure is very poor and the cost of transportation is high, he still makes 50–70 per cent profit from his business. He complains that the security agencies (police, customs and immigration) always demand money. On voice and accountability, he says that Nigerian democracy allows you to talk, but the authorities will not hear your voice. He does not think the government is stable, due to the continuous ethno-political uprisings. For Ibrahim, government is not effective in any way: it does not keep promises, its efforts are inadequate, there is no human face, and it makes voters into victims. Quality regulations do not exist, and frowning while raising his voice, he laments that the middle class no longer exists. He says that corruption is an organized institution which negatively affects the poor masses in particular, while benefiting politicians, judges and the military. On poverty, he says that what little good infrastructure exists is not properly maintained due to corruption. The farms lack storage facilities, bank loans are difficult to get, and the hospitals lack the necessary equipment. He describes the hospitals as mere buildings, lacking all forms of amenities. Ibrahim says that although he can afford two square meals a day, many people and households he knows manage on only one meal a day. He frowns again, sharing that some families eat meat only once a week. He shares further that his Hausa background and culture is very dear to him because his people are very hospitable. They quell their sorrow with annual celebrations, festivals and frequent traditional events. More importantly, he says that his tribe respects other people very much, as they produce so many food crops for the Nigerian economy.

Blessing, a 26-year-old Christian woman student from Benue in north-central Nigeria feels that Nigerians can speak out, but many people are still quite scared of the potential for government brutality in the so-called democracy. Blessing says that the country is still unstable and erratic, and that the government is largely ineffective. She lives in the north-west, and expresses her fears of the Hausa-Muslim community when they go on ethno-religious rampages. She asserts that the roads are quite good in the north of the country, but the hospitals are ineffective, and the water and power supply too sporadic. Blessing believes that the older generation lived much longer than the later generation in Nigeria, using her grandparents as a case study. She thinks that most Nigerians do not have real jobs, saying that many informal job opportunities are temporary. She has been engaged in such jobs, and after five years in a low-paid job, she decided to go back to the university in order to be exposed to better opportunities. The most interesting thing about her culture is festive events in her hometown or village. She is proud of the fact that women do not sleep around after marriage in her village.

An exclusive interview with AbdulSalam, a man in his late forties, was very revealing. He is a Muslim from the south-west with a master's degree, but who has never had formal employment. He set up and runs a political magazine, which he says adds much joy to his existence. He says that the business environment in Nigeria has failed. Infrastructure and utilities are intermittent, and this causes delays in the ability to produce in good time. Regulatory services have some bureaucracy, but do not really affect his little business. He is affected by the inability to gain access to additional finance (US$500–1,000) that would help his business grow quickly. With regard to voice and accountability, he laments: 'You can talk, but it will not change anything or change government policies, while the corrupt people still get back to power.' On political stability, he argues that after fourteen years of uninterrupted democracy, the system has not changed; hence, government is not effective in any way. He wonders why government could not fix the electricity system, which greatly affects his production cost and eats into his profits. He asserts that he hardly makes any profit, and that this will not change unless his business grows and is able to enjoy economies of scale.

He thinks the country needs true federalism to attain regulatory quality, and that positions are never allocated on merit in Nigeria: 'Rule of law does not exist and corruption is a hydra-headed monster.' The infrastructures is poor, he says, the hospitals are filled with quacks, unregistered, nurses are untrained, new hospitals are not being built and the quality of life is sad. What pains him most is that most Nigerians have this unique formula of eating – 0–0–1, 1–0–0 and 0–1–0 – where 0 represents no food and 1 represents a meal, so people only try to have one meal a day. His eyes dampen, expressing pain at the situation. He complains that only one person might have a job in a whole family, while all the others members would rely on him or her. However, his love for Nigeria is based on moral teachings across the board: respect for elders, maintenance of family ties, brotherliness, moral support from the community, love and assistance from extended and immediate family, and many more factors which constitute the binding fabric of society. He strongly feels that moral culture can aid economic development, and thus continuity of the family system. These cultures preach against stealing, bad behaviour, rudeness, prostitution and homosexuality. Abiding by traditional norms in a leadership position will positively affect real development in Nigeria.

Ebele, a 26-year-old female Christian banker from the south-south of the country, is of the opinion that although regulations are in place in the Nigerian business environment, they are questionable and largely ineffective. She joins the others in saying: 'Unlike the days of the military where people could not even talk, here you can say all that is in you, but the government will not even see you, not to mention hear your voice; they are insensitive to the needs of the people.' The government cannot execute a simple project because corruption has either affected pricing or political rents have been paid. She says that corruption here is normal. She feels that poverty must have improved over the years, but is still not good enough for a country like Nigeria. She demonstrates passionately with her hands that agriculture has yet to be fully explored in the country, saying that the complete value-chain could put the youth in permanent employment. Ebele asserts that employment law is also very poor in Nigeria, and unfavourable to Nigerians. Employers exploit workers by giving them very poor remuneration. In the same vein, she says: 'Lots of low-paid jobs are available, people who are overqualified take them because they have no choice.' However, Ebele loves Nigeria. She says we are peace-loving people with rich and diverse cultures, who are blessed with many natural resources. She wants every Nigerian to give hope to children by turning them away from the street: 'Every child is your child,' she says, emotionally.

The final in-depth interview was with Audu, an investment banker from north-central Nigeria who is in his early thirties. His perception of the business environment is influenced by his work experience. He is quick to compare the business environment in Nigeria with that of the UK, giving examples of private equity and venture capital firms and the way they support new and existing businesses. He complains that it takes about twelve to eighteen months to register or get a full licence for a private equity company in Nigeria, which can naturally discourage foreign investors. Business development support and investment promotions for him can be rapidly implemented through an effective sales and marketing team in order to achieve organizational targets. On voice and accountability, he says the government is still resistant to freedom of expression, and gives an example of a former minister who was recently arrested for talking. Audu says that political stability is still very shaky in the country, electoral reforms are needed, and votes do not count:

> The government is not effective in any way, they cleared over US$11 billion from the foreign reserves and more billions of dollars are being stolen daily. The rule of law is still very subjective in the country and the size of government is too large. Over 42 ministers should be slashed by 50 per cent, reduce the size of legislature, identify two or three infrastructural projects that should be tackled fully, but it will take a warrior to achieve this.

He smiles as he makes the last point. The good thing about his culture is that it is rooted in family orientation, a leadership hierarchy within the family, respect for family, and good traditional food, art, music and literature. Audu's mum died a long time ago, but he goes to his village often to see his maternal grandma and, along with other relations, gives her money monthly. This gives him much joy, he says.

The above in-depth interviews illustrate real-life cases. The next sets of analysis are from secondary sources, which emerged in January 2012. The price of petrol per litre was NGN 65 (US$0.43), and the President of Nigeria increased it to US$1 per litre, arguing that the oil sector had to be liberalized, thus the need to remove the fuel subsidy. This resulted into a six-day national strike, and most importantly, the people's reappraisal of overall governance.

In the heat of this situation, several face-to-face discussions with the people and comments on social websites were gathered as qualitative materials. A comment on the situation from thenewsafrica.com on 24 October 2011 reads thus:

> *When a Nigerian pays NGN 65 (USD 0.43) for fuel rather than NGN 40 (0.27), he is subsidizing the incompetence of Government by NGN 25 (USD 0.17).*
>
> *When a Nigerian has to buy a generator and buy petrol and diesel because electricity generation is worse off, he is subsidizing the incompetence in Government.*
>
> *When a Nigerian has to drill a borehole, buy pure water or bottled water rather than get public portable tap water, he is subsidizing the inefficiency of Government.*
>
> *When a Nigerian has to maintain 3 phone-lines or 3 different internet subscriptions just because of call-quality or crippled bandwidth, he is subsidizing the failures of government regulation.*
>
> *When a Nigerian has to pay heavily to secure his life and property through personnel and gadgets, he is subsidizing the failure of government to protect him constitutionally.*
>
> *For bad roads, we subsidize by having to visit the mechanic more often than usual or sometimes with our lives.*
>
> *We can go on about the educational system, health sector, the environment, maritime, and so on.*
>
> *It is time for us to remove our own subsidy by making the government do what they are supposed to do.*

Nasir El Rufai, a former Minister of the Federal Capital Territory (FCT) Abuja, expressed his own grief online, saying:

> *Those giving economic arguments for or against fuel subsidy withdrawal miss the point totally. It is not about economics but about trust! The spending pattern and priorities of President Goodluck Jonathan since*

2010 is evidence of whom he cares for. Under his watch, we increased our debt stock by about USD 20 billion, ran down excess crude reserve from USD 6bn to zero, foreign reserves from USD 45 billion to USD 30 billion. Under the same president, USD exchange rate moved from NGN 140 to N160 as at January 2012. Debt stock has doubled to higher than 2005 levels. Interest rates over 20%! And all this is while nearly NGN 10 trillion (USD 66.6 billion) has been spent on government officials, trips abroad, and perquisites/subsidies to politicians! There is no power supply improvement; no minimal jobs created; no transport infrastructures; no agricultural output; but there are many private jets. Stationary, refreshment and snacks in the Presidency will consume about NGN 2 billion (USD 13.3 million), with NGN 1.6 billion (USD 10.6 million) spent by the president and the vice president in 2012. Does that make sense? Miscellaneous spending by the Villa (presidential palace) alone totals NGN 1.7 billion (USD 11.3 million) for food, honorarium, and something called 'welfare packages' – another security vote! In the 2012 budget, National Assembly intends to spend NGN 150 billion (USD 1 billion) on itself, the same amount as in 2011 to pay those huge allowances. It has not been reduced, so we will spend about NGN 320 million (USD 2.1 million) for every National Assembly member in 2012, as we did in 2011. Where is the shared sacrifice? Where is accountability? We must resist the NGN 8,000 (USD 53) tax being imposed on every man, woman and child to fund the fuel subsidy and insist that Federal Government cuts its own wastefulness! The issue with President Goodluck Jonathan is simply that of trust. He has wasted huge financial resources and put us in debt in the last 20 months. We must be wary! We cannot trust him with more money, as he will only waste more of it. That is the issue and he can only earn that trust through small steps.

Another Nigerian asserted:

We have lost everything we met on the land. Cocoa, palm oil, groundnuts, cotton, cashew, and rubber have been forgotten and are better produced by nations who came to learn from us. We have lost our moral compass, our society is fractured, and our statehood is threatened. Our citizens are in all prisons around the world. Some of them prefer foreign prisons to coming back to Nigeria. Our passport is treated with disdain everywhere you present it. Why should our Senate Leader earn NGN 600 million (USD 4 million) per annum?

Why should our senators earn NGN 30 million (USD 200,000) per annum? Why should our National Assembly gulp NGN 1.2 trillion (USD 8 billion) per annum while we try to save NGN 1.4 trillion (USD 9.3 billion) from subsidy removal? Why should our government be this big with special advisers on cassava and beans affairs? Do we need 36 ministers? Why would our president spend close to NGN 1 billion (6.6 million USD) on food while close to eighty percent live on less than a dollar a day? Why should he budget a billion for generators and diesel when he is urging us to believe in his power sector reform? Why does our President need six private jets? Why do our governors move around with twenty-vehicle convoys while David Cameron has just two vehicles and one outrider? Why should our politicians keep their salaries when Obama slashed his? Why should we continue to be wasteful when the handwriting on the wall says 'danger'? Why should we believe this government when it says the subsidy gain will be properly reinvested!?

LIFE IN MAKOKO – LAGOS STATE (SOUTH-WEST)

Figure 2.1   Poverty in Ijegun Egba Lagos, Nigeria

Figure 2.2   Poverty in Ijegun Egba Lagos, Nigeria

Several BECANS research benchmarks and indicators (Eboh and Lemchi 2010) show that Lagos State was the highest-performing among Nigeria's 36 states. Lagos is a coastal stretch of land along the Atlantic which was ceded to the British in 1861 and was the capital of Nigeria until the 1990s, but still remains the commercial capital of the country. The entire state is regarded as urban, but some believe that 5 per cent of the state may still be rural. Makoko is a suburb in Lagos where households live on the margins of the Lagos lagoon, but have been without running water for the last thirty years. Power supplies fluctuate in many areas, and are unavailable in most parts, where homes are built on the water with rough wood and without any real sanitation. Families manage to have one square meal a day even though they are dependent on fishing, their schools are substandard, they lack primary healthcare, and mosquitoes breed freely, causing frequent malaria among several other diseases. For years, they have lived this way. Ijegun Egba is another area with this level of underdevelopment (see Figures 2.1 and 2.2).

UMUNWALOKA VILLAGE – IMO STATE (SOUTH-EAST)

Nigerian president Umaru Musa Yar'Adua died on 4 May 2010. CNN immediately carried out a survey of Nigerians' perceptions of this tragic event, and Marcs commented as follows:

> We neither need condolence messages nor breaking news for the death of our President, because who cares? I think for Nigeria to stop losing people in that seat, they should liberate we the Biafra's instead of claiming one Nigeria while we are not. I come from a village called Umunwaloka Village in Nnenato community (Obibi-Ochasi), Orlu LGA Imo State, Eastern Nigeria. There, we cannot visit with our fellow kinsmen in another street anymore because gully erosion has divided us. The matter has been reported to the Nigeria government for many years even before I was conceived, but they pay no heed to that. Our farmlands have been eroded by floodwater, people have lost their houses to the erosion, and our little river (Ezize Okpii) has been covered with sand. Our natural ancient streams (Omurima and Okpii) have been eroded by the gully erosion, no access for the poor people to get drinking water anymore, yet we put on semi-happy faces as Nigerians.
>
> Let the death of this so-called good president (Umaru Musa Yar'Adua) be a stepping-stone for the Liberation of the Biafra's. My people are dying every minute of the most common thing in this world (water). You will be jailed if you talk of pipe borne water,

electricity, pension, or even subsidized education for kids in my area.
Who cares about who dies in Nigeria? My father died at the age of
77 in 2006 without smelling pension, even though he pays his tax
every year to the corrupt government. Who cares? (CNN Wire Staff,
6 May 2010)

VISIT TO SOKOTO, KANO AND KADUNA (NORTH-EAST)

I visited some northern Nigerian states in 2009 as part of the sensitization for my organization's staff and other stakeholders in Islamic banking. It also exposed me to understanding several perceptions, attitudes and lifestyles of the indigenous people. During my tour, I visited the tombs of Uthman Dan Fodio and other northern emirs in Sokoto. In the eighteenth century, Uthman Dan Fodio was a Fulani who challenged the powers of the Kanuri Empire and gave strength to the Sokoto Caliphate. He led the Islamic jihad in the northern part of the country and parts of the north-central region. I saw several men or Islamic scholars either sitting alone or with their students or wives and relations. They were camped on the long road past the tombs. They prayed for people who came to visit the tombs, and they expected to receive money voluntarily from visitors. That is all they did for their livelihood. They did not have other jobs and were not skilled in any way except in Quranic Arabic and maybe Islamic jurisprudence, which they learned informally from their sheikhs or senior clerics. They would usually not visit the hospitals even where they were available, would not attend formal educational institutions, and did not care what happened in the polity. All they wanted in life was to be able to fulfil their fundamental religious obligation – to observe *salat* (Muslim prayer) and fast in the month of Ramadan. Whatever happens to them, their families or the state/government is regarded as their predestination or the Will of Allah. Hence, they do not have a definition for poverty since everything is attributed to fate.

My experiences in the major cities of Kano and Kaduna were very similar. I went on market intelligence in Kano and Kaduna, visiting our offices and other financial institutions in the states. I ended up taking my lunch in the car, and each day in the traffic ten or twenty children, men and women in sound health surrounded the car asking for money. I wished I could just pass the remaining food to them. This experience was a daily occurrence. It was observed later that most of the children were in *madarasas* (informal Arabic-Quranic schools) and their scholars encouraged them to beg for alms since they had no means of survival and their parents were unable to support them.

Most of these *madarasas* are fee-free schools, and their scholars collect these monies from them at the end of the day as a form of payment.

VISIT TO SEVERAL LOCATIONS IN OSUN AND OYO STATE (SOUTH-WEST)

In March 2010, with USAID Markets we visited several cassava-producing states where a partnership has been developed between financial institutions, farmers' co-operatives and cassava off-takers. The states of Osun and Oyo belong to the south-west geopolitical zone. It was amazing to note that many of the farmers were well educated and spoke good English. It was evident that most had attended secondary school, while many had university degrees and some were retired civil servants. They sent their children to formal educational institutions with the proceeds from the sale of agricultural produce. They accessed funds from financial institutions to support their farm inputs, and used the medical facilities available in their locality while also relying on traditional or alternative medicines.

This empirical evidence advances the kind of economic thinking that is best suited to Nigeria. Would it make sense to crystallize this socio-economic experience into benchmarks and variables, with numbers attached to them? How best do we measure this culturally grounded circumstance other than through ethnographic studies? Would the Eurocentric neo-classical economic theories be of any use? Viewing these issues from these perspectives requires a completely new approach, one that is founded on the new and emerging economic thinking of integral development economics.

Integral Development Economics

Development economics may be seen as distinct from conventional neo-classical economics, as well as political economy. It is mainly applicable to under-developed or developing economies 'with varying ideological orientations, diverse cultural backgrounds, and very complex similar economic problems that usually demand new ideas and novel approaches' (Todaro and Smith 2009, p. 7). It is imperative that development economics also consider issues of socio-cultural, ethno-religious, political and very traditional elements from local economic perspectives. The theories of Marx and Keynes argue for government-engineered economic transformation where accurate information is gathered, rather than leaving development in the hands of market forces. Hettne (1995) mentioned that development should involve structural transformation with recognition of cultural, political, social and economic changes. He also referred to Marx, who maintained that capitalism is the first stage of any development before socialism can be applied, and that the failings of capitalism thwart the development of just and sustainable economies. Todaro and Smith also observed that the heterogeneity of the under-developed economies with their complex development processes would require the combination of other relevant concepts and theories from traditional economic analysis and considering the development process experiences of Africa, Asia and Latin America. Cypher and Dietz (2009) stress that 'this specialized field is mainly about regime change and search for optimal growth path or at least superior to the existing allocation of resources and current efficiency levels'. Hettne (1995) observes that the development economic model would suffer if no political structure was willing to support it. Development economics is expected to integrate political economy rooted in sociology, politics and law (Amadi 2008, p. 3), while Debraj (2007) asserted that this field of economics that studied the developing world made good use of economic theory, econometrics and social anthropology. They observed that two similar developing societies could evolve along different lines depending on past expectations, aspirations or actual history. In other words, Nigeria's development pattern will be different from that of Ghana even though they are both West African states with similarities in specific ethnic groups, and a very huge difference will also exist between Nigeria and South Africa because socio-cultural perceptions and the influences of colonialism or apartheid are absolutely different. Exactly the same economic development model may not work for these countries, but they may be quite similar when compared to Latin American economies. A country like Nigeria thus requires its own model, which would also serve as a guide for other sub-Saharan African countries. This overall model may perhaps be termed 'The Nigerian Socio-political and Economic Structure'.

Nigeria's economic growth and development pattern have been shaped by several interrelated social, political and economic forces from the days of colonialism to the present-day neo-patrimonial democratic structure. Whatever economic model Nigeria adopts will still be affected by the performance of governance indicators, including overall performance of development indicators with particular reference to GNI per capita and GDP, as well as the country's business environment and competitiveness in individual states. Figure 2.3 shows Nigeria's socio-political and economic structure, which highlights the principal indicators promoting poverty and unemployment in the country. Thus, whether Nigeria adopts a fully fledged Modernization Theory Model, a Dependency Theory Model, a Work System Model or the Islamic economic system, it will still be affected by the performance of governance indicators, development indicators, and the realities of 'business environment and competitiveness across Nigerian states' (BECANS; Eboh and Lemchi 2010). Poverty and unemployment are caught up in the interplay of these three overwhelming factors. Todaro and Smith (2009, p. 554) observe that ineffective government leads to market failure and a restriction of a country's ability to achieve economic development. Good governance indicators here include voice and accountability, political stability, government effectiveness, regulatory quality, rule of law and control of corruption (Kaufmann et al. 2008). Development indicators are limited to GNI per capita (atlas method – current US$) and GDP (current US$). BECANS indicators, as designed by Eboh and Lemchi and his co-researchers, include infrastructure and utilities, regulatory services, business development support, investment promotion and security. Addressing the lack of appropriate governance must be a priority for international organizations as it affects other development issues such as poverty, unemployment and a gap in co-ordination of services.

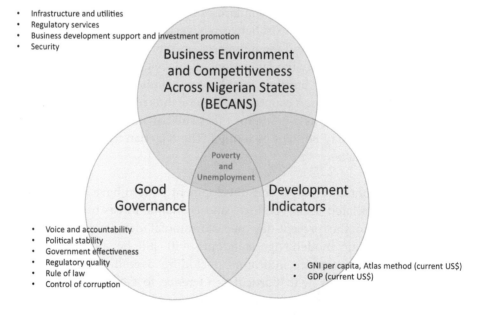

Figure 2.3   The Nigerian socio-political and economic structure
Source: Oshodi (2012b, 2012c).

Good Governance

The World Bank and IMF (2006) identified three broad categories on which 'good governance' can be based:

1. **state/bureaucratic capability** – this includes issues related to financial management and public administration;

2. **accountability and oversight of institutions to promote checks and balances** – this includes issues related to voice and accountability, transparency, the role of the media and civil society, the rule of law, executive constraints and democratic representation and participation;

3. **overall performance** – this includes control of corruption, service delivery, and policy outcomes.

The World Bank has been more concerned about the positive effect good governance might have on poverty reduction, especially in sub-Saharan Africa, in line with the Millennium Development Goals as contained in the Poverty Reduction Strategy Papers. The World Bank's governance indicators are: voice and accountability, political stability and violence, government effectiveness, regulatory burden, rule of law and control of corruption. The United Nations Economic and Social Commission for Asia and the Pacific views governance as the process of decision-making and the process by which decisions are implemented (or not implemented). On the other hand, the major characteristics attributed to good governance are: it is participatory, consensus-oriented, accountable, transparent, responsive, effective/efficient, equitable, inclusive and follows the rule of law. It ensures that corruption is minimized, the views of minorities are taken into account, and that the voices of the most vulnerable in society are heard in decision-making, while also being cognizant of the present and future needs of society.

Manor (2000) observed that the devolution of formal political authority could enhance the transparency, responsiveness and accountability of government for people at the local level. Johnson and Start (2001) felt that governments should create 'market rights that provide the poor with an opportunity to engage in market relations, but not necessarily the benefits that markets would provide'. Kaufmann et al. (2006) measured governance using the World Bank's indicators and observed that 60 per cent of all cross-country comparisons resulted in highly significant differences, and that nearly one third of countries had experienced substantial changes in at least one dimension of governance between 1996 and 2006. They observed that previous difficulties in measuring the complicated issues of governance have in recent times improved in Nigeria.

Kaufmann (2004) finds that governance constraints, and corruption in particular, are a key determinant of a country's global competitiveness. According to Grindle (2002), the issue of good governance calls for improvements in virtually all aspects of the public sector. Particular areas in need of improvement are: institutions which set the rules of the game for economic and political interaction; the decision-making structures which determine priorities among public problems and allocate resources to respond to those problems; organizations that manage administrative systems and deliver good services to citizens; human resources that staff government bureaucracies, and finally, the interface of officials and citizens in political and bureaucratic arenas. Grindle (2002) perceived that governance issues should be country-specific and that realistic strategies needed to be in place to gradually implement these rather broad elements in a bid to reduce poverty. Grindle (2002) further noted that concern with good governance in the Poverty Reduction Strategy Papers often lacked depth in delineating a clear diagnosis with clearly relevant remedies. The World Bank identified six main indicators which are used to measure good governance across countries. The review adopts the World Bank's definitions, which are from various sources. These definitions are extracts from World Bank research titled *Governance Matters VI: Aggregate and Individual Indicators 1996–2006* (Kaufmann et al. 2007).

VOICE AND ACCOUNTABILITY

The Bertelsman Foundation (in Kaufmann et al. 2006) measured voice and accountability with a country's stateness, political participation, stability of democratic institutions, and political and social integration. The OECD Development Centre (in Kaufmann et al. 2006) observed that voice and accountability are best measured by hardening of a regime. The Economist Intelligence Unit (in Kaufmann et al. 2006) measured the indicator with orderly transfers, vested interest, accountability of public officials, human rights and freedom of association. Freedom House (in Kaufmann et al. 2006) favoured political rights and civil liberties. The World Economic Forum (in Kaufmann et al. 2006) identified government transparency on policies, freedom of the press, ethical contract awards, no influence of the legal system on political issues, and effectiveness of the national parliament/congress. Global Integrity (in Kaufmann et al. 2006) noted that the subject could be measured with six variables: civil society organizations, media, public access to information, voting and citizen participation, election integrity and political financing. Gallup (in Kaufmann et al. 2006) simply asserted that confidence in honesty of elections is appropriate to measure the subject.

The University of Binghamton Cingranelli-Richards Human Rights Database (CIRI) and University of North Carolina Political Terror Scale (PTS) (in Kaufmann et al. 2006) identified restrictions on domestic and foreign travel; freedom of political participation; imprisonment because of ethnicity, race or political and religious beliefs, and government censorship as ways to measure voice and accountability. The International Fund for Agricultural Development (in Kaufmann et al. 2006) identified policy and legal framework for rural organization, and dialogue between government and rural organizations. Latinobarometro (in Kaufmann et al. 2006) mentioned satisfaction with democracy and trust in parliament. The International Budget Project (in Kaufmann et al. 2006) identified open budget initiatives as the measure for the subject. Political Risk Services (in Kaufmann et al. 2006) disregarded the military in politics and stressed democratic accountability, which should show government responsiveness to the people in free and fair elections and the ability of government to remain popular. The Institute for Management Development (in Kaufmann et al. 2006) said it was measured in terms of transparency of government policy. Global Insight (in Kaufmann et al. 2006) identified (1) institutional performance – assessment of how mature and well established the political system is, and how far political opposition operates within and outside the system, and (2) responsiveness – how well the population and organized interests can make their voices heard in the political system where representation is fairly and effectively handled.

POLITICAL STABILITY

Business Environment Risk Intelligence (in Kaufmann et al. 2006) identified several indices that best measure political stability, which surrounds the political risk index. This includes: dependence on/importance to a hostile major power; negative influences of regional political forces; social conditions such as wealth, distribution and population; factionalization of the political spectrum and the power of those factions; factionalization by language, ethnic and/or religious groups and the power these possess; the restrictive (coercive) measures required to retain power; the organization and strength of forces for a radical government; societal conflict involving demonstrations, strikes and street violence, and the instability which results from non-constitutional changes, assassinations and guerrilla wars.

On political stability, Global Insight (in Kaufmann et al. 2006) mapped out an analysis that illustrates the effects of domestic risk varying with a country's GDP. It observed that a military coup d'état reduces the GDP growth rate by 2 per cent during any 12-month period; an increase in scope or intensity of one or more insurgencies/rebellions reduces the GDP growth rate by 3 per cent during any 12-month period, and an increase in scope or intensity of terrorism reduces the GDP growth rate by 1 per cent during any 12-month period. A political assassination or similar event reduces the GDP growth rate by 1 per cent during any 12-month period. An increase in scope or intensity of one or more civil wars reduces the GDP growth rate by 4 per cent during any 12-month period. An increase in scope, intensity or frequency of rioting reduces the GDP growth rate by 1 per cent during any 12-month period.

The Political Risk Services International Country Risk Guide (in Kaufmann et al. 2006) identified government stability, internal conflict, external conflict and ethnic tensions as the main measures of political stability. Global Insight Business Risk and Conditions (in Kaufmann et al. 2006) identified civil or political unrest as threats to investors, and the number of sources of terrorism which may target or affect businesses.

GOVERNMENT EFFECTIVENESS

On the issue of government effectiveness, the World Bank (in Kaufmann et al. 2006), the African Development Bank (in Kaufmann et al. 2006) and the Asian Development Bank (in Kaufmann et al. 2006) identified policies to improve efficiency of the public sector, budget management, efficiency of public expenditure and the management of public debt as measures. The Business Environment and Enterprise Performance Survey (in Kaufmann et al. 2006) stressed the effect telecommunication, electricity and transportation have on the growth of businesses. The Bertelsmann Transformation Index (in Kaufmann et al. 2006) identified consensus-building, governance capability and the effective use of resources as ways to measure government effectiveness. Global Insight (in Kaufmann et al. 2006) associated measures with domestic political risk, and further observed that an increase in the government's personnel turnover rate at senior levels reduces the GDP growth rate by 2 per cent during any 12-month period. In the same vein, a decline in government personnel quality at any level, and a deterioration of government capacity to cope with national problems because of institutional rigidity of gridlock, reduce the GDP growth rate by 1 per cent each during any 12-month period. The Economist Intelligence Unit (in Kaufmann et al. 2006) identified quality of bureaucracy/ institutional effectiveness and excessive bureaucracy/red tape as measures of the subject. The World Economic Forum (in Kaufmann et al. 2006) identified the following measures: competence of public sector personnel; quality of the general infrastructure; quality of public schools; time spent by senior management dealing with government officials; public service vulnerability to political pressure, and wasteful government expenditure. The Institute for Management Development (in Kaufmann et al. 2006) measured government effectiveness based on the following: the rate at which governments adopted economic policies to fluctuations in the economy; whether or not public services were independent from political interference; whether the implementation of government decisions was effective or not; whether government bureaucracy negatively or positively affected business activities; whether or not the distribution infrastructure was efficient in delivering goods and services; whether or not the political system could meet the present economic challenges they were facing, and finally, consistency in the direction of policies.

REGULATORY QUALITY

Both the African Development Bank (in Kaufmann et al. 2006) and the Asian Development Bank (in Kaufmann et al. 2006) measured regulatory quality with trade policy, competitive environment, labour market policies/factor and product markets. The World Bank and European Bank for Reconstruction and Development (in Kaufmann et al. 2006) identified information about and interpretation of laws and regulations; unpredictability of changes of regulations, and the effect of labour regulation, tax regulation, custom, foreign currency and trade regulation on growth of businesses. Global Insight (in Kaufmann et al. 2006), which analysed the factors surrounding regulatory quality, observed a 2 per cent reduction each in export/import volume due to worsening in the export/import restriction/regulation during any 12-month period depending on assessment time. The European Bank for Reconstruction and Development (in Kaufmann et al. 2006) measured the subject with liberalization, trade and the foreign exchange system, and competition policy. The Economist Intelligence Unit (in Kaufmann et al. 2006) identified unfair competitive practices, price controls, discriminatory tariffs, excessive protections and discriminatory taxes.

The World Economic Forum (in Kaufmann et al. 2006) measured regulatory quality with the following indices: burdensome administrative regulations;

discriminatory tax system; import barriers/cost of tariffs as obstacles to growth; limited competition in local markets; ease of starting a company; ineffective anti-monopoly policies; negative effect of competitiveness on environmental regulations; artificial effect of government subsidies on industry, and the complexity of the tax system. The Heritage Foundation (in Kaufmann et al. 2006) measured the subject with foreign investment and banking/finance activities. The World Bank (in Kaufmann et al. 2006) identified the business regulatory environment, manufacturing and products markets and trade policy. Political Risk Services (in Kaufmann et al. 2006) looked at government's attitude towards investment, which included risk to operations, taxation, repatriation and labour costs. The Institute for Management Development (in Kaufmann et al. 2006) measured regulatory quality with exchange rate policy, protectionism, competition legislation, price control, legal regulation, access of foreign financial institutions to the domestic market, foreign and domestic access to the capital market, competitive advantage, legal framework, public sector contracts, personal/corporate taxes, political system agenda, labour regulations, and the effects of legislation and subsidies on economic development.

RULE OF LAW

Afrobarometer (in Kaufmann et al. 2006) measured the rule of law with fear of crime at home and trust in the courts of law and police. The Asian Development Bank (in Kaufmann et al. 2006) identified issues of property rights as the main measure of the subject. The World Bank and European Bank for Reconstruction and Development (in Kaufmann et al. 2006) identified the court system as it related to being fair, affordable, enforceable, honest and quick to protect property rights, and the effect of organized crime, the judiciary and street crime on businesses. Business Environment Risk Intelligence (in Kaufmann et al. 2006) identified enforcement of contracts, direct financial fraud, money laundering and organized crime. Global Insight (in Kaufmann et al. 2006) identified losses and costs of crime; scope, intensity or frequency of kidnapping of foreigners, which reduces the GDP growth rate by 1 per cent during any 12-month period, and enforceability of government contracts and private contracts. The Economist Intelligence Unit (in Kaufmann et al. 2006) measured rule of law with violent crime, organized crime, fairness of the judicial process, enforceability of contracts, speediness of judicial process, confiscation/ expropriation, intellectual property rights protection, and private property protection. The World Economic Forum (in Kaufmann et al. 2006) identified the additional costs that common and organized crime impose on businesses, money laundering issues, quality of the police, influence of the political structure, citizen and firms on the judiciary, legality of government actions, and official/unregistered firms and tax evasion. Global Integrity (in Kaufmann et al. 2006) identified executive accountability, judicial accountability, rule of law and law enforcement as measures of rule of law. The International Fund for Agricultural Development (in Kaufmann et al. 2006) identified access to land and water for agriculture. Political Risk Services (in Kaufmann et al. 2006) identified law and order. The former is 'an assessment of the strength and impartiality of the legal system while the latter is an assessment of popular observance of the law'. The Institute for Management Department (in Kaufmann et al. 2006) identified tax evasion, justice, and personal and private property security, insider trading, and patent and copyright protection. Global Insight (in Kaufmann et al. 2006) measured the subject with judicial independence and crime. The former is the ability of the state and outside actors to influence or distort the legal system, which affects expected investment; the latter has to do with how businesses are damaged by crimes such as kidnapping, extortion, street violence and burglary, as they affect foreign investors.

CONTROL OF CORRUPTION

The World Bank and European Bank for Reconstruction and Development (in Kaufmann et al. 2006) measured corruption based on the following indices: irregular/unofficial additional payments firms pay to public officials to get things done, the frequency of these unofficial payments, and the consequence of unofficial payments imposed by public officials. Transparency International (in Kaufmann et al. 2006) identified frequency of corruption, frequency of household bribery, and the extent of major and petty corruption. The World Economic Forum (in Kaufmann et al. 2006) identified: public trust in the financial honesty of politicians, the extent to which legal contributions to political parties are misused by politicians, diversion of public funds due to corruption, the frequency of extra payments made by firms for public utilities, tax payments, loan applications, the awarding of public contracts that influence law, policy regulations, decrees and favourable judicial decisions, and finally, illegal firm-imposed extra payments used to influence governmental policies. The World Bank (in Kaufmann et al. 2006) identified transparency, accountability and corruption in the public sector. Political Risk Services (in Kaufmann et al. 2006) measured corruption within the political system, as it distorts the economic and financial environment, reduces the efficiency of government and business and leads to inherent instability in the political system. Global Insight (in Kaufmann et al. 2006) saw corruption as 'an assessment of the intrusiveness of the country's bureaucracy'. This is about the degree of red tape and the activities of corrupt officials and other groups.

The Good Enough Governance Agenda

Grindle (2002) proposed a 'good enough' governance agenda, which seeks to promote government reforms in a more realistic way and focuses on improving governance in those areas that matter most for the overall development process. She emphasized the following:

- Minimal conditions of governance are required to allow political and economic development to happen.

- Elements of different regimes may work for different reasons, and those aspects that work should be encouraged.

- Legitimacy should not be seen in absolute terms, and varies considerably even within a specified state.

- There needs to be concern for incremental, progressive change and ways in which reformers can institute change with regard to what alliances need to be built and what trade-offs need to be made.

- The state should intervene to produce core public goods, and where it can perform well, but should not tackle a wide range of issues, reforms and so on at once. Priorities for state intervention/ involvement are important, and some level of state capture may be tolerated to achieve other goals.

- There are no moral absolutes, thus implementation is likely to be patchy and uneven.

- It is important to recognize what is working, rather than focusing mainly on governance gaps and action on the ground in the contextual realities of a specific economy.

This concept is seen as a more realistic alternative to the World Bank-championed good governance imposed on countries without acknowledging current country-specific socio-political and economic circumstances. Good enough governance means that interventions believed to contribute to economic and political development need to be questioned, prioritized and made relevant to the conditions of individual countries (Grindle 2005). Grindle further mentioned that the concept directs attention to the minimal conditions that governance should put in place to allow the mechanism of industrialization to be set in motion. Stern (1991) observed that the state's role should not necessarily focus on production, but rather on health, education, protection of the poor, the infrastructure and providing the right environment for entrepreneurial activity to flourish. Killick (1990) raised the issue that minimal governmental interventions may constitute what the government does best. The types of policy instruments that would give governments a comparative advantage should be assessed. Rodrik (2004) referred to the good enough governance agenda when he stressed that developing countries may initially only need some improvements in their institutional environments in order to set growth in motion. Court and Hyden (2001) have shown that corruption as such does not present an insurmountable obstacle to development. They went further to point out that a number of states have achieved considerable developmental success despite serious problems with corruption.

In the contemporary world, fostering economic transformation and guaranteeing minimal levels of welfare are necessary (Evans 1995). Evans also tried to bridge the gap between developmental states and predatory states which results in an intermediate state with some semblance of bureaucratic organization, but without the degree of corporate coherence enjoyed by development states. Kohli (2004) observed that the relationship between state and economic development should at least achieve 'some minimal level of development probably necessary for the construction of modern states'. He further mentioned that 'cohesive-capitalist states' are ideological and their organizational characteristics help to define goals narrowly, and therefore 'concentrate resources on a narrow set of priorities'. Oshodi (2009) showed that good governance indicators directly affect the performance of development indicators in Nigeria and India, hence the need to further appraise the make-up of two major development indicators, GDP and GNI.

Development Indicators in Nigeria

Nigeria and the international community have mainly adopted the quantitative economic growth indicators described below to measure economic growth, and assume that increased economic growth will have a positive effect on poverty and inequality reduction where 'pro-poor' policies are developed in tandem with economic growth. The Nigerian socio-political and economic model in Figure 2.3 focuses on GDP and GNI as two important development indicators within the realm of classical economic theory as acknowledged by Western-designed international organizations. GDP is the aggregate market value of goods and services produced in a country in a given year, including the aggregate of all expenditure that year, such as consumption expenditure by households, investment expenditure by businesses, government expenditure and net exports (exports less imports), using the expenditure approach (flow of product). Using the income approach (flow of cost), GDP is calculated as the aggregate of all income earned in a year, such as wages earned by workers, rent earned by property owners, interest earned by lenders and profits earned by firms. Nominal GDP is measured in actual market prices; real GDP measures the volume of goods and services, adjusted for inflation, and is used for comparisons between countries. Thus, GDP measures all that a country produces internally regardless of who produces it. GDP measures the total value for final use of output produced by an economy, by both residents and non-residents.

GNI, on the other hand, is the value of a country's income and that of its people, derived as GDP plus net receipts of primary income – that is, compensation of employees and property income from abroad. Thus, it is the total income earned by a country either inside or outside the country. Todaro and Smith (2009, p. 14) see GNI as a traditional economic measure of development where growth of income per capita is used to determine a nation's ability to expand its output at a rate faster than the growth rate of its population. They further mention that 'levels and rates of growth of "real" per capita GNI (monetary growth of GNI per capita minus the rate of inflation) are used to measure the overall economic well-being of a population' in terms of how much real goods and services are available to the average citizen for consumption and investment. Todaro and Smith (2009, pp. 43–6) review the World Bank's income-based country classification using GNI to measure the overall level of economic activities, which is often used as a summary index of the relative economic well-being of people in different nations. GNI is 'calculated as the total domestic and foreign value added claimed by a country's residents without making deductions for depreciation (or wearing out) of the domestic capital stock' (Todaro and Smith 2009). GNI comprises GDP plus the differences between the income residents receive from abroad for factor service (labour and capital less payments made to non-residents who contribute to the domestic economy) (Todaro and Smith 2009).

Table 2.1   Economic development indicators

Development Indicators	2000	2005	2007	2008
Population, total (millions)	124.77	141.36	147.98	151.32
Population growth (annual %)	2.6	2.4	2.2	2.2
GNI, Atlas method (current US$ billions)	33.45	87.69	143.29	175.62
GNI per capita, Atlas method (current US$)	270	620	970	1,160
GNI, PPP (current international US$ billions)	140.77	215.51	274.28	293.10

Source: Derived from World Bank development indicators.

Table 2.1 shows that Nigeria's population growth rate reduced from 2.6 per cent in 2000 to 2.2 per cent in 2008, while GNI per capita (Atlas method in current US$) was at a very low level of US$270 in 2000 and increased dramatically to US$1,160 in 2008, thereby propelling Nigeria from a low-income economy to a low-middle-income economy. The GDP growth rate was highest in 2007 at 6.4 per cent, with a high figure of US$212.08 billion in 2008.

Figure 2.4 and Table 2.2 show Nigeria's GDP and GNI performance from independence in 1960 to date. These two indicators underwent a slight rise around 1980 and started to skyrocket by 2005. What caused this sharp increase? Was it relative political stability? Did good governance indicators perform better, influencing development indicators? Did confidence grow among local and foreign investors? Did the country generally produce more? Did debt forgiveness by the international community contribute to it? Did this GDP/GNI performance have any significant link with real poverty reduction among the majority in Nigeria? Does the country still require an integral economic development model to further accelerate development indicators, or can it do without it? Should more efforts be devoted to issues related to basic neo-liberal and Keynesian economic theories in a manner that addresses specific challenges of poverty reduction? Olusegun Obasanjo, Nigeria's president from 1999 to 2007, implied in 2007 that the full scope of GDP in Nigeria and most African countries was inadequately captured because of unknown socio-economic structures in this region (Oshodi 2010). Obasanjo's views require further analysis.

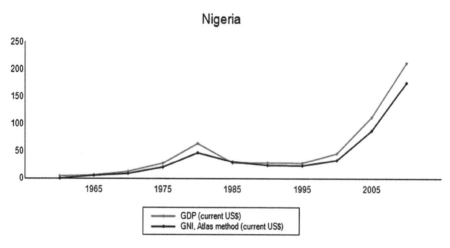

Figure 2.4   Nigeria's 50-year GDP–GNI relationship
Source: Derived from World Bank Development Indicators.
Scale: US$ billions.

Table 2.2   Nigeria's 50-year GDP–GNI relationship

	1960	1965	1970	1975	1980	1985	1990	1995	2000	2005	2008
GDP (current US$)	4.20	5.87	12.55	27.78	64.20	28.41	28.47	28.11	45.98	112.25	212.08
GNI, Atlas method (current US$)	—	5.58	8.91	20.78	47.18	30.46	24.15	23.59	33.45	87.69	175.62

Source: Derived from World Bank development indicators.

The BECANS Model

The good governance and development indicators are World Bank-driven research, and largely look at overall country performance. Business Environment and Competitiveness Across Nigerian States (BECANS), on the other hand, is Nigeria-specific research conducted by a local research team, which rated individual states in Nigeria based on the BECANS benchmark. The indicators in the BECANS model include infrastructure and utilities, regulatory services, business development support, investment promotions and security.

These indicators or dimensions are called the BECANS benchmark. The objective of BECANS is to promote evidence-based reform of Nigeria's business environment, thereby focusing on sub-national jurisdiction (Eboh and Lemchi 2010, p. 7). The concept of BECANS is based on the premise that the responsibility for shaping the country's business environment is shared between the three tiers of government: federal, state and local. States and local government in Nigeria provide and manage basic public amenities such as roads, water supply, sanitation, primary healthcare and other social welfare provision. States in the country are more specifically responsible for property allocation and registration, tax administration, contract enforcement and the administration of justice, to mention just a few areas. Eboh and Lemchi observed that without commensurate business environment reforms within individual states and local government, the macroeconomic and institutional reforms of Nigeria's federal government structure would not produce the desired impact on employment and poverty.

The BECANS model seeks to tackle the security challenge in Nigeria since it largely affects the country's ability to encourage more business activities and thus create more employment in Nigerian states. Eboh, Lemchi and their co-researchers examined the Nigerian business environment index in 2007 (known as BECANS-I) and post-2007 (known as BECAN-II), comparing the relationship or performance of the overall BECANS dimension or benchmark.

According to Eboh and Lemchi (2010, p. 23), business environment denotes the full range of public policies, institutions, regulations and administrative systems within which people and firms operate. They stressed that the government's provision of necessary social services largely affects the management, productivity and competitiveness of each firm, and its ability to make and implement decisions. The research team felt strongly that creating a conducive business environment in Nigeria would have a huge impact on job creation considering the fact that the majority of employment providers in the country are small-scale businesses that have been the worst hit by the poor business environment. They observe further that two thirds of Nigerians live and work in rural areas where they struggle with intermittent electricity supply, inadequate or inaccessible roads, poor or no water supply and ineffective public services, which generally hurt the livelihoods of rural people. More specifically, Eboh and Lemchi lamented that a 'bad business environment is the reason for the slow progress of economic diversification to the non-oil sector in Nigeria and is the main factor affecting why real growth improvement in the past half-decade has not reduced employment, poverty and the living standard of Nigerians'.

Eboh and Lemchi (2010, p. 24) identified the key task of BECANS as follows:

- Develop a model of benchmarks and indicators for assessing the business environment at the state level.

- Collect and scrutinize empirical data for evaluating the benchmark and indicators.

- Apply the data on the benchmarks and indicators to gauge the performance of individual states.

- Prepare and disseminate a business environment scorecard of Nigerian states, including associated reports and policy briefs.

- Facilitate the use of business environment scorecards/reports in policy dialogue and advocacy.

- Promote the use of the business environment scorecards/reports as an evidence base for state government to prioritize reforms.

- Provide regular feedback on the business environment at the state level.

Eboh and Lemchi reviewed relevant literature relating to the concept of the business environment and competitiveness in a bid to justify the underlying reason for the developing the BECANS indicators. They referred to Gareth (2004, in Eboh and Lemchi 2010), who paid attention to the range of policy, regulation, legal and institutional factors incentivizing the private sector to promote economic activities. The World Bank (in Kaufmann et al. 2006), Oshodi (2009), Grindle (2002) and Khan (2005) attributed private sector performance to overall governance matters. Kohli (2004), Evans (1995), Fritz and Menocal (2006), Hellman et al. (2000), Johnson and Start (2001), Joseph (1983) and You and Khagram (2005) preferred state efforts to direct the business environment, but feared state capture, which is common in developing states. The *World Development Report* also stressed sound governmental policies as determinants of an effective business environment. Eboh and Lemchi (2010, p. 26) further observed that while microeconomic stability is a precondition for sustained growth, a country's economic competitiveness is beyond fixing inflation, interest rates and fiscal deficits. Eboh and Lemchi attributed external and internal factors as responsible for business environment performance, hence affecting economic growth, poverty reduction and sustainable development. The external factors affecting firms include the infrastructure, regulations, labour markets and microeconomic policies such as monetary, fiscal and financial measures, while the internal factors are managerial skills, entrepreneurship ability and cost.

More specifically, Nigeria's poor business environment has led to stagnated real economic development even though the GDP–GNI relationship illustrated in Figure 2.4 shows improvement in economic growth. UNIDO (2002) observed that the productivity of Nigerian workers was only 10 per cent of that in Botswana, and 50 per cent of that in Ghana and Kenya. Eboh and Lemchi referred to similar research conducted by Iarossi et al. (2009) which showed that labour productivity, measured by the average value added per worker in the manufacturing sector, was about US$3,980 for Nigeria, compared to US$24,938 for South Africa, US$13,504 for Brazil, US$11,607 for China and US$13,078 for Kenya. Iarossi et al.'s research also showed that in Nigeria, a 1 per cent increase in productivity (measured in terms of total factor productivity) led to a 0.41 per cent increase in employment. This shows the need to improve the business environment for individual firms in order to reduce unemployment and poverty. Eboh and Lemchi estimated that one in five Nigerians were unemployed, and Iarossi et al. (2009) mentioned that only 10 per cent of the 6 million new entrants into the country's job market found a job, and that employment growth had been unable to keep pace with expansion in economic activities in the key sectors during 2000–2007.

Poverty in Nigeria

The World Bank ranked countries based on their GNI per capita, then further classified them as: low-income countries, lower-middle-income countries, upper-middle-income countries, high-income Organization for Economic Cooperation and Development (OECD) countries and other high-income countries. Countries with a GNI per capita of US$875 or less are low-income countries, those with a GNI per capita of US$876–3,465 are lower-middle-income countries, those with a GNI per capita of US$3,466–10,725 are upper-middle-income countries and those with a GNI per capita of US$10,726 or more are high-income countries, with a few countries classified as 'other high-income' economies. Todaro and Smith (2009) noted that there are special distinctions for upper-middle-income or newly high-income economies with advanced manufacturing sectors as newly industrialized countries.

This neo-liberal school of thought perceives that the higher a country's GNI, the more likely it is that it will rise out of poverty. Whether or not this notion is feasible in Africa is an argument that is examined in Chapter 5. Figure 2.4 demonstrates the 50-year GDP–GNI relationship in Nigeria, with the performance showing that these two development indicators started to improve dramatically from 2002, although in-depth interview analysis and the comments from Nigerians above show that poverty has not reduced much in Nigeria. How can poverty best be measured in Africa, and in Nigeria specifically? The World Bank measures poverty by the percentage of a country's population that lives on less than US$1 per day. This US$1 is not based on the conventional conversion rate, but rather on purchasing power parity (PPP). Todaro and Smith (2009, p. 46) asserted that this is 'calculated using a common set of international prices for all goods and services produced, valuing goods in all countries at US prices'. They further defined it as 'the number of units of a foreign country's currency required purchasing the identical quantity of goods and services in the local market as US$1 would buy in the United States'.

The UN Development Programme coined the Human Poverty Index (HPI), based on three goals or the end product of development: longevity is measured by life expectancy at birth; knowledge is measured by a weighted average of adult literacy (two thirds) along with mean years of schooling (one third), and standard of living is measured by real per capita GDP adjusted for the differing PPP of each country's current currency, reflecting the cost of living and considering the assumption of diminishing marginal utility of income (Todaro and Smith 2009). In other words, HPI is measured in terms of 'life' (the fraction of people unlikely to live beyond 40 years of age), of basic 'education' (measured by the percentage of adults who are illiterate) and of overall 'economic provisioning' (measured by the percentage of people without access to safe water plus the percentage of children who are underweight for their age).

Real poverty in Nigeria or among the Nigerian people is defined in several ways, mainly being appraised within the context of classical economic theories where benchmarks are measured against several indicators. This book examines some of these quantitative figures and identifies some real-life and rather qualitative perceptions of poverty, drawing on data from the Nigerian Bureau of Statistics (NBS), the African Institute for Applied Economics (AIAE) and other international institutions. Ajakaiye and Adeyeye (2001, in Eboh and Lemchi 2009) saw Nigerians living on two thirds of the mean monthly household expenditure of poverty. The Access to Financial Services in Nigeria survey conducted by Enhancing Financial Innovation and Access (EFInA 2010) reviewed poverty in the country by examining personal monthly income. It found that the average monthly income of Nigerians was less than NGN 8,000 (US$53), while 39 per cent of the population either indicated 'no income' or 'refused to answer'. It also found that 34 per cent of those who earned less than NGN 5,000 (US$33) per month were from the north-west, while 40 per cent of those who earned over NGN 100,000 (US$666) per month were from the south-south. EFInA also found that 46 per cent of the adult population represented the most asset-poor in the country on of a ten-tier living standard measure (LSM).

POVERTY OF SOCIAL INFRASTRUCTURE AND PHYSICAL INFRASTRUCTURE

There are several kinds of poverty that affect Nigerian households, individuals, states and geopolitical zones. There is however a unique kind of poverty that affects Nigerians with low incomes, middle incomes and high incomes – infrastructural poverty. The country suffers from years of infrastructural decay and outright lack of essential amenities. Infrastructure can be divided into two broad categories: social infrastructure and physical infrastructure. Social infrastructure includes investment in education and health, and is thus more relevant to the goal of poverty reduction than physical infrastructure (Jerome and Ariyo 2004, in Eboh and Lemchi 2009; Jahan and McCleery 2005, in Eboh and Lemchi 2009; Ogun, in Eboh and Lemchi 2009), according to one school of thought. A second school of thought considers that a combination of social and physical infrastructure is necessary to achieve poverty reduction, while a third school of thought maintains that investment in infrastructure has no effect on poverty reduction (Ogun, in Eboh and Lemchi 2009), based on the theoretical position that investment in infrastructure is necessary for economic growth, but has little relevance to poverty reduction. It also considers that actual infrastructural benefits are significantly lower than are anticipated. Finally, it believes that predatory governance structures and institutions in developing countries with corrupt leaders do not make concrete infrastructural investment decisions, thereby lowering the contribution to growth that will benefit the poor (Ali and Pernia 2003, in Eboh and Lemchi 2009). In particular, the patrimonial leadership structure in Nigeria encourages leaders to over-price infrastructural projects so that they can enjoy huge rent from these contracts. Hence, corrupt actors absorb far more than 50 per cent of the infrastructural projects or contract costs.

In their BECANS model, Eboh and Lemchi (2010) measured social infrastructure using the following indicators: primary school enrolment, number of students per teacher, approved capital budget for education as a percentage of the total capital budget for a particular year, approved capital budget for health as a percentage of the total capital budget for a particular year, infant mortality rate, HIV prevalence among pregnant women aged 15–24, number of patients per doctor and the proportion of the population with access to improved sanitation in both urban and rural settings. Eboh and Lemchi (2010) regarded physical infrastructure as 'infrastructures and utilities', believing that improving access to infrastructure is very important for poverty reduction since it promotes job creation. They also noted that inadequate infrastructure and utilities such as energy, transport, communications, water and sanitation constrain the productivity, growth and competitiveness of firms.

Eboh and Lemchi's research illustrated the performance of geopolitical, zones and states on their respective benchmarks and measures. The highest-performing geopolitical region in Nigeria was the south-west, while the north-west was the lowest-performing. Oyo State in the south-west was the highest-performing state, while Zamfara in the north-west was the lowest-performing. The infrastructure and utilities benchmark classed the south-west as the highest-performing geopolitical zone, while the north-west was the lowest-performing. In the same vein, Delta State in the south-south geopolitical zone was the highest-performing state, while Kebbi State in the north-west was the lowest-performing.

Unemployment in Nigeria

The International Labour Organization (ILO) defines the unemployed as members of the economically active population who are out of work but available for and seeking it, including people who have lost their jobs and those who have voluntarily left work (World Bank 1998, p. 63, in Obadan and Odusola 2000). Unemployment is defined as individuals seeking jobs remaining unemployed, and is expressed as a percentage of the total available workforce.[1] One in five Nigerians are unemployed, and only 10 per cent of the 6 million new entrants into the country's job market find employment (Iarossi et al. 2009, in Eboh and Lemchi 2010). Nigeria's 'economy recorded 7.5 per cent expansion in 2011 that was faster than the global and regional average, this growth, which did not impact positively on the lives of the majority, might neither improve the employment rate and living standards of Nigerians in 2012' (Nnodim 2012). In the same vein, 'recent data from the National Bureau of Statistics placed the

---

1   http://www.investorwords.com/5838/unemployment.html (accessed 9 September 2013).

country's misery index at 34 per cent, a development which analysts described as 'horrible and terrifying"' (Nnodim 2012). Employed Nigerians are still exposed to poverty, spending two thirds of their mean monthly earnings on household expenditure (Ajakaiye and Adeyeye 2001, in Eboh and Lemchi 2009).

There are several neo-liberal data sets on unemployment in Nigeria which show trends over a period just like those of many other development indicators, but this book will examine qualitative research conducted by EFInA in 2011. EFInA commissioned Real Edge Research Options to examine the low-income population in Nigeria and to develop ways to encourage financial institutions to provide appropriate and affordable financial products that would best suit their needs. In February 2011, 28 focus groups of approximately 10 people each (a combined total of 271 respondents) were sampled from the six geopolitical zones of Lagos, Benin, Enugu, Kaduna, Nasarawa and Yola. The research showed that the respondents included those employed in the formal and informal sectors as well as those unemployed. The following respondent discussions are extracted directly from EFInA's publication on the research findings.

A respondent from Benin, a male aged 26–40, asserted: 'I work as an agent for those who want to rent houses and I also do my tailor work.' Another male respondent from Enugu in the same age bracket mentioned that 'during the trade fair (which is just once a year), I go to the venue to do some part-time job'. A man from Benin said: 'I am a brick layer but also cut timber in the bush.' A woman from Lagos said: 'I sell provisions [beverages], but in our village, people are building houses every day so I sell sand, gravel and sometimes I help people sell their land and they give me 10 per cent of the money.' A woman from Kano said: 'I am a civil servant but I sell recharge cards [mobile telephone air time] and soft drinks when I get home in order to make ends meet.' A man from Yola mentioned that 'as elections are around the corner, politicians send their agents to different words to give out money so that we can vote for them'. A man from Lagos asserted that he was paid NGN 15,000 (US$100) a month as a driver, and a sales clerk from Lagos said she was paid NGN 8,000 (US$53) monthly. A young woman from Kano aged 15–25 said she was a businessperson, but went to her parents for money when business was slack, while a man from Kaduna explained that his friends lent him money when he was in need. EFInA's research concluded that the average monthly income of NGN 5,000–40,000 (US$33–267) was spent on food, shelter and clothing, which are the key priorities of those on low incomes. This research showed that many Nigerians were not truly employed, since they were not on a fixed income that could meet their most basic needs and they largely belonged to the informal sector. Others that were employed still largely lived in poverty because their earnings would probably only meet their transport costs for the month.

Conclusion

Economic development in Nigeria has been viewed mainly in terms of the growth of the country's development indicators, especially GDP and GNI performance over time as captured by the World Bank and other international and national agencies that align with this neo-classical economic pattern. These agencies argue in favour of good governance indicators as preconditions for economic growth and development, and consistently measure the six good governance indicators: voice and accountability, political stability, rule of law, control of corruption, government effectiveness and regulatory control. Another school of thought prefers the good enough governance agenda, which stresses only those areas of governance that are sufficient to drive minimal economic development and reduce poverty. Unemployment as a major cause of poverty was reviewed using a rather qualitative approach, since unemployment figures are unable to tell the full story. Many Nigerians in the informal sector who claim to be employed are not gainfully employed; rather, they scrounge for part-time job opportunities that come by chance. This shows that in reality, unemployment in Nigeria may be much higher than the World Bank estimate of 50 million in its working age data.

Most importantly, this chapter shows some personal perceptions of poverty that stretch across the geopolitical zones, which means that Nigeria is still quite far from real sustainable development. Indigenous economic research using the BECANS benchmarks included infrastructure and utilities, regulatory services, business development support, investment promotion and security. It found that the enlarged socio-political and economic model for Nigeria encompassed the six good governance indicators, the two development economic indicators and the BECANS benchmarks, which traced poverty and unemployment to their intersection. Most previous research simply identified poverty or defined poverty based on the World Bank and UN US$1 per day yardstick, and more recently on the Millennium Development Goals 2015 target.

The next chapter will explain the African socio-economic world – African economic thought, the political history of Nigeria, the indigenous financial system and the redefinition of poverty in a typical African context.

3

The African Socio-economic World

Introduction

The previous chapter introduced the realities of economic development issues in Nigeria, stressing concerns about governance, poverty and unemployment. This chapter looks at African achievements, analysing the overall context of the research design in a manner that fits with the African cultural economic environment. Non-Africans and even some Africans say that nothing good will come out of Africa except misery and human disasters, forgetting that Africa, at least in its external context, has been caught up in Western neo-liberal socio-economic thoughts. This leads to confusion, because the people still have allegiance to their indigenous ways, which are a combination of traditional and both Christian and Islamic ways. In the fourteenth century, one of the greatest works in human history, combining philosophy, sociology, economics and religion, emerged from the African continent. Readings show that Adam Smith, David Ricardo, Karl Marx and John Maynard Keynes would have studied the work of Tunis-born Ibn Khaldun (1332–1406). In the lower part of the Sahara, indigenous Africans may not have written tracts on the specialization or division of labour or the prohibition of interest and property rights, but they practised it in their daily farm and market activities on the platform of rotational contribution while land was available for communal and family use. Rather than being mutually enriched by the triple heritage of the indigenous lifestyle, the Islamic way of life, and the ways of the colonizers who brought Christianity, Africa is trapped. To move on within the globalized world of the twenty-first century, a moral integral balance is urgently needed.

The Economic Theory of Ibn Khaldun

The greatest known scholars in economics are believed to have come from Europe. In the twenty-first century, students across the globe have made reference to the works of Adam Smith, David Ricardo and Karl Marx, and more recently outstanding economists like John Maynard Keynes, Sir Henry Roy Forbes Harrod, Evsey Domar and William Easterly. The world appreciates their contributions to economic theory and knowledge in general. The Arabs and Africans also lay claim to great works in science, mathematics, sociology, history, philosophy and economics based on the works of Al-Jabbar (Algebra) and Ibn Khaldun, among others. Abdurahman Ibn Khaldun was born in Tunis on 27 May 1332. His father was a scholar who exposed him to the intellectual world. He memorized the whole Quran by heart, learned the Hadith (the deeds and sayings of the Prophet Mohammed), philosophy, jurisprudence, grammar and poetry, receiving certification for his studies. At the age of 19 he began serving the government of Ibn Tafrakin, the ruler of Tunis, where he was exposed to the realities of court politics and deficiencies in governance. In 1352, when Abu Zaid, the Emir of Constantine, defeated and annexed Tunis, Ibn Khaldun escaped. He moved around North Africa, joining the Council of Ulama (scholars) in Fez, the capital of Morocco, continuing to study while participating in politics. He faced several political challenges, was imprisoned, and escaped to Spain, becoming a chief justice before he moved back to Tunisia due to growing political differences and shifting loyalties. At the age of 45 he started his famous work *Muqaddimah* ('An Introduction to History') south of Constantine at Fort Salama, later moving back to Tunis in order to access more material for his work. He moved to Egypt at the age of 50, becoming a chief Maliki judge, later taking a teaching position at Bein al-Qasrein, where he lectured on the Hadith and the Al-Muwatta of Imam Maliki. He completed his *Muqaddimah* and wrote about *asabiya* (social solidarity) and its role in the rise and fall of states. He died at the age of 74 on Wednesday 17 March 1406, and was buried in the Sufi cemetery outside Bab an-Nasr in Cairo (Hozien 2009).

Ibn Khaldun worked on economics and economic surplus, emphasizing the need for less government expenditure on mercenary armies to increase economic surplus by shifting resources to education and human development. He was against taxation and tariffs, which obstruct trade and production. He also did not support state involvement in trade and production. He believed that government bureaucrats could not be adequately motivated in the business environment, and would therefore not clearly understand commercial activities.

In his *Economic Theory of Ibn Khaldun* (1993), Dr Selim Cafer Karatas observed that Ibn Khaldun systematically analysed the functioning of an economy placing high importance on technology, the concept of specialization in foreign trade with economic surplus, and the government's role in stabilizing policies to increase output and employment. Karatas (1993) observed that Ibn Khaldun predicted the survival of the state in his *Muqaddimah*, where his theory encompassed the empirical and theoretical power explaining the consequences of government policies for production, trade, investment and specialization.

THE STATE

According to Ibn Khaldun, the primary role of the state is the establishment of law and order, which should provide a favourable environment for economic activities. However, trade and production are dependent on the enforcement of property rights, the protection of trade routes and overall security. Government policies should favour economic activities. Karatas (1993), in his review of Ibn Khaldun's work, mentioned that government should take a minimum amount of the surplus through taxation to provide the minimum services and essential public works. He said that 'if state tries to over-expend its bureaucracy and its mercenary army by over-taxing the economic surplus, the specialization, the production, the trade and the economic activities will be reduced making economic surplus to shrink'. Ibn Khaldun preferred the state to provide adequate public works, which would make it convenient for entrepreneurs to expand their business activities, thus increasing employment. The state should provide essential public amenities such as trade centres, roads, and activities which encourage trade and production. Ibn Khaldun noted that if the state involved itself in business activities, not only would all motivation and zeal be lost, but the size of the army and bureaucracy would also be increased. In other words, he saw government's role as lying in the area of stabilization policies. Karatas (1993) observed that Ibn Khaldun envisioned greater production and maximum efficiency when trade embedded in specialization was offered via profit-seeking entrepreneurs who would bear the risk and share the profit or loss in business deals or wealth-creating activities.

SPECIALIZATION AND ECONOMIC SURPLUS

Ibn Khaldun emphasized the benefit gained when entrepreneurs are able to exercise specialization in production and trade. He further singled out specialization as the major source of economic surplus. Specialization is then a function of population, trade, production and minimum taxation. Ibn Khaldun viewed the subdivision of crafts to be an efficient skill necessary to achieve efficiency in production lines. This specialization should increase with population growth, leading to even greater efficiency in producing surplus goods. The effectiveness and skill of the production line acknowledges creation and transfer almost unconsciously. Karatas (1993) acknowledged that increased production was the result of the specialized co-ordination of multiple functions through teams, rather than individuals. Karatas (1993) summarized Ibn Khaldun's justification for specialization and production line co-ordination as: 'The combined labour produces more than the needs and necessities of the worker.' Amazingly, Adam Smith captured this when he wrote: 'the value of the materials which he works upon, that of his own maintenance, and of his master's profit'. This may also be related to John Heron's (1996) co-operative inquiry and Peter Reason's (2003) human enquiry, where the co-researchers' knowledge exchange and knowledge creation increased what would have been gained through the research of only one person. More specifically, Ibn Khaldun stated that 'through cooperation, the needs of a number of persons, many times greater than their own (number) can be satisfied'. Karatas (1993) explained that the provision of co-ordination and co-operation of factors in production is a function that must be performed by entrepreneurs driven by market forces. Furthermore, Karatas emphasized that Ibn Khaldun believed that where there is law, order and security of peace, greater specialization can be achieved when the population grows with minimum taxation and free trade. Karatas (1993) observed that Adam Smith said that specialization is a function of the market, and that the greater the market, the greater the specialization. In summary, Karatas said that a greater population implies a larger market for products through specialization.

In a study conducted on labour and its sentiments, Ibn Khaldun theorized that profit is the value realized from labour, with labour being a function of demand and supply.

SUPPLY AND DEMAND

Ibn Khaldun felt it obvious that the prices of goods and services are determined by supply and demand. Thus, excessive supply of goods in relation to demand drives prices down, while scarcity of supply of goods increases them. However, he attributed low food prices to some unfortunate situations caused by weather conditions which affect food production. Karatas (1993) observed that Ibn

Khaldun created the concept of long-run cost of production in accordance with Marshal's thinking.

MONETARY POLICY

Ibn Khaldun stood against the manipulation of currency by rulers, noting that although it would give them opportunities to build palaces for themselves and live in luxury while establishing larger armies, they would consume more state resources, which would remove economic incentives, causing inflation and loss of the people's confidence in the currency, thereby raising moral and ethical questions. Ibn Khaldun said that the supreme policy of the state is to protect the purchasing power of money, which is a form of justice. He therefore proposed that an independent monetary agency should be under the authority of the chief justice or a God-fearing and ethical person who would not tamper with the value of currency. Ibn Khaldun did not see any value in the quantity of money as a measure of a country's wealth, but rather the purchasing power of money under a stable monetary policy, which gives confidence to the people using that currency. In other words, what states need is less government expenditure on luxury buildings and ammunition, lower taxes, and a stable currency for trade and production (Karatas 1993).

FIXED PRICES

Ibn Khaldun argued against price fixing of goods by the government, as well as the government's role in commercial and agricultural activities. He asserted that the government buys commodities from the farmer at fixed prices by force, then resells them at much higher prices at optimal times, making abnormal profits simply because it has the power to tamper with prices at all stages. Ibn Khaldun spelt out the consequences of this type of arrangement:

- Farmers will not be able to sell their produce at a good price.

- This repeated process kills farmers' incentives and motivation to produce in the future.

- Government's trading activities in this regard may lead to the destruction of civilization.

- Price fixing is more dangerous to the state engaging in commerce directly, and is thus harmful to the subjects in the long term.

PROPERTY RIGHTS

Karatas (1993) observed that the protection and enforcement of property rights needed to be defended as a matter of justice for civilization's survival. People will naturally be deterred from acquiring property where they do not have rights, hence more infringement of property rights means people will lose interest in buying property. This, according to Ibn Khaldun, will also cause a decline in economic activities. Karatas (1993) noted that Ibn Khaldun saw an apparent strong relationship between property rights and justice. Ibn Khaldun said that men persist only with the help of property, and the only way to acquire property is through cultivation, the way to cultivation is through justice, and justice balances mankind. Thus, violation of property rights is an unjust act. Ibn Khaldun said:

> people who collect unjustified taxes commit an injustice; those who infringe upon property rights commit an injustice; those who take away property commit an injustice; those who deny people their rights commit an injustice; those who, in general, take property by force, commit an injustice; and injustice ruins civilization.

The work of Ibn Khaldun is indeed Africa's best success story, and should be celebrated every day. He laid the foundation for a moral socio-economic path, a path that has yet to be fully explored by African societies. Ibn Khaldun's work is thoroughly African. He borrowed a great deal from the classical sources of Shariah, especially in his interpretation and analysis of real-life situations that have stood the test of time.

The Pre-colonial Political History of Nigeria

The economic theories of Ibn Khaldun never filtered down to the people of sub-Saharan Africa. The northern part of sub-Saharan Africa had a very organized socio-political structure, and its economic antecedents were based on simple Islamic commercial jurisprudence. In the south of Nigeria, predominantly populated by Christians and those adhering to traditional religion, there was a mix of the economic principle which started from a purely traditional or indigenous economic approach and later morphed partly into the Western economic style. Nigeria's present triple heritage (Mazrui 1986) economic system developed gradually from its socio-political history.

THE PRE-COLONIAL POLITICAL HISTORY OF NORTHERN NIGERIA

In the eleventh century, Islam came to northern Nigeria, and spread southwards by the sixteenth century. That century witnessed an invasion of northern Nigeria by Muslim conquerors from the central Sahara known as the Kanuri of Borno. A Fulani-led jihad of Uthman Dan Fodio in the eighteenth century challenged the powers of the Kanuri Empire and strengthened the Sokoto Caliphate. These ruling dynasties ruled from the north-west and north-east of the region. Islam spread deep into the middle belt, but was resisted in the south. Several minority tribes in the northern and middle-belt settlements practised Islam, and may even be seen as ethnic Muslims. The socio-political structure was based on Islamic law – Shariah. Power was centred on the Sultan of Sokoto, and all other sub-regions respected and paid tribute to him. The sultan is the political, judicial and administrative head of the whole region, and has several assistants. The principal assistant is the vizier, the chief of staff. Other regions within this caliphate had emirs, who also have several assistants, such as the waziri, who is also like a chief of staff, the hakimi (fief-holders) in charge of maintaining law and order and collecting taxes in the state, and the alkali, acting as a judge and mainly handling civil and family Shariah issues. Royalties in this region are passed from the bottom to the top, thus lower officers in the administration channel agricultural produce and taxes from the waziri to the emirs, and eventually to the sultan. This highly organized setup helped build socio-economic orderliness into the system.

THE PRE-COLONIAL POLITICAL HISTORY OF SOUTH-WEST NIGERIA

The Yorubas dominate the south-west of Nigeria. They are a people divided by various leaders and tribes who have a strong affinity for their traditional religion from the Middle Ages. Oduduwa, who is believed to be the founder of the Yoruba kingdom, came from Makkah in Arabia when the region was cleansed of idols in the sixth century. Some aspects of the Islamic religion, culture and language may have been adopted during this period; however, Islam was more likely introduced and accepted by them in the sixteenth or seventeenth century by traders from the middle Sahara or from the north. Islam's influence only extended to certain towns like Eko (Lagos), Epe, Ikorodu, Ijebu, Kabba and Egba, among others. There was no sign of Christianity until the early nineteenth century, when some Yoruba slaves from the Americas returned with it. The Yoruba had a fragmented leadership from the beginning, and political settlements and sub-towns had engaged in several bitter wars with different leaders wanting to expand the kingdom or empire. Oduduwa did not form a co-federal political unit, but rather appointed his sons and close kinsmen to be obas (kings) and chiefs (kingmakers and subordinates) across the Yoruba land. Succession to the throne was hereditary, and members of various ruling families nominated an heir to the throne at the death of the oba. Traditional religion is very important in the Yoruba kingdom, showing much respect to Oluwa or Olodumare (the Supreme Being), some of His ministers being Ogun (the god of iron), Shango (the god of thunder), Esu (the devil) and Osun (the god of the river). The ifa (religious priest) is believed to have very good knowledge of these gods and goddesses, thus he appeals to them when necessary. Law enforcement is also carried out traditionally or spiritually, thus secret cults and societies such as the Ogboni and Egungu play major roles. The gods or secret cults' deities may immediately punish anyone who lies or breaches a contract after swearing an oath.

THE PRE-COLONIAL POLITICAL HISTORY OF SOUTH-EAST NIGERIA

The south-eastern region of Nigeria is dominated by the Igbo people, from the Niger-Congo family, and has over 200 groupings. It is a highly fragmented political settlement with a few dozen people per village. There is no centralized system, and there are no chiefs and no urban settlements. Villages are comprised of family members and close associates who share common ancestral, commercial and religious commitments, as well as a common ancestral shrine. The eldest man in each family holds the title of ofo. The ofos from different families in the little villages form the council of elders, with the oldest of them leading the ofo council. They deliberate on socio-political issues and make suggestions or recommendations, but have no authority to enforce anything since the individual family members can reject or accept their decisions. A major powerful political authority in this region is the ozo, a title-holder. This position is not hereditary, but commands the respect of the elders, families and other villagers because of wealth. The ozo's material achievement earns this prestige and authority, which almost every Igbo man wants to attain. In times past, the ozos were the warlords and great farmers. Thus, individual financial success was the main source of power in the Igbo lands. The Igbos are a very religious and traditional people, and Ala, the goddess of the earth, is one of their deities. The traditional priest or spiritualist has the final say in matters of the rule of law, while the council of elders can advise on necessary punishments.

THE PRE-COLONIAL POLITICAL HISTORY OF SOUTH-SOUTH NIGERIA

The kingdom of Benin lies towards the south-south of Nigeria, and has a long history related to the Yoruba kingdom. The first Oba of Benin was a grandson of Oduduwa, the founder of the Yoruba people. This empire extended to Lagos in the south-west and Nupe in the north-central region at some stage in history. The Oba of Benin exercises legislative, executive and judicial powers, but in practice depends on his chiefs out of respect for custom and tradition. The oliha is a special royal priest who performs sacrificial offerings and crowns every new oba during coronation ceremonies. Under the authority of the oliha is the Uzama, a class of seven chiefs whose titles are hereditary. There is a warlord called the Ezomo and another class of 19 non-hereditary chiefs called the Eghaeyo-n ore and headed by the Iyasere. The detailed administration of village and justice is in the hands of 29 hereditary chiefs called Eqhaevo-n ogbe. In reality, the Oba of Benin cannot unilaterally take any decision without consulting and agreeing with his chiefs. He cannot ignore his senior chiefs in the administration of the state. If he does so, it is believed that the wrath of the gods would descend on him. Income for the Oba of Benin comes from voluntary gifts from the chiefs and the people, and those who want favours from him, especially chieftain titles and land. The chiefs and oba are also the judicial heads, and very serious offences such as treason, witchcraft and homicide are handled by the oba.

Further down the south-south region of Nigeria are highly fragmented and diversified political settlements along the Atlantic coast, riverside areas and creeks. They include the Ijaw, Ibibio, Anang, Efik and a many other tribes. Several villages within a relatively small radius speak different languages. There are enormous tribes, ethnic groups and cultures among these people, and they frown on inter-village marriages. They are mainly involved in fishing, and live their entire lives around the waters. There is no real leadership, no defined economic structure and their religious beliefs are traditional and affiliated to sea gods.

The Indigenous Informal African Financial System

The economic system in northern Nigeria is primarily based on the Islamic economic system, as discussed in Chapter 6. In the south of Nigeria, the predominant economic and financial system is based on co-operative rotating contributions popularly called *esusu*. This rotating contribution encompasses agricultural co-operatives, local market communities and traditional religious groups, including witchcraft and secret societies. More recently, the modern society has now adopted several forms of *esusu*. Interestingly, *takaful* (Islamic insurance) and *qardh-hassan* (Islamic interest-free loans) have been merged into the informal *esusu* model.

ESUSU

Esusu, the institution of rotating savings, dates back to the sixteenth century from the Yoruba lands in south-west Nigeria. It was carried to the Caribbean and part of the Americas during the slave trade era. It is called *esu* in the Bahamas, *susu* in Tobago, *sou* in Trinidad (Seibel 2001a; Seibel 2001b; Sawani and Patterson 2001). *Esusu* is also called *ajo* in the Yoruba lands, *isusu* or *utu* among the Igbo people, *osusu* among the Edo from south-south Nigeria, *adashi* among the Hausa from northern Nigeria, *dashi* among the Nupe from north-central Nigeria, and the Ibibio people call it *etibe* (Microfinance Nigeria 2010). In Ghana it is called *anago susu*, in the Ivory Coast *nago*, in Southern Togo *yesyes*, and in Central Togo *jojuma* (Seibel 2001a). A similar rotating savings system in the Horn of Africa is called *iddir*, and in Panama it is referred to as *caja de ahorros* (Sawani and Patterson 2001). Sawani and Patterson also asserted that major West African communities in the United Sates also practise *esusu*. *Esusu* and *iddir* are also closely linked with informal *takaful*. *Esusu*, *iddir* and informal *takaful* are periodic contributions, usually from people of the same socio-economic class, with interest not being charged if any member borrows from the fund for the purpose of consumption. Traditional *esusu*, as practised by the Yorubas, allows people to contribute regularly into a pool which is collected monthly by the members in a rotational manner. The groups usually consist of five or more members. Contributions may be daily, weekly or monthly, with the members taking turns to collect the money. They may choose to borrow without interest from the fund in certain periods to meet pressing socio-economic needs. These monies can be used to meet needs involving education, health, trade, domestic issues and even capital projects like the construction of houses.

Esusu-like arrangements are used across Nigeria by farmers, and are referred to as co-operatives. A group of ten farmers, for example, will work on each others' farms in a rotating manner, which saves them the cost of additional labour. This arrangement is also adopted for constructing homes for members. Seibel (2001a) observed the same practice in Liberia, where men worked as a group, working on each other's fields in turn, and carrying out all necessary tasks together. He noticed the same practice in Ivory Coast in 1985 and in Ghana in 1979. Seibel (2001a) said that in Ghana, he noticed a group of women jointly producing palm oil which was later sold in the market, with the proceeds being allocated to one member of the group at a time.

There is evidence of traditional secret societies, including practices of witchcraft, especially in southern Nigeria, where members may contribute a valuable asset, either living or non-living, to please the gods or spirits in turn. This is a way some of the indigenous deities are maintained or sustained. Failure to contribute may have negative effects on the member or his or her clan.

Rotational savings as practised in different parts of Nigeria have been transforming gradually to align more with the principles of conventional economics and the Islamic economic system. An in-depth interview with Chief Jerry Gushop (Marfa Mangu – 'Chief of the Chief') from Jos in north-central Nigeria revealed that rotational contribution is used in various forms in his environment. He confirmed that men help themselves on their farms, working together and sharing specializations in a rotational manner. He said that members of the same church also contribute money together, and members may borrow at 5–10 per cent interest. Church members also help each other to cultivate their farmland in turn at a very small cost, usually to cover feeding and transportation for the day, but would cultivate the pastor's land free of charge. Chief Jerry shared that farmers now form co-operatives of 10–50 members, which they register with the local council. This allows them to borrow from the conventional financial institutions, where each member serves as collateral for the others. This reduces the likelihood of default, while the bank has confidence in the co-operatives. He confirmed that people working as civil servants and some in corporate organizations use a form of rotational contribution which allows them to borrow at 10 per cent interest, with the interest being shared among members at the end of the year.

Another in-depth interview with Alhaja Fatima from Lagos shows that the women of the *asalatu* group (prayer session) that meets every weekend contribute a fixed amount each at every meeting. Members who are unable to attend the meeting will still need to forward their weekly contributions. Members take turns to collect bulk contributions monthly. They may borrow without interest on a very short-term basis for a maximum of one month, and the money must be returned before the next person collects on her turn.

Mrs Mayowa from Lagos is the collector of *esusu* or *ajo* from ten members every month, the members also taking turns in conducting the collection. She shared that some members have double contributions, which allows them to collect the total contribution twice a year. She also said that among market people it is common for the collector in an *ajo* to collect a daily commission when there is a daily collection, and many collectors do this on full-time basis. Members are not allowed to borrow from their own version of *esusu*.

Informal *takaful* is in practice not much different from *esusu*. Members contribute with the purpose of helping themselves to meet their financial needs. Contributors may never need to collect their contributions if they do not have any pressing financial needs, but the money may be invested in low-risk business transactions or in a Shariah-compliant savings account. Members can engage in business ventures using the *takaful* fund on profit/loss-sharing basis. In this case, members of the *takaful* fund have to agree on the business proposal for which their money will be used since they also share in the risk. Informal *takaful* is becoming common among Muslim student societies, mosque members and Islamic organizations in general. In Lagos, there are a handful of cases where Muslim middle-class friends or colleagues set up *takaful* funds to generate capital for business propositions while borrowing on a short-term basis to meet financial needs. They borrow on either a *qardh-hassan* (interest-free loan) basis where the loan is for consumption purposes, or on the basis of *mudarabah* or *musharakah* (investment partnership) for business purposes.

In Nigeria, *zakat* has remained informal since its inception. It was well co-ordinated in northern Nigeria during the Sokoto Caliphate, and has managed to remain informal thereafter. *Zakat* contribution is usually taken to the imam (Muslim cleric) to give to any member who needs it. Other people identify those they know with needs and give it to them. Many Islamic organizations, especially in southern Nigeria, co-ordinate *zakat* within their organization to make it more effective. Some organizations give out *zakat* money to their members in the form of *qardh-hassan*, which they eventually return. This money may be used for business or personal consumption. In northern Nigeria, state governments co-ordinate *zakat*. The introduction of Islamic banking in Nigeria can be seen as an opportunity to institutionalize *zakat* and make it more effective on a national scale.

There has been a significant change in the way rotating savings have evolved in Africa, with no predetermined pattern. Seibel (2001a) identified patterns of change in these ways:

- from labour, in kind or premonitory currency to cash;

- from non-financial to financial groups;

- from rotating to non-rotating patterns;

- from saving only to savings-driven credit.

Seibel (2001a) noted that the first phase is that of rotating work groups, which can offer services for a wage while allocating the total to one member at a time. The second phase may simply abandon the rotational pattern by keeping the income in a joint savings fund for emergencies, joint activities or distribution during certain periods. The third phase is where the co-operative turns into a credit association, using the savings as a permanent fund to provide loans to members. The fourth phase is where the fund becomes very large and commercialized, lending at high rates of interest while demanding collateral. In this case, interest becomes the incentive for saving.

The informal African financial system has over time been largely influenced by what Ali Mazrui calls the African triple heritage. In Nigeria, *esusu* takes three main forms in the twenty-first century. One version maintains the indigenous concept, where there is no interest payment for borrowing from the contribution and the primary purpose for contributing is to meet members' bulk financial needs. The second is where groups, including religious organizations, may contribute and accept interest from their members, or they may take wages by working on each others' farms. This represents a neo-classical economic approach imported from the West. The third version is based on the Islamic economic system, which allows what may be called *takaful esusu*, which meets the financial needs of members and allows the payment of *zakat* and other forms of gifts to support them. The religious affiliations of Nigerians influence the kind of *esusu* they adopt. This, however, calls for a close scrutiny of Mazrui's triple heritage.

The African Triple Socio-economic Heritage

It was the inevitable that the Nordic world and the African, especially that part of it which constitutes the Yoruba world – should meet at the crossroads of Sweden. That I am the agent of such a symbolic encounter is due very simply to that my creative muse is Ogun, the

god of creativity and destruction, of lyric and metallurgy. This deity
anticipated your scientist Alfred Nobel at the very beginning of time by
clearing a path through primordial chaos, dynamiting his way through
the core of earth to open a route for his fellow deities who sought to be
reunited with us, mortals.
(Wole Soyinka 1986, in Anagwonye 2009, p. 160)

These are the words of Wole Soyinka at the Nobel Banquet in Sweden, where he demonstrated his African faith in Ogun, the god of creativity, destruction, lyrics and metallurgy, and the role this ancient Yoruba god has played in his life. It is not common for Nigerians with a formal education to align with their African heritage in a Western country, simply because they feel the religion of their forefathers is primitive and lays more emphasis on Christianity than Islam. It is this way of thinking that has influenced Africans' economic choices. A Nigerian from the north would not recognize any culture outside the Islamic way of life, with even the Christians from the north dressing and behaving like their tribespeople. Those from the south-west are a mix of Muslims and Christians with a touch of traditional religion thrown in. In reality, many Muslims and Christians still secretly communicate with traditional deities, either directly or through traditional priests. Those from the south-east and south-south are predominantly Christians who nevertheless have very strong relationships with traditional deities. Southern Nigerians shy away from their traditional heritage in public, largely preferring British ways. Even many Muslim Yorubas with formal education openly prefer the British way of life.

Whereas it took a thousand years to disseminate cultural change among the Jews, many Africans today undergo cultural change within a single generation. Africa is indeed at war – a war of cultures between indigenous Africa and the forces of Western civilization (Mazrui 1986). Mazrui feels strongly that perhaps the curse, or warning, of the African ancestors contained in Chinua Achebe's *Things Fall Apart* is beginning to materialize. They understand it as a sign from their ancestors calling Africans to rethink their recent past, their present and their future in a bid to reconstruct their future for good. Tsenay Serequeberhan wrote in his *African Philosophy*: 'In the name of the universality of values, European colonialism violently universalized its own singular particularity and annihilated the historicity of the colonized.' He continued, 'Western philosophy – in the guise of a disinterested, universalistic, transcendental, speculative discourse – served the indispensable function of being the ultimate buttress of European conquest' (Serequeberhan 1999, pp. 4–5), adding: 'For the colonizer who refuses in refusal – in the very act of refusing – radically changes the directionality of his or her horizon of life possibilities' (Serequeberhan 2000, p. 10). Colonization for many Nigerians did not offer anything exceptional for the people, but protected the motives and interests of the colonizers. The British purposely distorted the indigenous lifestyle, saying it was inferior to that of the rest of the world, and offered Western education to southern Nigeria. However, those in the north preferred to maintain their simple and nomadic lifestyle based on Islamic heritage. In 1951, when laying out the strategies of his political party known as the Action Group, Chief Obafemi Awolowo said, 'It is our belief that the people of Western Nigeria particularly, and of Nigeria in general would have life more abundant when they enjoy – freedom from British rule, freedom from ignorance, freedom from disease, and freedom from want,' which were the needs of the people then who were in the hands of the British. It is even worse in northern Nigeria, where ignorance and poverty throughout British rule was normal. There were no adequate hospitals, and the few railway lines they had were mainly to transport coal and agro-commodities to the ports to be shipped to Europe. Mazrui observed: 'European colonial rule in Africa, in fact, was more effective in destroying indigenous African structures than destroying African culture.'

THE SOCIAL DIVIDE CREATED BY THE COLONIZERS

The Nigerian hinterlands were seized by the British in 1897, and the eastern region was conquered in 1894 and declared the Niger Coast Protectorate. By 1900, the northern part of the country was declared the Protectorate of Northern Niger, which later became Nigeria. The colony of Lagos was joined with the hinterlands and the Niger Coast Protectorate, becoming the Colony and Protectorate of Southern Nigeria.

Nigeria was divided into the Northern and Southern Protectorates from 1900 to 1914, with each protectorate under a different administration. The political structure of northern Nigeria was well organized under the Sultan of Sokoto, with all emirs governing under him. All the British had to do was rule the north indirectly via the sultan, since resistance was very low. What was of primary concern to the Hausa-Fulani-dominated north was the protection of their religion, Islam, thus they rejected Western education since they thought it would push them away from the Islamic way of life over time. The people from the northern part of the country could also be seen as 'ethnic Muslims', since the only real culture they knew was Islam. The British passed orders to the sultan, and the emirs carried out these policies without questioning their leaders.

The British helped the south-west Yoruba people to achieve political tranquillity by putting a stop to several battles between different political settlements. The British supported obas and traditional leaders who submitted to their rule and power, while those who resisted were defeated in battle or sent into exile. Indirect rule in the south-west was challenging for the colonial masters compared to the north, but it was still achieved.

The south-east and south-south of the emerging country, apart from the kingdom of Benin, was the most challenging since there was no real leadership. The British created new leaders, or warrant chiefs, in Igbo lands whom the people largely rejected and later replaced by locally elected councils. The south-south people of the riverside areas were hardly recognized, either because they had no organized political structure that could be inherited, or they were just not visible to everyone. Instead, the approach adopted in the south-east was adopted.

Indirect rule was more prevalent in the north, with the sultan and emirs strengthened and given more power, especially in the field of revenue collection. In the south, Christianity and education were the main instruments the colonial masters used to buy the people over, apart from creating new chiefs where the existing ones were not co-operating with them. The north was loyal to British colonialism, but the region can almost be seen as a landlocked sub-state, with only the River Niger and River Benue in its south. Revenues were low in this region, and the people were not very enterprising. The people in the south were open to Western education and accepted Christianity at the expense of their traditional religion. Even Muslims among the Yorubas had to change their names to English and biblical names just to attend Western schools, usually opting for further education in Europe and America. Their educational and entrepreneurial abilities, interest and their exposure made them challenge the authority of the colonial masters. Nevertheless, revenue was high in this region; trade with the rest of the world was normal, with Lagos and Port Harcourt expanding international trade. Cocoa was being largely produced in the south-west, and palm kernel in the south-east. Income was high, and the British enjoyed good revenues and taxes in these regions.

The British observed that the north was economically challenged, and decided to set up a common treasury for the Northern and Southern Protectorates so that high revenues from the south could be used to subsidize the administration in the north. In 1914, Lord Lugard amalgamated the two regions by creating a single treasury. By 1930, the state was divided into three regions: the North, above the River Niger and River Benue, and the West and East, both below the two rivers. The British mainly ruled from the Colony of Lagos and started to centralize the federal civil services and other government agencies. The colonialists created poor governmental and economic structures that only protected their immediate economic interests. Mazrui wrote about the distribution of Africa's mineral resources and the way it was being controlled by the British, Muslims and Westernized Africans, calling it the 'aesthetics of imperialism'.

TRIPLE ECONOMIC MANIPULATION

Nigerians found themselves at the intersection of a triple economic heritage, the indigenous economic heritage, the socio-economic Islamic heritage, and the colonial or Western heritage. In the words of Mazrui, the best embodiment of the modern African triple heritage (indigenous, Islamic and Western) is Nigeria. Richard (2004, p. 15) also referred to Mazrui's triple heritage thesis based on the notion of Africa as a 'cultural bazaar' – a place of exchanges, mixtures and métis sages, while the cultures of Africa have long been ignored and despised. On this note, Semou Pathe Gueye, in his *African Renaissance as an Historical Challenge*, raised the question of whether or not it is an economy which can reach a sustainable and consistent GNP without any attention to the necessity to improve the quality of life of the majority of the people. He went further, saying that 'a genuine social policy can be ensured only by the sustainable, dynamic, and "socialization" of misery and poverty. But how do you harmoniously combine economic and socio-cultural efficiencies?'

The economic junction of these heritages could then be established on Lessem and Schieffer's moral economic core. This moral economic core is founded on the foundation of 'religion and humanity', and underlies the Four Worlds, starting with Southern indigenous wisdom and moving to the Eastern moral cores of Hinduism, Buddhism and Confucianism, and from there, Catholicism as captured under distributivism, and the Christian West with its Quaker and Protestant impulses for economic renewal. The moral drive is lodged at the centre of a world, for example in the case of Islamic economics (Lessem and Schieffer 2010b), as illustrated in Figure 3.1. For pluralistic Nigeria, the moral sentiment would be the ethical thoughts from Western-influenced Christianity based on classical and neo-classical economic theories, and the moral elements in the indigenous African financial system based on the *esusu* model, with moral theories as embedded in the Islamic economic system.

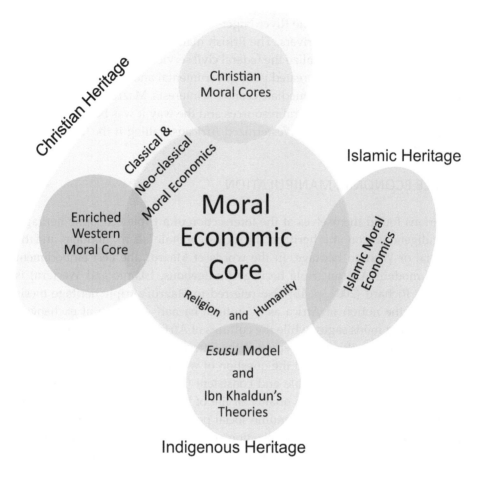

Figure 3.1   The Nigerian Triple Moral Economic Heritage Model
Source: Derived from Lessem and Schieffer's Moral Economic Core Model.

Figure 3.1 shows the Nigerian Triple Moral Economic Heritage Model based on Lessem and Schieffer's Moral Economic Core Model. The indigenous heritage contains the *esusu* model and Ibn Khaldun's 'green' economic thoughts that have stood the test of time for centuries. The Christian heritage is comprised of the enriched Western moral core and the Christian moral core as embedded in the overall classical and neo-classical moral economics. The Islamic heritage extends from the East towards the South and into the enlarged moral economic core, which shelters religion and humanity. This combined heritage was described by Mazrui as follows:

The most successful Semitic religion in the world is Christianity;
the most successful Semitic language is Arabic; the most successful
people globally are the Jews. Contemporary Africa's triple heritage
of indigenous, Islamic and Western legacies is just the modern
culmination of much older triple heritage – of indigenous, Semitic and
Greco-Roman influences on Africa.

The purpose of determining a common moral element in the three heritages is not to indulge in a mere academic exercise, but to create an economic path that will help develop Nigeria and other African states – at least in this century – to reduce poverty considerably. Within the background of this triple heritage, it is necessary to examine other generic economic development factors that contribute to poverty and unemployment in Africa.

Economic Development in Africa

The influence of the triple heritage is evident in several African states, and very pronounced in Nigeria. The inability of Africans to interfuse the moral core of these heritages has led to serious poverty since there is a heavier tilt towards one heritage rather than an integral balance in the middle (Lessem and Schieffer 2010b). UNCTAD carried out a study on economic development in Africa and examined the generic causes of poverty, unemployment and economic inequalities in Africa in the light of a shift from structural adjustment to poverty reduction. UNCTAD (2002) reviewed the World Bank's estimates of people living below the poverty line of below US$1 per day PPP, estimating that in sub-Saharan Africa the number increased from 217 million in 1987 to 291 million in 1998. UNCTAD adopted the World Bank definition of poverty, but used a different methodology. It used both a household survey and national account data to determine that poverty has increased consistently in Africa since 1965–9, rising from an average of 55.8 per cent to 64.9 per cent in 1995–9.

We may wonder whether there was such extreme poverty in the eighteenth and nineteenth centuries when the Sokoto Caliphate ruled northern Nigeria, the Alaafin ruled the Old Oyo Empire or when the Oba of Benin Empire controlled most parts of the present south-south region of Nigeria. There may not have been neo-classical measures of poverty, but indigenous people have property rights and could either farm on their own land or farm as tenants on the land of others, paying their property owners and kings with farm produce. They grew large families which played the role of specialized labour on the farms, and conveniently applied the *esusu* or rotational contribution/participation model to cultivate their land. No doubt, there were inter- and intra-ethnic wars, yet the history books do not tell us of poverty in ancient Africa among the ancient Nigerian people. What, then, is the course of poverty in Africa? Neo-liberal multilateral organizations have now agreed that 'while economic growth is considered essential for poverty reduction, this may not necessarily or automatically drip down to the poor; (UNCTAD 2002). They also observe that although macroeconomic and structural stability are necessary to promote rapid and sustainable growth, this will have a temporary negative effect on the poor. These organizations have now instigated certain polices as prerequisites, not only to achieve rapid growth and improve income distribution, but to also serve as poverty reduction strategies.

While acknowledging the soundness of all the research carried out on the measures of poverty across the world, and specifically on poverty issues in Africa, there is a need to take a look at another direction based on the experiences of those who live in typical African states. Nigeria's GDP may be catching up with that of South Africa, but the poor in South Africa hardly suffer from the infrastructural poverty which afflicts even wealthy Nigerians. There are records of the deaths of both rich and poor Nigerians in road accidents due to the terrible road infrastructure, while every Nigerian family must have a generator to enjoy basic amenities because the power supply is intermittent. South Africa is largely free from such poverty. While in Nigeria a household of six members or more may live in one room, Libya has not had the same experience. Instead, Libyans may have suffered from poverty of human rights, political exclusion in the Gaddafi era, or what they term autocratic governance. Botswana's economy seems comparatively better, but because of the spread of HIV/AIDS, its people suffer from the poverty of poor health. In the Democratic Republic of Congo, political instability has resulted in a shortened average lifespan for its people over the decades.

Most African countries suffer from a combination of many poverty indicators illustrated in Figure 3.2. In southern Sudan, Mali, Niger and northern Nigeria, many cannot afford one meal a day, while many university students in Nigeria barely have two good meals a day. Most importantly, Africans suffer from ethno-religious poverty, or the poverty of loss of their valuable indigenous heritage. For Mazrui (1986), the Islamic and Westernized Christian heritages have compressed the indigenous African socio-economic heritage, which may have caused more confusion for the continent, trapped in between the three heritages. Uthman (2009) summarizes poverty as material and physical deprivation, political and social exclusion, and cultural, religious and educational deprivations. Badr-El-Din (2003) made a distinction between absolute and relative poverty. Absolute poverty is the inability to meet basic needs, while relative poverty is related to income inequality.

From a purely economic perspective, it is generally believed that Africa, unlike China or Japan, does not have any proficient indigenous model, so Westernized neo-classical economic and political theories are promoted in the region on the assumption that they will be as effective as they have been in Europe and North America. Many have also argued that the Islamic economic system is only a theory that may have existed hundreds of years ago, so it cannot fit into the ethno-linguistically diversified African states. How likely is it, then, that Islamic finance can reduce the impact of poverty in Africa within the context of the continent's overall socio-economic position? Alternatively, should the question be changed to how best to use Islamic banking and finance to solve the challenge of poverty? Analysing this would require the fusion of the literatures and realities of individual African states.

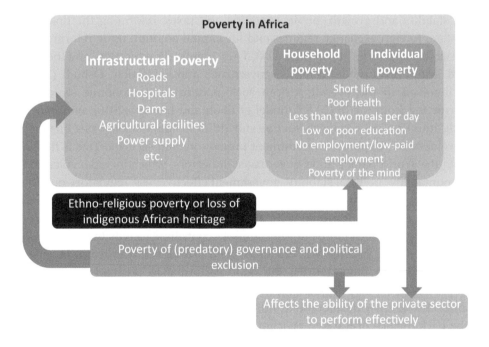

Figure 3.2   Redefining poverty in Africa
Source: Oshodi (2012b, 2012c).

Conclusion

There has always been much talk of the poor performance of Africa's development and governance indicators compared to other regions. Many notable writings have also focused on Africa's poor performance on the Millennium Development Goals and the inability of the region to meet the 2015 targets. Others have stressed the National Economic Empowerment and Development Strategy (NEEDS) designed to implement economic and institutional reforms, poverty alleviation, wealth creation, employment generation and value reorientation. A lot of research has also gone into the Human Poverty Index (HPI) based on three goals or products of development. Overall, there is a shift from structural adjustment to poverty reduction strategy papers, borrowing from UNCTAD (2002), where new elements of poverty reduction programmes are identified under country ownership and participation, policy aspirations of the poor, conditionality and poverty reduction. UNCTAD examined stabilization adjustment and poverty on the basis of three major subjects.

The first was macroeconomic and adjustment policies and poverty, such as: stability and growth, public spending and taxes, reforming the financial system, foreign exchange regimes and the capital account, trade reforms and agricultural policies. Secondly, UNCTAD identified education and health, and lastly, institutional reforms, governance and correction. Oshodi (2009) is involved in the overall African socio-political and economic structure, borrowing from the BECANS model of Eboh and Lemchi (2010), with major indicators that include: infrastructure and utilities, regulatory services, business development support and investment promotion, and security. This is tied in with the World Bank's good governance indicators, which include: voice and accountability, political stability, government effectiveness, regulatory quality, rule of law and control of corruption. This is further infused in the neo-liberal approach to economic growth, GNI per capital and GDP. The performances of or interplay between these huge benchmarks contribute heavily to poverty and unemployment. Poverty and unemployment are indeed trapped in between these forces. In other words, the poor performance of good governance indicators negatively affects the ability of development indicators (GNI, GDP and other known development indicators) to perform (Oshodi 2009), while the performance of the two benchmarks obstructs the ability of the business environment and competitiveness indicators in various African states to drive poverty reduction. It is also common in Africa that secure part-time or full-time employment does not mean the absence of chronic poverty. There may, however, be a need for the redefinition of poverty outside the US$1 or US$2 per day rule.

The next chapter spells out moral economics from the Jewish moral economic system to the Islamic moral economic system, while covering several other moral economic cores identified by Lessem and Schieffer.

4

Moral Economics

Introduction

The previous chapter looked at the economic and financial models that emerged from the African soil and redefined poverty in new lights that are more integrally realistic rather than following the purely empirical norm. The issues of poverty and unemployment are as old as man himself, and may be viewed within the context of the expulsion of Adam and Eve from the Garden of Eden. They found themselves in a strange environment where they needed to work hard for food. They were indeed faced with hardship as their family size started to multiply, thus more work had to be created so that the family could have enough to eat. This small family grew into a village, and into several settlements across the Earth. Known resources may have been limited from village to village, which must have led to the need to create rules that would guide resource management under a morally structured approach.

God intervened in this regard and sent messengers and prophets with divine guidance from among the people to take charge of the management of moral behaviour, moral exchange of goods and services, and moral relationships between fellow mankind which further developed the moral relationship between God and man. In this regard, God promised man His Pleasures in this world, and most importantly, the hereafter, where man is able to achieve morality on Earth based on the dictates of His messengers. Adam Smith, Karl Marx, Ronnie Lessem and Alexander Schieffer spell out morality in their socio-economic approach to development. Overall, in integral terms, there is lopsidedness in global economic inequalities, where the West and North prey on the East and South, and the South is unable to pull itself out of the depths of this immorality game. It is this imbalance that gave birth to a new 'moral economic core', in the words of Lessem and Schieffer (2010a).

The Moral Economic Core

The detailed work of Lessem and Schieffer (2010a) on integral economics in a 'moral economic core' (see Figure 4.1) asserts that ethical and moral economics have their foundation in religion and humanity. Plotting the contributions of this faith-based economic system in the Four Worlds Integral Framework, Lessem and Schieffer mentioned that 'respect for creation is seen as the starting point in this endangered world, thus justice and peace including economic justice have to flow as a natural result from a genuine and appropriate concern for creation' which is placed in the Southern indigenous moral core with its origin from Africa. Hinduism, Buddhism and Confucianism represent the East in this moral economic core. According to Lessem and Schieffer, Hinduism's morals are based on an economic system and political arrangement that are elevated in such a way that individual self-realization is promoted. In Buddhism, human development seeks to understand how lower and higher desire motivates us, such that energies are shifted from competition to co-operative efforts to solve global challenges and the achieve a nobler goal. For the Confucians, Lessem and Schieffer assert that 'all things in the universe – self, family, business, and nation – contain competing tendencies that must be balanced'.

The original and moral elements of Catholicism are placed in the North of the Four Worlds. The main moral values in this system are based on the belief that the creator is the owner of work, and man only shares in that activity. Therefore, for there to be progress, 'greater justice, wider brotherhood, and a more human ordering of human relationships, all of which are greater than technical advances' are essential to build an ethical and moral economic system. Lessem and Schieffer plot the Christian core in the West of the Four Worlds, mentioning that original blessing rather than original sin is to be recognized here, and adding that no single culture is the sole path to the source. In Lessem and Schieffer's work, the Islamic moral economic system maintains a comfortable position at the centre of the Four Worlds. Maintaining moderation and balance in material dealings, reasoned pursuits and spiritual quests are the most significant indicators of man's nobility outside of righteousness. Order, proportions, refinement and beauty are a by-product of this moderation.

Developing ethical and moral economic principles, to fend off the evil of interest, requires the detailed and practical aspects of economics, banking and finance to be strong for a developing African economy like Nigeria. At the same time, they must examine the factors of production, consumption, competition, and the spirituality of ethical and moral economics.

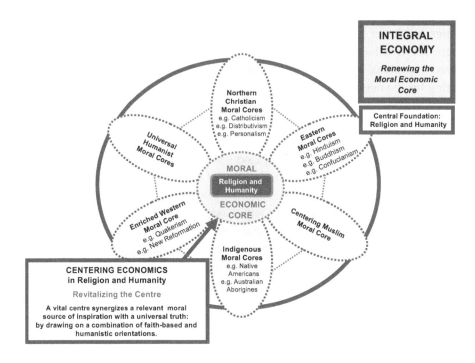

Figure 4.1   The moral economic core
Source: Lessem and Schieffer (2010a).

In practical terms, ethical and moral economics are embedded in the concept of the Islamic economic system which illustrates the ethical aspects of financial transactions within the moral economic framework.

Jewish Moral Economic Theory

We now turn specifically to the Jewish heritage, whence came the Christian and the Muslim. In the beginning, clans, villages and several political settlements across the regions of the world, realized the need to manage household resources in relation to needs, so they tried several methodologies. This art of management was called different things in different languages all over the world. However, the Greek word *oikonomia*, which means the art of household management, was accepted into English language and called 'economics'. Centuries before this time, the Jews had developed their version of household and community management based on ethical principles, which was the foundation of Judaism and the bond that united the Jewish community.

Sauer and Sauer from the Action Institute observed from several readings that there are five basic axioms of Jewish economic theory: participation in the creative process, protection of private property, the accumulation of wealth, caring for the needy, and limited government (see Figure 4.2).

PARTICIPATION IN THE CREATIVE PROCESS

Jews believe that 'man is created in God's image', which means that God is the creator of the world and man is also creator of the world. Sauer and Sauer (2011) quoted the Babylonian Talmud Shabbat 10a, where it was mentioned that man was given the divine essence to partner with God in the act of creation. They further quoted the Midrash, which says: 'all that was created during the six days that God created the world still requires work' (Genesis Rabba 11:6). In other words, the world that God created is not perfect, and man is required to fine-tune this creation through the use of several forms of resources, hard work, and innovation. Sauer and Sauer asserted that in Judaism, work, creative activities and innovation are the channels through which man exercises his divine image of God. This explains the zeal which Jews put into all that they lay their hands on. They find it necessary to refine the works of God, adding improvements and ornaments to make the works more convenient to live in. This may also be reflected in the manner in which Jews interpret or perceive subjects in the Torah and their overall interest in global socio-economic and political issues. This has also largely put the Jews in a leadership position due to the enormous efforts they inject into perfecting God's creation.

PROTECTION OF PRIVATE PROPERTY

Jews believe that private property rights are an integral part of their moral economic system, and hence should be well protected. Man can only create and improve what God has already designed, thus the need to be innovative when advancing the material world. Man's motivation and fulfilment in the use of God's creation is for him to have access to and ownership of private property. Sauer and Sauer (2011) refer to two of the Ten Commandments that say: 'You shall not steal; and you shall not convert anything that belongs to your neighbour.' The moral economic thought here is that all forms of stealing, deception, unethical business practices and the use of false weights are unacceptable. On the other hand, coveting the private property of others attracts very serious punishment; the Rabbis related this to the flood experience during the time of Noah, which was the result or punishment of those who coveted the private property of others. In the same vein, all forms of deception in business transactions are unethical. The rabbis need to further define what deception in modern business transactions looks like.

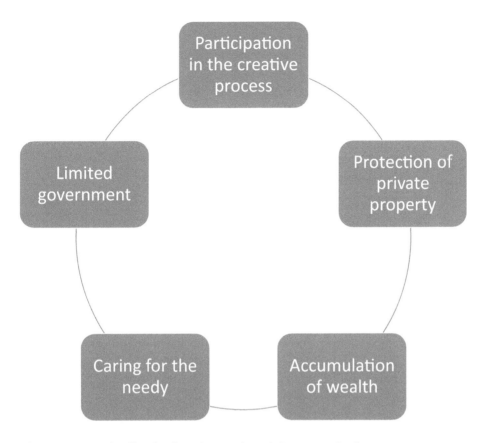

Figure 4.2   The five basic axioms of Jewish economic theory

THE ACCUMULATION OF WEALTH

The Jews believe that the accumulation of wealth is a virtue, not a vice. They believe it should be the reward for refining the creative process while maintaining private property. The outcome of a combination of these efforts would be expected to create and increase wealth. On this subject, Sauer and Sauer (2011) referred to the Talmud, which teaches that 'One who benefits from his own labour is greater than one who fears heaven' (Berachot 8a and Avot 4:1). They also observe that in the Torah, reward in the form of great wealth is given to productive and virtuous workers, and is also reflected in the riches of Abraham, Isaac, Jacob and Solomon. The moral aspect of this economic belief system is that the accumulation of wealth should be honest. Sauer and Sauer (2011) noted that the Talmud sages considered the refusal to benefit from one's labour through accumulating wealth as dangerous, leading to madness. Sauer and Sauer made particular reference to idleness, as contained in the writing of Maimonides, which says that 'whomsoever has in his heart that he shall indulge in the study of Torah and do not work but rather be sustained from charity defames the Lord's name, cheapens the Torah, extinguishes the light of faith, causes himself ill and removes himself from the word to come' (Mishnet Torah Laws of Oaths and Vows 8:13). The Jews consider it necessary to support the poor members of the society by engaging in a gift-giving obligation called *tzedakah*, which is very different from income redistribution.

CARING FOR THE NEEDY

Tzedakah in Jewish economic thought literally means 'justice'. Deuteronomy 15:7–8 says: 'You should not harden your heart or shut your hand from your needy brother.' Sauer and Sauer (2011) asserted that man's role in this world is to work, innovate and create in the process of evaluating the material world, giving out charity to those that are in need. Sauer and Sauer (2011) further explained Maimonides as reflected in *The Guide for the Perplexed*: 'we do not perform an act of Tzedakah when we fulfill those duties towards our fellow men which our moral conscience imposes upon us; for example when we heal the wounds of the sufferer'. Sauer and Sauer (2011) explained that the Jewish economic system distinguishes between the man-to-man relationship and the God-to-man relationship. *Tzedakah* belongs to the man-to-man relationship, which is based on moral law rather than legal principle. Yehuda HaKohen (2009) stressed the need for the Jewish state to maintain a high moral standard while building a society where no one goes hungry and where people behave with genuine love and concern for one another. He quotes Vayikra 25:35: 'If your brother becomes impoverished and his means falter in your proximity, you shall strengthen him – proselyte or resident – so that he can live with you.' HaKohen also referred to the verse at the end of Malachi which says that the sages recommend that this charity be at least 10 per cent of a person's regular income.

LIMITED GOVERNMENT

Jewish moral economic theory sees government as inefficient in directing business activities. It is believed that government will use its power to subdue the zeal of the entrepreneur. Sauer and Sauer (2011) examined the work of Rabbi Sacks, which refers to Frederick Hayek's warning in *The Road to Serfdom* mentioning that when government controls resource allocation and maps out the workings of the economy, there will be a risk of increasing oppression of the people, particularly the entrepreneurs. HaKohen (2009) asserted that it is necessary for the Jews to create an economic system founded on Torah values, which encourage free enterprise and limit governmental intrusion while promoting communal responsibility that inculcates social mindfulness in societies.

On the issue of interest, Ingrid Rima (2009) analysed the belief of ancient Hebrews that 'happiness is not dependent on wealth and the pursuit of riches would lead to sin'. Thus, they follow strict moral and ethical guidance from the Book of Moses and other Hebrew Prophets of God. They believe that 'charging interest to fellow Hebrews for the use of money or goods was strictly forbidden as usury'. Rima observed that this became a moral standard in the economic behaviour of ancient Jews.

The Jews combined these five axioms and developed their moral economy based on the Torah and supporting sources of Jewish theology. The morality embedded in it is very similar to other religious thoughts carved out of Judaism, such as Christianity and Islam, while the Roman moral economic thoughts are trapped between the content of the Torah and the New Testament. This leads to another moral economic system, the Buddhist moral economic system, which is now having some minor influence in Nigeria among the traditionalists, or herbalists, who combine Asian and African natural herbs for spiritual healing.

The Buddhist Moral Economic System

Siddhartha Gautama, also known as Buddha, was born in 563 BCE in Lumbini near the Nepalese-Indian border into a royal family, living a very comfortable life in the palace court. At age 29, he went on an excursion outside the palace territory and saw a feeble old man, a person suffering from diseases, a cremated corpse and a holy hermit. This new exposure opened up his mind to the realities of life and to the hermit holy man, who was later a great influence in his life, future and the birth of Buddhism. In his *Introduction to Buddhism*, Thomas Knierim (2002) observed that in April/May 528 BCE, Buddha was meditating under the Bodhi tree in Bodh-Gays, south of Gaya in the state of Bihar, India, when he experienced the Great Enlightenment, which revealed to him the path of salvation from suffering; he spent seven weeks there until he fully realized Buddhahood. He later died from food poisoning at the age of 80 in 483 BCE.

Knierim (2002) identified the Four Noble Truths in Buddhism: life means suffering; the origin of suffering is attachment; the cessation of suffering is attainable, and there is a path to the cessation of suffering (see Figure 4.3).

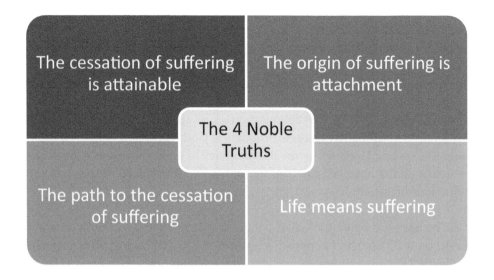

Figure 4.3   The Four Noble Truths in Buddhism

1.   **Life means suffering** – Human beings, and the world we live in, are not perfect, which means we have to endure physical and psychological suffering. This means man cannot get everything he deserves and will pass away one day.

2.   **The origin of suffering is attachment** – Suffering is attached to transient things and the ignorance thereof. Transient things include physical objects around us, ideas and objects of our perceptions, while ignorance is the lack of understanding how our mind is attached to impermanent things which end up being lost. Suffering follows loss (Knierim 2002).

3.   **The cessation of suffering is attainable** – Suffering can be ended by human activities through simply removing the cause of suffering.

4.   **The path to the cessation of suffering** – A path exists to put an end to suffering, which is a gradual corridor of self-improvement extending over many lifetimes, where rebirth is subject to karmic conditioning (Knierim 2002).

Knierim further identifies the Noble Eightfold Path, which describes the way to the end of suffering as outlined by Buddha. This indeed is the ethical and mental development guideline.

Table 4.1 shows the Noble Eightfold Path. *Right view* is the cognitive aspect of wisdom that helps us understand imperfect worldly objects and ideas while grasping the nature of the law of karma and karmic conditioning. *Right intensions* are a commitment to ethical and mental self-improvement. *Right speech* falls under ethical conduct, which is the guideline for moral discipline. Knierim (2002) quoted Buddha's explanation of right speech as abstinence from false speech, abstinence from slanderous speech, abstinence from harsh words that offend others, and abstinence from idle chatter which lacks purpose or depth. *Right action* refers to abstinence from harming sentient beings, especially the taking human life or suicide; abstinence from taking what is not given, such as stealing, robbery, fraud, deceitfulness and dishonesty, and abstinence from sexual misconduct. *Right livelihood* means living in a righteous way while wealth is being acquired legally and peacefully. Buddha does not support dealing in weapons, dealing in living beings, working in meat production or selling intoxicants. *Right efforts* are described as a prerequisite for the other principles of the path. Mental energy is the force behind right efforts, which happen in both wholesome and unwholesome states. *Right mindfulness* emanates from perception, and is the mental ability to perceive things with clear consciousness: 'The mind posits concepts, joins concepts into construct, and weaves those constructs into complex interpretative schemes' (Knierim 2002). *Right concentration* is the development of a mental force, occurring in natural consciousness at a somewhat low level of intensity. In Buddhism, this is practised through moral prescription, mediation and non-violence (Knierim 2002; Pryor 1991; Schumacher 2001).

Table 4.1   Buddhism's Noble Eightfold Path

Right View	Wisdom
Right Intention	
Right Speech	Ethical Conduct
Right Action	
Right Livelihood	
Right Efforts	Mental Development
Right Mindfulness	
Right Concentration	

The Buddhist Four Noble Truths and Noble Eightfold Path have been applied to economics in several forms. Income redistribution in an ideal Buddhist state places great stress on gift-giving, especially to monks and monasteries (Pryor 1991). Pryor observed that 'through the law of karma, there is a distributive cycle of cosmic proportion' which is complemented by moral virtues of compassion and generosity. Pryor examined the Buddhist energy of virtue as a positive externality, and mentioned that the only hope for prosperity is in the regeneration of humankind through promotion of loving kindness, compassion, sympathetic joy and equanimity, or equitability. Regarding economic policies, Buddhism is generally based on ten royal precepts of kingship: generosity, morality, liberality, non-opposition, non-anger, forbearance, non-hurtfulness, self-restraint, gentleness and liberality. Pryor (1991) made reference to the Buddhist ruler King Ruang, who passed economic policies such that taxes should never be more than 10 per cent for crops, and less in periods of drought. He also ensured that the state provided interest-free loans to those who wanted to engage in commerce, with no profit taxes on business transactions. The Buddhist moral economic system distinguished between human needs and wants. Needs are limited to basic consumables or necessities – food, clothing, shelter and medicine (Knierim 2002; Pryor 1991; Schumacher 2001). Buddhists should have just enough to fulfil their basic biological needs after disposing of their entire wealth to the monasteries, while luxury consumption should be relinquished. Buddhism is a doctrine of the middle way. A very modern Buddhist intellectual sees capitalism and communism as paths leading to general materialism and spiritual sickness. In practice, there are two major schools of thought among Buddhist economists – one aligns somewhat with capitalism, while the other leans towards socialism. The socialist prefers nationalization of land through class struggle and eliminating private property. Both schools favour some degree of minimal redistribution of income to cover minimal consumption needs, while others argue that what is most important is the overcoming of self. On the role of government activities in the economy, there is no consensus between the two schools. Those who incline towards capitalism prefer little or no government intervention in business policies, while those who lean towards socialism prefer total government control of business activities and policies.

With regard to labour, Schumacher (2001) points out that the fundamental source of wealth is human labour, which is seen by Buddhists as a chance for man to utilize and develop his faculties, overcome his self-centredness by working in teams, and to be a part of supplying the goods and services necessary for existence. Buddhists believe that there are two forms of work: one enhances a man's skill and power, and the other turns man into a slave or some sort of mechanical tool. Schumacher (2001) asserted that Buddhists do not see the essence of civilization as the multiplication of wants, but in the purification of human character. Extravagance in Buddhism is an act of violence, and Schumacher (2001) noted that even the sale of antique paintings from Europe to the USA, if financially motivated, could be seen as violence since it represents economic gain based on non-renewable fuel. This is termed a parasite on capital instead of income.

Buddhist sociologists and economists see a lot of morality embedded in the Buddhist socio-economic system and its stress on consistent meditation, non-violence and justice. They believe that every aspect of conventional economic thought has a non-violent version, and that literature in this field is expected to grow as much as that covering the Islamic economic system. More than a century after the death of Buddha, the great philosopher Aristotle was born. Most of his works were lost, but what remains has consistently influenced generations globally.

Aristotle's Moral Economic Masterworks

Aristotle was born in 384 BCE. The son of Nicomachus, he was a student of Plato, and was the genius who tutored and inspired Alexander the Great. Rima (2009, p. 6) reviewed the works of Aristotle and observed that he was concerned about the kinds of wealth-getting activities necessary and honourable for man to undertake. Aristotle was particularly bothered about ethics and morals and how some of mankind's economic activities could negatively affect the well-being of the majority of families. Rima (2009, p. 10) observed that Greek thinkers believed that the real purpose of man's existence was to live a good life, which was best achieved within the city-state (*polis*). Thus, for Aristotle, the individual's ethical and moral activities determined the economic status of a state, while Plato felt that this limited the development of economic thought, so he preferred the state to take the lead in development. Rima further looked at the work of Xenophon (*c.* 431–352 BCE) titled *On the Means of Improving the Revenue of the State of Athens*, which addressed the issues of taxes on foreigners to increase revenue and increased production of silver on the assumption that the value of metal would never be lost. Rima (2009, p. 11) quoted the essence of the Stoic philosophy led by the Roman emperor Marcus Aurelius (121–180 CE): 'Be satisfied with your business and learn to love what you were bred to do, and as to the remainder of your life, be entirely resigned, and let the gods do their pleasure with your body and soul.'

Aristotle's moral economic thought centred on the art of gaining wealth through appraisal of several issues. He tried to answer the question of what sort of wealth-getting activity was necessary and honourable for individuals to undertake. He classified the art of wealth accumulation into two areas: household management and retail trade.

PROPERTY IS A PART OF THE HOUSEHOLD

Aristotle said that before we start to examine state management, it is essential to first look at the management of households. He viewed the art of acquiring property as an essential element in household management, and since man needed to live, and indeed live well, he required necessities to achieve this status. This household consisted of freemen and slaves, and must have instruments to make them work or live better. These instruments might be living instruments or lifeless instruments, and they helped to maintain life, the household, the community and then the state. Such property and instruments were elements of true riches, which led to an unlimited good life. However, he also noted that a minimal amount of wealth was essential for man to live a good life.

THE ART OF ACQUISITION

Aristotle observed that another type of wealth accumulation is the art of acquisition. Rima (2009, p. 11) quoted Aristotle: 'Of everything which we possess there are two uses: both belong to the thing as such, but not in the same manner, for one is proper and the other the improper or secondary use of it.' Aristotle gave an example of a shoe, which basically has two uses: it can serve the primary purpose of a shoe, or it can be given out in exchange for money or other goods through bartering. Aristotle said that using a shoe for barter is an unnatural use. This rule, he said, was applicable to all possessions. Aristotle viewed retail trade within the context of exchange by barter, which was not a natural way to get wealth. He saw barbarous nations as those that exchanged with each other the necessities of life. He gave another example of the exchange of wine for corn, and termed such barter trade as contrary to nature.

Aristotle, as captured in Rima's summary of the masterworks, said:

> For the various necessities of life are not easily carried about, and hence
> men agree to employ in their dealings with each other something which
> was intrinsically useful and easily applicable to the purposes of life, for
> example, iron, silver, and the like. Of this the value was first measured
> simply by size and weight, but in process of time they put a stamp upon
> it, to save the trouble of weighing and to mark the value.

In other words, Aristotle preferred the use of money (iron, silver, gold and so on),
which has intrinsic value, for the purpose of exchange or trade rather than barter.

THE NATURE OF MONEY

Aristotle saw bartering as an unnatural method of wealth accumulation, and
favoured unitized pieces of valuable metals that could be referred to as money.
He went further to say that:

> the most hated sort, and worth the greatest reason, is usury, which
> makes a gain out of money itself, and not from the natural object of
> it. For money was indeed to be used in exchange, but not to increase
> at interest. And this term interest, which means the birth of money
> from money, is applied to the breeding of money because the offspring
> resembles the parent. Wherefore of all modes of getting wealth, this is
> the most unnatural.
>
> (Politics, c. 300 BCE, in Rima 2009)

For Aristotle, earning money from money is usury, and is an unnatural means
of wealth accumulation. In the same vein, money should only be a medium of
exchange, and not a commodity in itself.

Aristotle was a scholar, and his work remains relevant in today's socio-
economic models. However, a question may arise as to the practical import
of Aristotle to the world of his time. He was the tutor of Alexander the Great,
whom many Islamic jurists believe to be Zul-qarnain, which literally means
'the two-horned one' in the Quran, Suratul Al-Kahf (18:83–98). The Quranic
commentary of Yusuf Ali (1983, p. 753), which explains the attributes of Zul-
qarnain, says: 'Zul-qarnain illustrates how power and opportunities should be
used in the service of God: he punished the guilty indeed, but was kind to
the righteous; he left primitive people their freedom of life; and he protected
industrious people from grasping neighbours.' Alexander the Great is indeed
the greatest practical success of Aristotle outside his *Politics*. The world was

growing more familiar with the works of Aristotle and other great philosophers during the time when Christ introduced his own teaching.

Biblical Moral Economics

Contemporary scholars have started to look at how the biblical version of moral economics can be related to modern economic development theories. There is a general notion that the classical and neo-classical economic models align with Christianity. This volume looks at the classical biblical teaching only in terms of the concept of poverty, unrighteous wealth, money and interest or usury.

POVERTY

Poverty was evident at the time of Christ, and he encouraged many to sell their property in order to be able to give more to the needy. Acts 5:34–7 says:

> *Neither was there any among them that lacked: for as many as were possessors of lands or houses sold them, and brought the prices of the things that were sold. And laid them down at the apostles' feet; and distribution was made unto every man according as he had need. And Joses, who by the apostles was surnamed Barnabas (which is, being interpreted, The son of consolation), a Levite, and of the country of Cyprus. Having land, sold it, and brought the money, and laid it at the apostles' feet.*

In Luke 18:22, after Jesus had read the Ten Commandments, it says: 'Now when Jesus heard these things, he said unto him, yet lackest thou one thing: sell all that thou hast, and distribute unto the poor, and thou shalt have treasure in heaven: and come, follow me.' Christian theologians argue whether it is allowed for Christians to own private property, and many answer yes, since they can hold property on behalf of Jesus, who is the real owner of their property.[1] The followers of Christ asked about the kind of poverty challenges they would face if they did not hold on to their property, and Christ's reply was: 'But seek ye first the kingdom of God, and His righteousness; and all these things shall be added unto you. Take therefore no thought for the morrow, for the morrow shall take thought for the things of itself. Sufficient unto the day is the evil thereof' (Matthew 6:33–4). These verses have several interpretations in the twenty-first century. The important fact here is that the biblical moral economic structure is based on a very high degree of charity to the needy. The 10 per cent monthly tithe

---

1   http://kingwatch.co.nz/Christian_Political_Economy.htm (accessed 9 September 2013).

is the most effective alms giving by Christians to support the Church and the needy. This is specifically laid out in Deuteronomy 14:22, which says: 'Thou shalt truly tithe all the increase of thy seed that the field bringeth forth year by year.'

UNRIGHTEOUS WEALTH

Christ placed a lot of emphasis on unrighteous mammon. 'Mammon' is a Syriac word for money and the idol of wealth.[2] Christ said that wealth earned by not hurting people was righteous, but the kind of wealth gained by enslaving people through forced labour or unethical working conditions was unrighteous wealth. Those Christ asked to sell their property may have come by it through unethical means. Unrighteous wealth is obtained through deception, theft, manipulation or dishonesty.[3] There are four ways to repent from unrighteous wealth. First, restore capital or return the money to the rightful owners. Second, make restitution by giving out much more of that item, money or goods as charity. A typical example is Zacchaeus, the tax collector who 'stood and said unto the Lord; Behold, Lord, the half of my goods I give to the poor; and if I have taken anything from any man by false accusation, I restore him four folds' (Luke 19:8). Third, give to the poor, especially where one is unable to locate those who were cheated or where the unethical wealth came from. Finally, even up the distribution of capital due to income or economic inequalities in the society. In Christianity, it is not advisable to hand out money to people in cases where it would lead to waste. In such situations, it is better to train potential recipients so that they will be able to manage capital, and not squander it in pointless consumption.[4] In other cases, they can be provided with the necessary factors of production.

DEFINITION OF MONEY

In his publication *The Legitimacy of Non-interest Banking in Nigeria*, Abdul Rahman Oshodi (2010) examined the opinion of Church scholars, The Scholastics (1100–1500 CE), and asserted:

> the Church scholars, familiar with the available writings in existence, echoed Aristotle. Thomas Aquinas argued that money is a measure, and usury 'diversifies the measure' placing extra demands on the money mechanism which harmed its function as a measure. Henry of Ghent wrote that: 'Money is medium in exchange, and not terminus.'

---

2   http://kingwatch.co.nz/Christian_Political_Economy.htm (accessed 9 September 2013).
3   http://kingwatch.co.nz/Christian_Political_Economy.htm (accessed 9 September 2013).
4   http://kingwatch.co.nz/Christian_Political_Economy.htm (accessed 9 September 2013).

Alexander Lombard noted, 'Money should not be able to be bought and sold for it is not extreme in selling or buying, but medium.'

PROHIBITION OF USURY

Quoting from the website Kingdom Watcher:

> *The Old Testament prohibits interest on loans to the poor, because they are a form of charity (Ex 22:24; Lev 25:35–37). The poor person will have to use the money borrowed for consumption goods so there will be no profit, which can be used to pay interest. This prohibition on interest was erroneously extended by Christians to business loans (Matt 25:27). Interest on commercial loans for the use in trade or business is not forbidden.[5]*

Specifically, Exodus 22:24–5 reads:

> *And my wrath shall wax hot, and I will kill you with the sword; and your wives shall be widows, and your children fatherless; if thou lend money to any of my people that is poor by thee, thou shalt not be to him as an usurer, neither shalt thou lay upon him usury.*

Leviticus 25:35–7 says:

> *And if thy brother be waxen poor, and fallen in decay with thee; then thou shalt relieve him: yea, though he be a stranger, or a so-journer; that he may live with thee. Take no usury of him, or increase but fear thy God; that thy brother may live with thee. Thou shall not give him thy money upon usury, not lend him thy victuals for increase.*

Oshodi (2010) referred to the work of Pope Leo the Great (440–461 CE), who laid the cornerstone for later usury laws when he forbade clerics practising usury and condemned laymen for it. Oshodi (2010) mentioned further that in 850 CE, the Synod of Paris excommunicated all usurers. The 2nd Lateran Council (1139) declared that unrepentant usurers were condemned by both the Old and New Testaments. Pope Urban III (1185–1187) cited Christ's words, 'lend freely, hoping nothing thereby' (Luke 6:35). Oshodi concluded by saying that usurers were required to make monetary restitution to their 'victims'.

---

5   http://kingwatch.co.nz/Christian_Political_Economy.htm (accessed 9 September 2013).

Vast amounts of such moneys were involved in death bequests. The heirs of usurers were also required to make restitution.

Ingrid Rima's work examines *Summa Theologica* ('Summary of Theology' or 'Highest Theology') by Thomas Aquinas (*c.* 1225–1274), written in 1269–90 CE, which saw cheating in trade and usury on loans as unethical and immoral acts. Under cheating in trade, *Summa Theologica* asked four questions:

- whether it was lawful to sell a thing for more than its worth;

- whether a sale was rendered unlawful through a fault in the thing sold;

- whether the seller was bound to reveal a fault in the thing sold;

- whether it was lawful in trading to sell a thing at a higher price than was paid for it (Rima 2009, p. 17).

Under the sin of usury, *Summa Theologica* asked:

- whether it was a sin to take money as a price for money lent, which was to receive usury;

- whether it was lawful to lend money for any other kind of consideration, by way of payment for the loan;

- whether a man was bound to restore just gains derived from money taken in usury;

- whether it was lawful to borrow money under a condition of usury. (Rima 2009, p. 18).

Rima also observed that the Bible accepts some kinds of usury, but Jews to Jews may not collect usury except from non-Jews. So, is usury ethical and moral to some people and not to others? The answer to this question is the foundation of the Islamic economic system.

The Foundation of the Islamic Moral Economic System

The Islamic moral economic system is based on *fiqh al-muamalat* – Islamic commercial jurisprudence derived from the Shariah, Islamic law:

> *The very objective of the Shariah is to promote the wellbeing of the people, which lies in safeguarding their faith (din), their self (nafs), their intellect (aql), their posterity (nasl), and their wealth (mal). Whatever ensures the safeguard of these five serves public interest and is desirable, and whatever hurts them is against public interest and its removal is undesirable.*
>
> *(Al-Ghazali, quoted in Chapra 2008c)*

This system seeks to promote a moral, socio-economic system that eliminates undue profits in business transactions and a bias-fee social structure. The Islamic economic system:

> *is a socialism which is not based on the competition of capital or class war, as socialism is in the West today, but on the moral principles guaranteeing fraternity between the classes and fostering mutual security and cooperation for all the good and felicity of their members, instead of crime and transgression. It is relatively easy to appreciate such Quranic socialism based upon brotherhood and institutionalized in Zakat, and charity.*
>
> *(Haykal 1976)*

> *Islamic socialism, meanwhile, brought together two powerful indictments of capitalism within contemporary Islamic discourse: its social dysfunctionality, and its power to disorder the moral universe, finding their inspiration, respectively, in modern notions of society and social function, and in pre-modern ideas of the harmony that should exist in human interactions, reflecting the balance of the God-given universe.*
>
> *(Tripp 2006)*

This system appreciates values, rules and behaviour; removal of poverty; moral and material education; good governance, and the well-being of all (Chapra 2008c). The crystallization of this moral economic system further defined the concept of Islamic banking and finance based on the principles of the avoidance of interest, uncertainty, gambling and unethical concern. It is also based on the philosophy of risk and reward in business transactions, asset-backed dealings, the quest for justice and Shariah guidance. The system thus 'has a built-in tendency to prevent concentration of wealth and power' (Budd 1986).

Haykal (1976, p. 550) described this economic system as 'Islamic socialism', and observed:

> the socialism of Islam is not the socialism of capital and distribution but one founded upon fraternity in the spiritual, moral, and economic spheres of life. A person's Iman (faith) is not regarded as completed until that person wishes for his fellow being that which he wishes for himself, it can be deduced safely that no Iman is complete unless its subject has urged the feeding of the hungry and has spent privately and publicly of what God has provided, with a view of serving the commonwealth. The more altruistic a person becomes, the closer he comes to realizing internal peace and happiness. This is indeed social justice as it relates to Islamic economic system.

Chapra (1976, pp. 149–50, in Khurshid et al. 1980) mentioned that some of the essential functions of the Islamic welfare state with respect to the economy may seek to eradicate poverty and the real value of money, maintain law and order, ensure social and economic justice, arrange social security and foster equitable distribution of income and wealth, and harmonize international relations while ensuring national defence. In the same vein, Haykal (1976, p. 551) said that this economic system is the highest that has ever been reached by man in any period, and that Islamic civilization is not only truly worthy of mankind, but also the only one that can guarantee man's happiness.

There are three basic elements in Islam: *Aqidah* – faith and belief; *Akhlaq* – morality and ethics, and *Shariah* – Islamic practical law.

Aqidah consists of six main articles:

1.   belief in One God;

2.   belief in all the Prophets of God, including Moses and Jesus;

3.   belief in the Divine Books: Zabour of David; Tawrat of Moses and Injil (the New Testament) of Jesus;

4.   belief in the Angels of God, including Jubril (Gabrael);

5.   belief in resurrection – the Day of Reckoning;

6.   belief in predestination.

Akhlaq has to do with the relationship of man with man, such as interest and the well-being of fellow humankind; love, sincerity and care; compassion and patience, and consideration and flexibility.

Shariah is the Islamic law, which is comprised of the Quran (words of Allah – the Creator) and the *Sunnah* (sayings and deeds of the Prophet Mohammed). *Fiqh* is the knowledge of the legal rules pertaining to conduct that have been derived from specific evidence (Nyazee 2000), the understanding of Shariah. There are five sources of Islamic law: the Quran, the Sunnah, Ijmah (consensus), Qiyas (analogy) and Ijtihad (interpretation).

The Quran is a divine book revealed to Prophet Mohammad over a 23-year period, which contains the works of other Prophets and Messengers of God such as Adam, Noah, Ibrahim (Abraham), Dahood (David), Sulayman (Solomon), Musa (Moses) and Isa (Jesus). Allah also gave Mohammed – popularly called 'the Prophet' (of Islam) – other rules and regulations that guide man in his social, political and economic life which are all embedded in the religion called Islam – a complete way of life. For example, the Quran says 'O you who believe, do not consume *riba* (interest) doubled and redoubled so that you may be successful' (Q3:130). It also says: 'Allah has permitted trading and forbidden *riba* ' (Q2:275). There are so many rules like that, but Mohammed exemplifies the explanation of all these laws in a very practical manner. The manuscript of the Quran was compiled during the Prophet's time, and can be easily and completely memorized because of the rhythm and smooth flow in its recitation.

Thus the Sunnah (literally 'well-known path') is the sayings and deeds of the Prophet. His sayings are called the Hadith. His acts are those authentic behaviours of the Prophet that gained legal status. His tacit approvals are some actions and deeds of this followers and companions which he saw or knew about but on which he did not comment. This silence amounts to tacit approval.

The Prophet gave his last major sermon on Mount Arafat, Makkah to over 115,000 Muslims in the 10th year of the *Hijra* (624 CE), and started to address economic issues before the core religious matters. He said:

Allah has forbidden you to take usury, therefore all interest obligation shall henceforth be waived. Your capital is yours to keep. You will neither inflict nor suffer any inequality. Allah has judged that there shall be no interest and that all interest due to Abbas Ibn 'Aal-Muttalib be waived.

Thereafter, he touched on the Five Pillars of Islam and many other religious morals. This shows the priority Islam gives to moral economic justice as a precondition for a good social system.

Ijma literally means 'agreement on a matter'. Technically, it is consensus or agreement among independent Islamic jurists about the interpretation of the Shariah. A practical example is the definition of *riba* (interest), which was perfected in the 1970s when Islamic jurists around the world firmly agreed on its definition, and which became the most important element in the Islamic economic system.

Qiyas, which literally means 'estimating and measuring', is a method of reaching a legal decision where some evidence, rules or precedents are evident in the Quran, Sunnah or Ijma. In this case, there will be a common reason why the new case does not have a legal rule in itself, but has an underlying rationale in the legal rules. Thus if there arises a situation in practical banking and finance, such as hedge funds, which never existed during the Prophet's time, jurists will critically analyse the subject and see whether it complies with the principles or elements of Islamic finance, such as avoidance of interest, uncertainty, gambling and unethical concern. In cases where such financial deals are based on reward/risk-sharing, investment must be asset-backed, morally just, and Shariah governance must be present.

Ijtihad literally means 'exertion, effort or striving', and technically means 'the efforts an Islamic jurist makes in order to deduce from the law something that is not evident from the original sources' (Abbasi 2009a). Many scholars are of the opinion that there should be no more *jtihad* after year 1258 or the period of the Abbasid Dynasty (150–1258 CE). The opposite of this is *taqleed*, which means 'imitation'. An illustration is the penalty charge on late payment, which is given to charity on behalf of the defaulter and does not form part of an Islamic bank's income.

THE FOUR SCHOOLS OF THOUGHT

There are four main schools of thought in the interpretation of the Quran and Sunnah, and they have slight differences in some of their interpretations. These schools are defined using the names of the four Imams – religious leaders who spread across different regions in Africa, the Middle East, Europe and Asia: Abu Hanifa al-No'man, referred to as the Hanafi School; Malik Ibn Anas referred to as Maliki School; Muhammed Ibn Idris al-Shafi'l, referred to as Shafi School, and Ahmad Ibn Hambal, referred to as Hambali School. The Hanafi School is mainly followed in Russia, Kazakhstan down to Afghanistan, Pakistan, part of India, Iran, Iraq, Turkey and part of Europe. The Maliki School covers North and West Africa, a small part of Saudi Arabia, and Kuwait. The Shafi School covers part of India, Bangladesh, Malaysia, Indonesia, Sudan, Ethiopia, Somalia, Tanzania and some parts of Southern Africa. The Hambali School is predominantly followed in Saudi Arabia. These schools are globally accepted, and they generally have an impact on the ways Muslims all over the world practise Islam. The same applies to Islamic jurisprudence covering Islamic finance. However, *ijma*, or consensus, among these schools is very common in Islamic finance.

THE NATURE OF MONEY IN ISLAM

In classical economics, there are four factors of production: money which is expected to earn interest, land expected to earn rent, entrepreneurs expected to make profit, and labour expected to earn wages. Abu-Saud (1976, in Khurshid et al. 1980) found in his study that most economists define money by its four classical functions: means of exchange, measure of value, medium of deferred value, and store of value. He mentioned that Patikin, Tobin, Gurley and Shaw, Pigou, Metzler, and Haberler are among the economists who do not include fiat money and its attributes of wealth. Milton Friedman, Martin Baily, William Pesek and Thomas Saving ignore the 'money as debt' argument and flatly state that money is a part of what we economically call relevant wealth and of net worth. Pesek and Saving admit that money is not totally identical with other goods. Don Patikin took up the Pesek-Saving theory and tried to show it was fallacious. He collaborated with Kalechi on the latter's view that money is a component of wealth. Abu Saud summed up his argument by saying:

> *money can be a quasi-commodity having a demand and a limited supply, there will be some undeniable difference between the usual commodities and money.*

- *Money has a technical (or artificial) property of yielding its owner real income simply by holding it without exchanging it against other goods.*
- *It has no carrying cost, no production cost, cost (almost so) and no substitute having complete liquidity.*
- *Demand on money is not genuine as it is derived from demand for goods that money can buy.*
- *Money is exempt from the law of depreciation to which all goods are subjected.*
- *Money is the product of social convention having a purchasing power derived mainly from the sovereignty as against the intrinsic value of other goods.*

This volume will therefore limit consideration of money within the framework of Islamic economics to a means of exchange.

THE EMERGENCE OF DEBT

Seventeenth-century goldsmiths stored gold for people and issued receipts, in which people developed much confidence. This public confidence led people to start trading in receipts without redeeming gold from the goldsmiths. As a result, bankers pumped masses of artificial receipts into the economy and they earned interest. The public confidence also led to a consistent reduction in the reserve ratio, and 100 per cent backing by reference to gold became unnecessary. In 1913, the US Federal Reserve Act gave privately owned Federal Reserve Banks permission to operate a 'reserve ratio' and created non-asset-backed artificial money. In 1931, the Bank of England stopped exchanging notes for gold since the artificial money was no longer backed by it. In 1944, the Bretton Woods agreement de-linked all currency from gold except the US dollar, which was later delinked in 1971 by President Nixon. Chapra (2008b) observed that the 2008 economic crisis was a function of the emergence of credit default swaps (CDSs), which are a way of insuring debt. He also mentioned other collateralized debt obligations (CODs) that mixed prime and subprime debt, lacked transparency, leading to fraud, and supervisory failure. In Islam, pure debt is prohibited since it has to do with lending for a fixed return which could be used for economic activity or exploitative purposes. This does not align with the Islamic concept of equity and justice.

DEFINING RIBA – FINANCIAL INTEREST

Allah says in the Quran:

> *O you who believe, fear Allah and give up what remains of your demand for interest if you are indeed a believer. If you do not, then you are warned of the declaration of war from Allah and His Messenger [Mohammed]; but if you turn back you shall have your principal. Deal not unjustly and you shall not be dealt with unjustly.*
>
> *(Quran 278, verses 278–9)*

Jabir bin Abdullah reported that the Prophet cursed the receiver of interest and the payer thereof, the one who records it and the two witnesses thereof. He said they are all alike in guilt. *Riba* literally means 'increase in' or 'addition to' anything. Technically, it is what the creditor charges the debtor at a fixed rate on the principal earned (Afzalua 1979). Muhmud Abu-Saud (1976, in Khurshid et al. 1980) quoted Samuelson, and said that interest is the price or rental for the use of money. Don Patikin said it is one of the forms of income from property, the other forms being dividends, rent and profits. Keynes held that the monetary rate of interest is the percentage of excess of a sum of units of money concentrated for forward units of time over spot or cash price of the sum thus contracted for forward delivery. Hanson (1973) saw it as a payment for the use of capital. Doi (1983) said it is any amount on capital or unfair gain in a transaction. Ali (1983) viewed interest as undue profit made not in the way of legitimate trade. Asad (1980) said that it signifies any unlawful addition to a sum of money by another person or body of persons. Zafar (1999) said that it is a pre-determined pricing of capital.

Interest is a form of payment for the use of capital funds (Uzar 1976, in Khurshid et al. 1980). It is the excess money paid by the borrower to the lender over and above the principal for the use of the lender's liquid money for a certain period of time (Saud 1976, in Khurshid et al. 1980). It is the price of money, opportunity cost of holding money, and the return for parting with liquidity (Central Bank of Nigeria 1999). Afzalua (1979) simply viewed interest as an evil to society, economically, socially and morally. El-Gamal (2006) observed in his study of *riba* that 'most conservative contemporary jurists do not consider all forms of what economists and regulators call interest to be forbidden riba'. He went further to mention two Islamic asset-financing instruments, *murabahah* (purchase and resale at mark-up) and *ijarah* (leasing), which are not interest-free. He argued further that the 'prohibition of *riba-al-fadl* (increase) illustrates definitively that there are forms of forbidden *riba* (illegitimate increase in exchange) that do not include interest'. 1st Ethical (2008) followed the path of most jurists by dividing *riba* into two main categories: *riba al-nase'ah* (delay/waiting) which involves charging a specific increase or profit on a specific amount lent for a given period. This includes *riba al-jahiliya* (a premium increased due to more time), *riba al-Quran* (a condition increased from the outset) and *riba Qard* (*riba* paid monthly on the capital at end of term). The second major type of *riba* is *riba al-fadl* (increase), which is the excess taken in the exchange of homogenous commodities and encountered in hand-to-hand purchase and sale. They can also be divided into *riba al-bay* (interest in business) and *riba al-Hadith* (interest from the Prophet). Islamic scholars thus agree that interest on loans or rent for the use of money is prohibited outright, but credit sale on mark-up bases is allowed.

THE INSTITUTION OF ZAKAT

There are five pillars in Islam: *Iman* (belief in One God), *Salat* (observing the five daily worship/prayer periods), *Zakat* (alms-giving), *Hajj* (pilgrimage to Mecca) and *Siyam* (fasting in the month of Ramadan). *Zakat* is a compulsory tax of 2.5 per cent of a Muslim's net annual wealth paid into a special treasury to redistribute wealth or assist the needy. Literally, the word means 'to grow and increase', since the purpose is to cleanse the wealth and souls of Muslims. Bashar and Dikko (2003) reviewed the work of Qardawi and mentioned that *zakat* implies cleanliness and cleansing. In personal terms, it means 'betterment and righteousness'. Siddiqi (1994) observed that the economic implications of *zakat* relate to savings, investment, income distribution, economic growth and social security. Tripp (2006) noted that *zakat* represents a key component of the moral economy since it epitomizes a number of ideas which help to define the economy. Practically speaking, financial institutions come into this programme by offering financial products based on *zakat* – term savings accounts or investment accounts which create long-term liabilities for them to provide Shariah-compliant assets and investments for economic development purposes, which also yield profit for the depositor and fee income for the bank. The 2.5 per cent *zakat* remittances go into a special *zakat* account that is used to assist the less privileged in society by channelling the funds through non-governmental organizations and charities. Since *zakat* is paid annually, liquidity will be consistently available and other charity-related projects like *waqf* (endowment) will be embarked on. *Waqf* are investments owned by the community and whose yields are used for communal needs only.

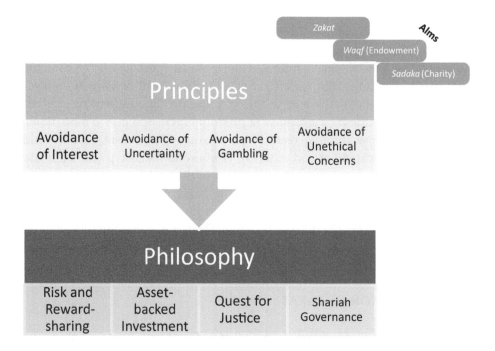

Figure 4.4   The principles and philosophy of Islamic banking
Source: Oshodi (2012a).

THE PRINCIPLES AND PHILOSOPHY OF ISLAMIC BANKING

The concept and practice of Islamic banking and finance all over the world are dependent on four main principles and philosophies (see Figure 4.4). The principles include the avoidance of *riba*, *gharar* (risky sale), *miysir* (gambling) and unethical concerns. The philosophies affirm risk- and reward-sharing, asset-backed investment, the quest for justice, and the practice of Shariah governance in transactions.

Riba is an excess, addition or undue reward for lending (Standard Bank 2009; *New Horizon* 2008a; Choudhury and Abdul Malik 1992). *Gharar* is something uncertain, probability, hazard, danger, peril or extreme risk (Standard Bank 2009; Afzalua 1979). Afzalua says further that there are two types of *gharar*: where elements of doubt, probability and uncertainty are involved in peril or risk, and where one of the parties in a transaction purposefully introduces an element of doubt as a result of deceit or fraud. *Miysir*, or gambling, is specifically mentioned in the Quran when Allah says: 'They ask you (O Mohammed) concerning wine and gambling! Say, in them is great sin and some profit for men; but the sin is greater than the profit' (Quran 2, verse 219). The Quran says further: 'all forms of gambling and betting are prohibited and are considered acts of impiety and abomination' (Quran 5, verse 3). Another traditional text is contained in the Hadith, where the Prophet says: 'the selling of foodstuff before receiving it and the selling of a thing which you don't have'. He also says: 'the sale of something absent for something present is also illegal and usurious' (Al-Quastalani V.4: 56, Chapter 46 Sahih Bukhari). *Miysir* literally means getting something too easily without hard labour, or receiving a profit without working for it, thus it is termed gambling (Afzalua 1979). The Prophet forbade the sale of *munabaha*: 'It is like gambling where two persons may agree to barter one thing or another without seeing or checking either of them' (V.5 Hadith no. 356 Sahih Bukhari). Unethical concern is anything the Shariah and *fiqh* term as unacceptable or interpreted as such by Shariah scholars.

In Islamic finance, *riba* relates to investments in interest-based transactions in conventional financial institutions such as banks, insurance companies and conventional bonds. Other forms include investments in alcohol or intoxicants, pork, cigarettes and tobacco, adult entertainment, arms and ammunitions, illegal trade, and any transaction or products the Shariah advisers judge unethical. The nature of business transactions in Islamic finance must share risk and reward, or profit and loss, by using Shariah-compliant financial modes or instruments such as *mudarabah* (partnership) and *musharakah* (joint venture). Other instruments, such as *qardh* (loan), *qardh-hassan* (good loan), *amanah* (trust), *wadiah* (safe-keeping), *murabahah* (purchase at mark-up), *ijarah* (Islamic leasing), *salam* (deferred delivery), *istisna* (build to order) and *sukuk* (Islamic financial certificates), can also be applied in a manner that ensures justice and fairness in transactions while spreading the risk among all parties. Depending on the method of application in business, these instruments ensure the investments embarked on are asset-backed and that principles of fairness are applied. Chapra (1992, p. 252) observed that official policies that concentrate the wealth and power in a few hands within communities are largely the result of an unjust economic structure.

Choudhury and Abdul Malik (1992, pp. 166–7) view justice within an Islamic economy as a social good in terms of consumption and production, which should be ethically adopted by the market system. They also stress that this financial system should 'produce goods that fully mobilize the resources of society towards productive transformation using of *zakat*, abolition of interest, and the establishment of *mudarabah* (investment partnership)'.

Justice entails equal reward and treatment for every individual in proportion to their contribution to society with the prevention of exploitation by the elite class (Bashar and Dikko 2003, p. 23). In other words, Islamic banking and finance must consider products and services that bring out the entrepreneurial skills and strength in the economically less privileged members of society with the aim of developing a better life for them and society at large. Finally, a Shariah board or advisory council/committee must be on ground in the Islamic financial institution to ensure end-to-end compliance with Shariah. This condition is most important, since its absence renders all other conditions void.

Studies of the Islamic economic system clearly mix Islam as a religion with Islamic commercial jurisprudence, economics, political economy, banking and finance, ethics and morals, and many more variables. It is these uncoordinated studies that have led Dr Mohammed Omar Farooq and many other researchers to judge that Islamic economics suffers from poverty of content and is unable to address issues of poverty at large. Farooq (2009c) asserted that the 'Muslim world owns a significant share of global poverty while there are lessons to be learnt from the experience and knowledge-base of the developed world to alleviate [the] Muslim world's pervasive poverty'. He also mentioned 'the rise of Islamic economics as part of a revivalist ethos of the twentieth century came with the promise to transform at least the Muslim world'. Islamic economics has yet to demonstrate what it claims, while Muslim-majority countries are among the poorest in the world, with the least education and human skills, perhaps with the exception of the oil-rich Gulf states. What tool will Islamic finance use to actualize its abstract model? Will borrowing from successful economic development models make it non-Shariah-compliant? Will it dilute the potency of this 'moral' economic structure? Should Islamic economics limit its practice to banking and finance? Can the Islamic economics model alone promote economic growth, development and good governance in any country, thereby reducing poverty? The answers require that we analyse the realities and performance of Islamic banking and finance in different countries.

Conclusion

The core foundation of religion is morality, which encompasses every aspect of the great religions of the world. Morality covers the man-to-man relationship, the man-to-God relationship and the man-to-society relationship through a variety of religious ethics and socio-economic moral theories. God sends messengers to every part of the world. Many are popular, especially those from the Middle East, but most of them are from Europe, Africa and Asia. While they may not be known except by people in their immediate environments, many are simply called philosophers, or great men and women who influenced history. All religions teach moral economics, and the most common factor is the prohibition of usury – a tenet universal to all the religions and philosophies examined in this chapter. Prohibition of interest or usury can thus be seen as the foundation of every religion, and their major pillar is the act of charity. Judaism, Christianity and Islam are based on exactly the same history, the difference being that Jews and Muslims do not believe that Jesus Christ is the son of God. Muslims say he is only one of the Prophets of God. Christians, on the other hand, do not believe in Prophet Mohammed, who is from among their brethren, from the lineage of Ismail. Buddha's teachings are not much different to those of Moses, Jesus and Mohammed, especially regarding his moral and economic thoughts. Everything Aristotle said on wealth-getting activities agrees with Islamic teachings, and his student, Alexander the Great, may have been portrayed in the Quran under the title Zul-qarnain.

The remainder of this book will develop the ideal socio-economic transformational model, tapping into the well-developed Islamic economic system, focusing specifically on poverty reduction in the continent of Africa, and exploring further the influence of the triple heritage. We will then look at the development of economic analysis, covering modernization theories, dependencies theories, world system theories and emerging economic theories in the twenty-first century.

5

Economic Thinking Leading to an African Context

Introduction

Chapter 4 covered aspects of moral economics across religions and ideologies, which are seen as the foundation on which this whole research is based. This leads to the relevance of moral considerations in the development of economic theories. Economic theories evolved gradually from the Physiocrats to modern-day Joseph Stiglitz and Ronnie Lessem. Early economic thoughts started to emerge around the mid-eighteenth century under classical economics, gaining favour with Adam Smith, Thomas Malthus, David Ricardo and Karl Marx. They then became neo-classical economics, which drew from the works of principal actors like Alfred Marshall and J.M. Keynes, thus leading to modernization theories. The 'Third World' countries grew uncomfortable with economic policies that seemed alien to their society, hence giving rise to dependency theories, which then split into dependency/neo-dependency theories and dynamic dependency theories. Argentinean economist Raul Prebisch led the way in this field, while Japan-moulded, state-led development quickly enveloped much of Far East. Immanuel Wallerstein, born in Columbia, engaged in ethnographic studies in Africa and opened the floodgates to a completely new view of economic development and what matters most to developing countries. From this, African World System Thoughts started to develop, from Africans in Africa. Dilip Mookherjee and his co-researchers explored the nature of development economics, where there is interplay between theory and empirical research, giving rise to new development economics in the twentieth century. Nobel Prize winner Joseph Stiglitz looked at market and government failures within institutions in developing countries. Sam Rima's Spiritual Capital Theory then added a completely new flavour to moral economics, while Ronnie Lessem and Alexander Schieffer drew from the Four World/GENE Model in designing Integral Dynamics.

Modernization Theories

Modernization theories emerged during the Industrial Revolution in Western Europe as countries transited from mainly agricultural economies to industrial ones. These theories continued to improve from the end of the Second World War up to the 1960s. They deal with the gradual modernization of societies and economies, and place further stress on both the process of change and reactions to it. Modernization theories assume that the economic development pattern experienced in the West and North are also expected in the East and South regardless of their socio-political setting, while they link economic growth to development on the bases of the effectiveness of capital, science and technology (Escobar 2008). Modernization theories may be further categorized into classical economic theories, and neo-classical economic theories.

CLASSICAL ECONOMIC THEORIES

Physiocracy

The Newtonian system recognizes that physical events obey certain laws which are universal, and calls for an inquiry into laws that govern human events and set forth ways of 'improving the social environment might be prescribed on the bases of these principles' (Rima 2009, p. 70). Rima mentioned that the Physiocrats scrutinized social processes in order to discover the causes and principles of regularities, just like Sir Isaac Newton (1632–1727) and many other physical scientists did in the realm of natural phenomena. The word 'physiocracy' came from the French word *physiocrate*, first used by Dupont de Nemours in 1776 after Quesnay's death. It literally refers to the law of nature, hence the need to conform to this natural order, which will ensure man's happiness. Not abiding by it will lead to catastrophic outcomes (Rima 2009, p. 73).

In the same vein, this philosophy suggests that it is not necessary and not desirable for governments to regulate, and that such legislational conflicts with nature are unnecessary because they conflict with nature and are thus exposed to failure – hence, the law of nature is supreme – leading to the foundation of *laissez-faire, laissez passer* ('let it be, let it happen'). This ideology thus became the foundation of the development of subsequent economic theories (Rima 2009, p. 73). The Physiocrats became concerned about laws that govern the distribution of wealth. France is regarded as the location of the first school of theoretical economics, and the beginning of a tradition of thought that is now called classical (Rima 2009, p. 70). François Quesnay, on the other hand, gave birth to economics by publishing *Tableau Economique* in 1758. He analysed the likely sources of disturbance as: a change in the proportion of income spent on agriculture, a change in the tax system, and an increase in the price of food that would improve the rate of return in agriculture (Rima 2009, p. 77). He described an economy as closed and stationary, where foreign trade is absent and savings are equal to the replacement needs of capital. He largely sought to explain the way net product is created and circulated among the three classes of economy, which is then reproduced the following year in order for the system to maintain itself. This period later witnessed writings from Adam Smith from Scotland, who was a key protagonist of the Scottish Enlightenment.

Adam Smith's The Wealth of Nations

Adam Smith, the master of classical economics, was born in 1723, and became an undergraduate at Glasgow and a Snell fellow at Balliol College, Oxford. At the University of Glasgow, where he lectured in moral philosophy, his teacher Francis Hutcheson (1694–1746) classified his subject into four branches: natural theology, ethics, jurisprudence and political economy. Smith became a Professor of Logic and then the Chair of Moral Philosophy. He later travelled to France as a tutor to the young Duke of Buccleuch in 1764, where he was exposed to the Physiocrats (Black 1971, p. 9). R.D. Collison Black wrote that a pension guarantee from the Duke of Buccleuch allowed Smith to devote the period 1767–76 to his work *The Wealth of Nations*, which became a classic, leading to contemporary economic theories; Rima (2009), however, noted that Smith never completed this book.

Smith's *The Theory of Moral Sentiments* (1759) reflects the grounding of classical political economy in moral philosophy, emphasizing human happiness and well-being (Rima 2009, p. 93). He sought to examine 'the happiness and perfection of a man, considered not only as an individual but as a member of a family, of a state, and of a great society of mankind' (Adam Smith, in Rima 2009). Rima (2009, p. 96) observed further that Smith's analysis of the social origin of moral judgement and standards was essential to individual and national interests that led to *The Wealth of Nations*. Smith opened up the theoretical framework and debate about the division of labour, the nature of money, and the impact of savings and investment on national economic progress. He also opened debate to issues around supply and demand, the development of foreign trade, and the adjustment of supply and demand to each other – which are necessary activities to human behaviour and which benefit humanity and society as a whole. Black (1971, p. 23) carefully examined

Smith's thoughts on labour, and observed that they represented the 'only universal, as well as the only accurate measure of value, or the only standard by which we can compare the values of different commodities at all times, at all places', thereby formulating the Wages Fund Theory (Rima 2009, p. 118). On the nature of money, Smith gave preference to gold over silver as the metal to be recognized as the standard, or measure, of value (Black 1971, p. 27), and largely maintained that the use of money eliminated the inconvenience of barter (Rima 2009, p. 103). During this period, Thomas Malthus emerged, who built on the works of Smith, but with more stress on population issues.

Thomas Malthus's Essay on the Principle of Population

Thomas Robert Malthus was born near Dorking in 1766, went to Jesus College, Cambridge in 1793, and became Professor of Modern History and Political Economy at the East India College at Haileybury. Malthus's book *An Essay on the Principle of Population* stressed that 'the power of population is indefinitely greater than the power in the earth to produce subsistence for man, without the voluminous mass of supporting evidence or qualifying allowance for prudential checks' (Black 1971, p. 75). On the same subject, Malthus said: 'the ultimate check to population appears then to be a want of food, arising necessarily from the different ratios according to which population and food increases' (Rima 2009, p. 127). However, this ultimate check is not the immediate check, except where there is an actual food crisis. Malthus also captured the term 'moral restraint' as a preventive check on population growth, specifically interpreting it to mean the postponement of marriage, coupled with sexual abstinence, until the time when one is financially capable of supporting a family while striving for proper education. He asserted that there would be economic inequalities, however, saying that people who are ambitious and who struggle to achieve through their efforts should be supported by the state, while criticizing the Poor Laws since they would encourage laziness at the expense of others. Generally, Malthus raised issues concerning the political economy of population behaviour and aggregate supply as it affects society's future improvement concerning speculation. Rent is differential surplus, according to Malthus in his theory of rent, which also aligns with that of Ricardo and overall classical economics.

David Ricardo's Principles of Political Economy and Taxation

David Ricardo was born to a Jewish broker in 1772, and although he lacked any academic background, he was prudent in practical business. He worked for his father at the Stock Exchange aged 14, setting up his own stockbroking firm at 21. He first wrote on monetary issues in 1809–10, which brought him in contact with James Mill, who encouraged him to continue writing. Hence, he published the first edition of his *On the Principles of Political Economy and Taxation* in 1817. He entered the House of Commons in 1819, while continuing his studies on economics. Ricardo sought to analyse 'the problem of Political Economy', where he determined the laws regulating the distribution of the national income between landlords, capitalists and labourers, and the changes in that distribution, particularly as they related to societal progress Black (1971, p. 126). He particularly viewed labour as both the measure and ultimate cause of value, and that it was no less a variable than that of gold or silver or corn. This very practical issue led him into the policy question of free trade of corn and the theory of comparative advantage (Rima 2009, p. 145). Ricardo recognized that defining prices would be facilitated if he could identify an appropriate measure of value that would not reflect wage and profit rate fluctuations; hence, he identified gold as the best measure. His analysis was largely abstract, but he was intellectually honest. Black (1971) observed that Ricardo's theory of differential rent is perhaps the best-known of all his theories, even though he did not originate it. He also developed the theory of comparative cost in international trade.

John Mill, Charles Babbage and other classical economists

James Mill and his son, John Stuart Mill (1806–1873), based their work on Ricardo's principles, which emphasize the theory of capital and its return. John Mill started to learn political economy from his father at age 11, and followed him into the service of the East India Company in 1823. He was Member of Parliament for Westminster from 1868 to 1886, by which time he had already developed a mature and independent attitude towards moral and social questions, publishing his *System of Logic* in 1843 (Black 1971, pp. 247–8).

Mill asserted that the laws of production reflect the dictates of nature, the laws of production of wealth are physical truths, and the law of distribution is partly a human institution (Rima 2009). Mill's description of the principles of political economy addresses institutional details with some application to aspects of socialism rather than Ricardian orthodoxy (Black 1971, p. 248).

Charles Babbage (1791–1871) anticipated the links between international trade and economic development. He recognized the invention of new machinery as promoting division of labour, and encouraged Britain to mainly manufacture machinery in line with the comparative advantage model. He has also been recently been acknowledged as the 'pioneer of the computer' (Lefauve and Hax 1992). Classical economists see growth in terms of increase in per capita income. Rima notes that they give recognition to the law of value, the law of wages, the law of capital accumulation, the law of population growth, the law of diminishing returns, the law of rent, the law of comparative advantage, the quantity theory of money and the law of markets.

Marginalism emerged as a critique of classical economics championed by Samuel Bailey (1791–1870), Nassau Senior (1790–1864), William Stanley Jevons (1835–1882), and later by Friedrich Engels (1820–1895), Francis Edgeworth (1845–1926), Knut Wicksell (1851–1916), Irving Fisher (1867–1947) and J.B. Clark (1848–1938). W.S. Jevons came up with diminishing marginal utility as the basis for value in exchange with emphasis on calculus for derailed analysis. Swiss-based Leon Walras and Austrian-based Carl Menger devoted a lot of effort to the reconstruction of the theory of value in the 1870s. They stressed marginal utility rather than cost of production as value in the exchange determinant. Johann Heinrich von Thunen (1783–1850) from Germany explained factor rewards as they relate to marginal increment contributions to total product (Rima 2009), then Karl Marx emerged with his law of motion.

Karl Marx's Inquiry into the Law of Motion

Karl Marx was born in Germany to a Jewish lawyer who converted to Lutheranism. He entered the University of Bonn aged 17 to study law, but transferred to the University of Berlin after his first year to study philosophy and history. He was greatly motivated by the works of Georg Hegel (1770–1831) in his pursuit to learn criticism. He later became a journalist, then editor of *Rheinische Zeitung*, a business paper sponsored by business interests. Pierre Proudhon, a French philosopher, seems to have encouraged him to interpret economic phenomena based on Hegel's philosophy. Marx was among those who formed the German Workers' Union, which joined other groups to become the International Communist League.

Karl Marx sought to promote a system that would succeed capitalism in his *An Inquiry into the Law of Motion*, in which he developed the theory of the development of the capitalistic system, spelling out social reforms aimed at the best interest of members of society. Marx was also influenced by Comte Henri de Saint-Simon (1760–1825), who called for the recognition of society, and Charles Fourier (1772–1837), who developed the theory of socialism. In 1848, Engels and Marx developed a statement of principles called *The Communist Manifesto*, which spelled out the theoretical basis of communism, provided a critique of utopian socialist movements and laid out strategies towards achieving socialist aims (Rima 2009). Interestingly, under the condition of simple production, Marx observed that money should only be a medium of exchange in order to circulate commodities. According to Marx, stable economic growth requires proportionate expansion of capital goods industries and consumers.

Sam Rima's *Spiritual Capital Theory* (2012) quotes Marx on his criticism of capitalism:

> *In capitalism, improvements in technology and growing levels of productivity boost the amount of capital wealth in society while concurrently thinning the economic value of this wealth, thereby lowering the rate of profit – a tendency that leads to absurdity, characteristic of crises in capitalism, of 'poverty in the midst of plenty,' or more accurately, crises of overproduction in the midst of under consumption leading to the possibility of deflationary tendencies. There comes a point in a consumption-based economy, when most essential life needs are met via production, and in order to prevent economic activity from reaching a level of equilibrium, more non-essential goods must be produced to keep the economy growing. However, these opulence (luxury) goods cannot be purchased by the working classes, as their labour value has not sufficiently increased to provide the disposable income necessary to buy such goods. Thus, in order to maintain a tall level of consumption, financial instruments are shaped to allow the 'proletariat' or masses to continue consuming using debt, which further undermines their economic well-being while enhancing that of the owners of capital at the working class's expense.*

More interestingly, Marx took a stand against all earthly and heavenly gods which do not acknowledge human self-consciousness as the highest divinity (Marx and Engels 1968 [1888]). Use value occupied a central place in Marx's theory of communism, which envisaged a society of the future where there would be no mediation through the market, as wealth would satisfy needs indirectly. It would see the restoration of the natural relationship between things and men. If a society based on use value were to prevail, the market would have to be abolished. Socialism or communism would replace the market with a rational plan worked out between the associated producers (Marx and Engels 1968 [1888]). Harvey (2010) wrote at the outset of his *Companion to Marx's Capital* that new knowledge arises out of taking radically different conceptual blocs, rubbing them together, and making revolutionary fire. Harvey went further than Marx's thoughts, writing: 'Capitalism had to grow within the interstices of the old society and bit by bit supplant it, sometimes through force, predation and seizures of assets, and at other times with guile and cunning.' At the beginning of the twentieth century, classical economics started to metamorphose into neo-classical economic theories.

NEO-CLASSICAL ECONOMIC THEORIES

Alfred Marshall's Principles of Economics

Alfred Marshall (1842–1924) laid the foundation of neo-classical economics by translating Mill's version of Ricardo's theories into mathematics. Marshall's interest in economics was out of concern to address the challenges of developing a better life for humans and addressing poverty-related issues, which may have been influenced by his desire to become a Church of England minister early in his life. He studied economics as a science of human behaviour rather than a science of wealth, observing the complexities of managing human behaviour or motives and developing limited variables to measure them with consideration for neighbourliness and charitable acts. His interest in poverty led him to try to find solutions to problems of human improvement.

Marshall saw his *Principles of Economics* as 'an attempt to present a modern version of old doctrines with the aid of new work, and with reference to the new problems of our age' – giving birth to neo-classicism (Rima 2009, p. 318). He observed that 'political economy or economics is the study of mankind in the ordinary business of life while examining that part of individual and social action that connects with the attainment and use of material requisites of well-being' (*Principles of Economics*, in Rima 2009, p. 319). Rima summarized the main features of Marshall's transformatory work as follows:

- *The assumption that the effects of human motives as they relate to behaviour in the marketplace can be measure in terms of sums of money.*
- *The explicit introduction of demand equations in the explanation of commodity values.*
- *The recognition that the technical coefficients of production are not fixed but vary with factor substitution cost at the margin which will further affect the marginal cost of producing commodity in the short term.*

- *An inquiry into the laws of return that govern the cost of production in the long term.*
- *Recognition that the real wage of labour is not a constant that depends on the cost of producing raw produce at the margin, and that there is a separate wage rate for each grade of labour that depends in the long run on the amount grade demanded and the amount of that grade demanded and the amount supplied.*
- *Recognition that the return to capital is distinct from that of organizations.*
- *Recognition that factor prices and commodity prices are interrelated, and that the theories of value and distribution are different aspects of a single problem.*

(Rima 2009, p. 343)

Rima observed that Marshall's views on price are not only based on production cost and marginal utility, but on the interaction between several other forces that influence the demand and supply of goods.

Augustin Cournot and other neo-classical economic theorist

Augustin Cournot's *Researches into the Mathematical Principles of Wealth* (1838) was not developed until the late 1870s, which gave birth to the development of the case of monopsony, or buyer monopoly, to parallel the traditional case of seller monopoly. *Economics of Welfare* by Arthur C. Pigou (1877–1959) and Dennis Robertson (1890–1963) contributed to the theory of monopoly pricing in the latter's, *Economics of Imperfect Competition* (1933). Italian-born Piero Sraffa (1898–1983) worked further on Marshall's external economies and laws of return. Edward Chamberlin (1899–1967) examined the determination of prices in markets where monopolistic and competitive elements are blended. Joan Robinson wrote *Economics of Imperfect Competition*, and Robert Triffin (1911–1993) published his *Monopolistic Competition and General Equilibrium Theory* in 1940. Joseph Schumpeter published *The Theory of Economic Development* in 1934 and in 1939, John R. Hicks published *Value and Capital*, F.A. Hayek published *Profits, Interest, and Investment*, Bertil Ohlin published *Studies in the Theory of Money and Capital* and Gunnar Myrdal published *Monetary Equilibrium*. Maurice Dobb's writings on his theory of wages in 1928 debased the relevance of the theory of value to the labour market.

Shortcomings in Marshall's theory of consumer surplus led to Pigou's *Economics of Welfare*, while in contrast to Marx's revolutionary path to socialism, Sidney and Beatrice Webb, H.G. Wells, George Bernard Shaw, Hugh Gaitskell, Hugh Dalton, G.D.H. Cole, H.D. Dickson and Evan Durban preferred the establishment of socialism by peaceful means. Abba Lerner's *Economics of Control* in 1944 led the way for Keynesian fiscal policy. Hobson and A.F. Mummery argued against Adam Smith's production imbalances, and asserted that investment, and thus production of consumer goods that exceeds consumers' aggregate capacity to purchase them, would lead to imbalance.

J.M. Keynes's economic thoughts

Another face of modernization theories emerged with John Maynard Keynes's critique of mainstream tradition in his *General Theory of Employment, Interest and Money*. His personal life influenced his perceptions. He worked for the British government in the Indian Office, married a Russian, learned philosophy and economics from Henry Sidgwick and Alfred Marshall, and experienced the two world wars during which deflation and unemployment were the norm. Neo-classical economists conclude that unemployment is a result of workers' unwillingness to accept a real wage which corresponds to their marginal productivity, so increases in employment can be achieved only by reducing monetary wages until they are equal in real terms to labour's marginal product. Rima observed that Keynes rejected this and argued that monetary wages are generally bargained or set by cultural and perhaps legal forces.

Both classical and neo-classical thinkers maintain that flexible commodity prices, wage rates and interest rates ensure that income will be saved and invested, thus preventing long-term over-production and unemployment. Keynes disagreed, arguing that interest rates do not automatically channel savings into investment since people require both asset and transaction demands for money. For Keynes, interest is the reward or benefit for parting with cash, rather than a reward for saving it, thus favouring a full-employment economy. Keynes was heavily engaged in public affairs, and in 1940 he wrote an essay on 'How to Pay for the War', followed by his plan for an international monetary authority in 1943. Although his full proposition was rejected at the Bretton Woods Conference in 1944, many of his ideas were adopted. Cypher and Dietz (2009) felt that even though Keynes influenced the conference, the IMF and World Bank never demonstrated a strong affinity for the Keynesian approach on economic issues, which meant that neo-liberalism remained victorious. Rima (2009, p. 457) asserted that Keynes was a brilliant English theorist who valued theory primarily as a guide to policy, and indeed brought a reawakening of 'political economy'. He died early in 1946 after working out the American loan arrangement.

A mix of neo-classical theories

The American Evsey Domar developed a growth equation based on the premise that growth problems were a function of the stability of the saving function and a fixed capital coefficient. He said that investments accompanied by technological changes with the deepening of capital and productive capacity would not grow as rapidly compared with the capital coefficient being constant or where capital-saving technological change was reflected. Harrod, in his 'Essay in Dynamic Theory' (1939), borrowed from the static Keynesian model, where desired savings should equal the desired investment. He wrote:

> *warranted rate of growth as that rate of growth which, if it occurs will leave all parties satisfied that they have produced neither more nor less than the right amount, or, to state the matter otherwise, it will put them into a frame of mind which will cause them to give such orders as will maintain the same rate of growth.*

Walt W. Rostow mapped out the five stages of economic growth: the traditional society, the pre-conditions for take-off into self-sustaining growth, the take-off, the drive to maturity, and the age of high mass consumption. Todaro and Smith (2009, p. 111) analysed Rostow's model and observed that the 'principal strategies of development necessary for any takeoff [were] the mobilization of domestic and foreign saving in order to generate sufficient investment to accelerate economic growth'.

This was further described in the Harrod-Domar Growth Model, also known as the AK Model since it is based on linear production function of output of K times a constant A. Solow's neo-classical growth model expected economies to converge to the same level of income where they had the same rates of savings, depreciation, labour force growth and productivity growth, thus building up capital from savings and investments. The Harrod-Domar Growth Model further developed Solow's model, and placed much emphasis on the importance of increased savings and investment in a certain proportion to GDP as preconditions for economic growth and development. Capital formation leading to consistent savings and investment by both the individuals and the state is a very big challenge.

Readings in modernization theories

Lessem and Schieffer (2010a) observed that modernization theories are mainly based on the assumption that 'social change is linear, standardized and unidirectional; they impose value judgment on development process; and that the rate of social change is slow, gradual and piecemeal – evolutionary rather than revolutionary'. Davis (1991) and Weber (1973) saw modernization theories as hurdles where trophies were given for rapid development and modernity. Davis also commented that the Chinese development pattern would have to be different from that of Europe's capitalist development because of differences in the modernization structure. Sklair (1991), Roberts and Hite (2000) and Hayter (1990) asserted that Western modernization theory has to be mimicked by the Third World as borrowing from the former was a solution for the latter, while Samir Amin favoured unequal development theories for different regions. Escobar (2008) noted that modernization theory was validated by the promise of capital, science and technology. Cypher and Dietz (2009) wanted developing states to search for an optimal growth path, or seek one that was superior to the allocation of resources and existing efficiency levels. Anghel and Glavan (2005) reviewed the effects of market imperfections and the private and social impact on poverty traps, while Hettne (1995) said that this model only sought to promote future performance of the capitalist economies, and that the mainstream pattern of development was Utopian because of its lack of long-term viability. He observed further that this unviability was a result of lack of political support for it. For Hettne, development studies should be problem-oriented with acknowledgement of global disparities in material resources and the socio-political settings necessary to change such societies; in this regard, dependency theories emerged.

Dependency Theories

Criticism of modernization theories started to emerge in the 1960s, especially from the developing world, and primarily from South America, where Dependency Theory originates. Critiques of Dependency Theory, though mainly from the North and West, maintained that it would allow resources from the poor periphery states to flow to the core economically advanced rich states to the detriment of the former, thereby spreading extreme poverty. Dependency theorists argued that the less-developed nations have unique features and characteristics that made them distinct from the developed nations, so the same economic pattern of development could not be realistic, in particular if the core states did not have weak competing economies around them in the beginning. The basis of dependency theories is that poor nations provide natural resources and very cheap labour in exchange for obsolete technology and unfavourable trade conditions and various forms of slavery. Hans Singer and Raul Prebisch's papers in 1949 opened up the dependency theory debate when they observed that trade conditions imposed by the rich countries led the less-developed economies into poverty traps, and this idea became the Singer-Prebisch Thesis. Dependency theories can be further classified into classical dependency and dynamic dependency.

DEPENDENCY AND NEO-DEPENDENCY ECONOMIC THEORIES

The Argentinian economist Raul Prebisch proposed some elements of trade protectionism for developing counties as a strategy to enable them to be self-sustaining, and clearly favoured import-substitution industrialization. In the 1970s, international dependency models came to the fore. Cypher and Dietz (2009) noted that the 1948 UN-formed Economic Commission for Latin America (ECLA) led Prebisch to learn and understand that apart from the laws of demand and supply, developing countries were still constrained by power relations and dissimilar forms of production between nations which international agencies do not take into account. In the Prebisch-Singer Hypothesis, Hans Singer from the Institute for Developing Studies at Sussex University viewed relations between the centre and periphery as detrimental and antagonistic rather than complementary and harmonious. Todaro and Smith (2009) observed that international dependence models saw less-developed economies as beset by institutional, political and economic rigidities in their domestic and international affairs, thus leading them to be trapped by the dominance of and dependency on rich, advanced nations.

The International Dependency Revolution gave birth to the Neocolonial Dependency Model, the False Paradigm Model and the Dualistic Development Thesis. The Neocolonial Dependency Model was born out of Marxist revolutionary ideology. The model held that the powerful West used a divide-and-rule ideology to prey on the economies of the Southern less-developed countries to enrich the North and West. According to the False Paradigm Model, expert advisers from international organizations and locals in power with a foreign academic orientation were biased or unwittingly built economic models that were largely inappropriate for the developing South. The Dualistic Development Thesis maintained that the superior and inferior could coexist within the same environment, thus promoting inequality.

These three International Dependency Revolution concepts were Western capitalist economic models that were promoted to the communal weak Southern states.

The American Clarence Ayres (1891–1972) saw development in poor countries as hampered by both technology and ceremonialism. He asserted that economic development and technological progress were synonymous, but the latter was being curbed by ceremonialism. Ceremonialism, according to Ayres in the work of Cypher and Dietz, includes ideologies that reinforce social stratification and social mores, a system of indoctrination and social patterns of ceremonial behaviour. Gunnar Myrdal (1898–1987) identified the forces of under-development and the solution to poverty in the study of changes in 'attitudes and institutions', so various classical, neo-classical and even dependency theories are not sufficient to enable real development to take place. Under the dependency model, Arturo Escobar found that the root of under-development was the connection between external dependencies and internal exploitation, and not necessarily the alleged lack of capital, technology or appropriate cultural values. Cardoso and Faletto (1979), from the Marxist dependency school, proposed the facilitation of foreign investment to curb dependency exploitation. E.B. Geleta (2005), from University College Cork, observed that capital and foreign investment penetration into the peripheries had little no effect on development since repatriated profits by the core simply made development impossible. Lessem and Schieffer (2010a) examined the works of Dos Santos on the structure of dependence, and stressed three forms of historical dependency: colonial, financial-industrial and technological-industrial.

Colonial dependence allows financial and natural resources to be exploited by the colonial masters from the periphery to the core for the benefit of the latter. Financial-industrial dependence allows the core to push huge capital to the periphery and is centred on the export sector with rigid socialization. Technological-industrial dependence allows internal production by capitalists to buy raw materials for the periphery at disadvantageous prices for the latter and to sell manufactured goods and expertise to the periphery at ridiculously high prices. Lessem and Schieffer concluded that the peripheral countries must adopt a self-reliant model rather than relying on foreign aid and technology from the core. Alvin So (1990) summarized the assumptions of the dependency school as a general process applicable to all Third World countries as an external condition imposed from the outside, analysed mainly as an economic condition, and seen as a component of regional polarization of the world economy. There are other neo-classical dependency models that view imposed economic theories as being unconscious or unbiased.

The Lewis Theory of Development is a classic Structural Change Model perception. Lewis's Two-sector Model argued that surplus labour from the traditional agricultural sector can be redeployed to the high-productivity modern urban industrial sector without any loss of output. There have been several criticisms of the model, such as that it makes assumptions about the rate of labour transfer and employment creation, assuming that full employment exists in urban areas and not rural areas, and that rural surplus labour will be exhausted over time while real urban wages continue to increase. Michael Kremer's O-Ring Theory of Economic Development focused on externality at work, issues of skills in certain environments, and the multiplier effect, which will positively or negatively influence a firm or economy at large. Another major element of this model was what is referred to as 'positive associative matching' – workers with low skills work together, and those with high skills work together.

Ziyyad Muhammed (2010b), from the Islamic Finance Institute of Southern Africa, in his analysis of the evils of the interest-based capitalist system, said:

> Countries have also felt the harmful effects of borrowing on interest. Poor countries in Africa and South America were forced to borrow from wealthier countries at high interest-rates that were compounded. This resulted in countries owing much more than they originally borrowed. When they realized this, it was too late and the wealthier nations began demanding mineral rights or ownership rights for natural resources in these countries in exchange for repayment.

Nigeria, for example, borrowed US$5 billion up to 1986 from international creditors, repaid US$16 billion, and still owes US$28 billion. The US$5 billion borrowed had become US$44 billion over fifteen years, Obasanjo lamented in 2000. How best, then, can dependency theory be illustrated?

DYNAMIC DEPENDENCE STRUCTURES

The North and West dominated the economic structures of Latin America, Africa, Eastern Europe and the Middle East, imposing only economic structures that would favour the core. The case was very different in the Far East, where countries colonized by Japan have performed extremely well over the past fifty years. Thomas Gold (1986) observed that the Japanese colonial state created a sound investment environment in Taiwan, where law and order, unified weights and measures, private property rights, modern infrastructural development, available capital, and effective human capacity development were present.

Lessem and Schieffer (2010a) described this dependence structure as a dynamic dependence model, and Cypher and Dietz (2009) called it structural transformation.

Karl Marx, and then Keynes, favoured government intervention in economic development, while Singer (1965) said that development was growth and change, where change addressed both social and cultural issues with and emphasis on poverty reduction. Lessem and Schieffer (2010a) attributed the extreme interest in culture, religion, morals and home-grown socio-economic transformation models to economic development rather than mere economic growth. These and many more indicators are what state-led development, or the developmental state approach, crystallized in the economic prosperity of Japan, South Korea, Taiwan, and now Malaysia, Singapore, China, Thailand and India. Developmental states or state-led development approaches were consciously or unconsciously designed by the Japanese soon after the Second World War, and spread through much of East Asia and later some South Asian states. This approach allowed the state to distort market forces mechanisms in order to allow rapid and consistent industrialization to take place. States designed a good mix of export promotion and import substitution and short- and long-term strategies to fuel rapid growth and development.

This approach largely resembles the Big Push Model. Developmental states show effectiveness when a pilot agency, which has been granted 'embedded autonomy' (Evans 1995), is on the ground while the state captures rent-seeking behaviours in addition to capital flight being discouraged (Evans 1995; Evans 2004; Johnson 1982; Beeson 2004; Wade 1990; Mkandawire 1998; Ó Riain and O'Connell 2000; Low et al. 2004; Fritz and Menocal 2006; Kohli 2004; UNCTAD 2005; Than 2004; Stern 1991; Jomo 2004; Clark and Chan 2004). State-led development has not been successful in Nigeria because the state has been characterized by neo-patrimonialism, which allows clientele networks and individuals to gain positions and then be rewarded with money or further positions (Mkandawire 1998; Callaghy 1987; Evans 1995; Kohli 2004; Gerald and Rauch 2005; Fritz and Menocal 2006). The Nigerian neo-patrimonial state, like other sub-Saharan African states, is observed to be mainly influenced by ethno-linguistic diversity – that is, too many ethnic groups, religious affiliations, family ties, traditional cultism and political diversities (Easterly and Levine 1997; Collier and Gunning 1999).

The successful development state needs to be both close to and distant from the business class it hopes to influence and nurture. In other words, the state has to be sufficiently embedded in society that it is capable of implementing its goals by acting through social infrastructure, but not so close to business that it risks 'capture' by particular interests and is thus incapable of acting in the wider 'national interest'. Ideally, the effective developmental state should be 'embedded in a concrete set of social ties that binds the state to society and provides institutional channels for the continual negotiation and renegotiation of policies' (Evans 1995). A developmental state is determined to influence the direction and pace of economic development by directly intervening in the development process, rather than relying on the uncoordinated influence of market forces to allocate economic resources (Johnson 1982).

One of the key elements of a development state that is an essential prerequisite for managing the development process is the existence of a 'pilot agency', like Japan's celebrated Ministry of International Trade and Industry (MITI) (Beeson 2004). The pilot agency is charged with the task of directing the course of development itself, and employs and devises a range of policy tools to ensure that indigenous business is both nurtured and managed in the overall 'national interest' (Wade 1990). The developmental state has two components: one ideological, one structural. It is the ideological–structure nexus that distinguishes developmental states from other forms of state. In terms of ideology, such a state is essentially one whose ideological underpinning is 'developmentalist', in that it conceives its 'mission' as ensuring economic development, which is usually interpreted to mean high rates of accumulation and industrialization (Mkandawire 1998).

This promotes long-term entrepreneurial perspectives among the industrial elite (which is comprised of key business groups which resist growth, compromising demands for special interest groups) and embedded local social groups (usually, although not necessarily, capital) through close associational ties between state bureaucrats and domestic social classes among other social class interests by retaining autonomy (Ó Riain and O'Connell 2000). Low et al. (2004) identified three features of the contemporary developmental state as: (1) autonomy from societal forces for its bureaucracy; (2) an extended debate about the market, and governmental failures, and (3) dualism between the international liberal arena and domestic interventionism. Fritz and Menocal (2006) placed more stress on why some states had been capable and more supportive of development than others, and identified several structures which were not immutable but could be deeply entrenched: clientelism, patronage, populism, neo-patrimonialism or prebendalism. They further observed that narrow interest groups more concerned with building clientelistic networks than improving their general economic condition usually captured state-led development in Africa and Latin America.

Stern (1991) noted that China placed much more emphasis on preventive measures, including education, the provision of pure water supplies and adequate sanitation, which constitute major developmental efforts on the part of the government. Evans (1995, p. 48) looked at developmental states as being defined by the willingness of state financial institutions to back industrial debt–equity ratios as a critical ingredient in the expansion of new industries under the state's embedded autonomy. Than (2004) examined the developmental state in Myanmar and analysed the methods of state intervention as including rapid accumulation of capital through increased savings and investment, exploitation of agricultural surpluses for public industrial investment, import substitution and industrial protection. Kohli (2004) brought out the similarities between developmental states and cohesive capitalist states under right-wing authoritarian regimes where rapid industrialization was prioritized as a natural goal, coupled with full employment, close ties with industry, discipline, repression of labour, penetration and control of rural society, and using economic nationalism as a tool for political mobilization.

UNCTAD (2005) observed that governance in Africa 'requires various institutional arrangements and interventions by state to generate, distribute and revoke economic rents and to coordinate instruments in a way that meets wider development goals. This implies ongoing interaction and bargaining between policy makers and local entrepreneurs.' A developmental state exists where the state possesses the vision, leadership and capacity to bring about a positive transformation of society within a condensed period of time (Fritz and Menocal 2007). According to Jomo (2004), the main feature distinguishing the developmental state is its pursuit of industrial policy – that is, the selective promotion of certain economic activities, usually through state intervention, but often involving direct means such as official endorsement or proactive responsiveness to collective private sector initiatives. Clark and Chan (2004) believed that governmental interventions in the economy inevitably create market distortions and inefficiency. The developmental state bears close resemblances to the Big Push Model.

The Big Push Model is another interesting approach, but may have been borrowed from the state-led development school. It generally looks at how to address co-ordination failures via some sort of government-led drive towards rapid industrialization. The Hausmann-Rodrik-Velasco Growth Diagnostic

Decision Tree Framework addresses peculiar problems or circumstances within an individual country by using a decision tree to analyse possible causes of economic stagnation or under-development in terms of major factors such as low return on economic activity and high cost of finance, as is the case in almost all African states.

World Systems Theories

Immanuel Wallerstein, born in Columbia in 1930, served in the US Army from 1951 to 1953, then returned to Columbia University to write his master's thesis on McCarthyism as a phenomenon of the American political economy, in which he drew on C. Wright Mills's distinction in *New Men in Power: America's Labor Leaders* (1948). Wallerstein wrote in his book *The Essential Wallerstein* (2000):

> *I initially thought that the academic and political debates were merely over the empirical analysis of contemporary realities, but I soon became aware that the very tools of analysis were themselves to be questioned. The ones I had thought seemed to me to circumscribe our empirical analysis and distort our interpretations.*

He went on to say that he called his new perspective World Systems Analysis, which involved two major intellectual decisions: the choice of unit of analysis, which was crucial, and that the only plausible unit of analysis was a world system, or more generally, a historical social system. In 1955, Wallerstein obtained a Ford Foundation African Fellowship to study in Africa and write a dissertation on the Gold Coast (Ghana) and Ivory Coast. He travelled across much of Africa, where he eventually adopted an ethnographic research style in order to appropriately interpret social realities. Wallerstein admitted that he had to fight epistemological battles in order to be allowed to proceed with his analysis of social processes as integrated, complex wholes (Wallerstein 2000). He highlighted five major divisions of our modern world as race, nation, class, ethnicity and gender.

World Systems Analysis emphasizes developmental issues and unequal opportunities across nations. It thus addresses both political and intellectual issues where theory and practice are interwoven (Wallerstein 2000; Martinez-Vela 2001; Lessem and Schieffer 2010a; Modelski 1995). Wallerstein observed that both modernization and dependency theories are not sufficient to explain new and complex socio-economic activities in advanced capitalist states. He noted that a third category of countries, termed 'the semi-periphery', could be identified between the core states and the periphery states. Lessem and Schieffer (2010a) and Martinez-Vela (2001) acknowledged the wide intellectual scope of Wallerstein's ideas, such as unequal exchange, core–periphery exploitation and the framework for global trade. Wallerstein, also an academic sociologist, was largely influenced by Columbia's rebellions in the 1960s and 1970s, the works of Wright Mills, in which he grasped historic sensitivity and macro-structures, Ferdinand Braudel's Annales thinking, Marx and dependency theories and his fieldwork in Africa (Wallerstein 2000; Martinez-Vela 2001; Lessem and Schieffer 2010a; Modelski 1995; Chirot and Hall 1982; Skocpol 1977). George Modelski (1995), from the Department of Political Science at the University of Washington, saw world system development as a product of an evolutionary process whose structural components included economic, political, social and cultural factors that would together undergo a constantly evolving process. He said it was the behaviour of the human species that yielded periodization of world history and served as a way of developing the world economy and politics. He summarized world system evolution as the 'story of humans learning to live with each other, and learning to do so in global proportions'.

AFRICAN WORLD SYSTEM THOUGHTS

Africans in Africa naturally recognize the world system without necessarily giving or recognizing it by the name 'World System Theory'. From the desert of the Sahara to the coast of Southern Africa, conscious academics, religious scholars, village farmers' co-operatives and members of poor households know for sure that the most important elements in their lives involve sustaining a happy, healthy and peaceful communal environment. Villages and various political settlements in African states, from the so-called 'primitive' era until the invasion of the slave traders and colonizers, enjoyed relative political and social peace, while communal land was for all to benefit from and land tenants had rights. Local communal leaders presided over disputes, and poverty hardly existed. Modernization and dependency theories have obstructed the flow of this 'indigenous peace'. The perception and thinking of Africans within the context of the world system is thus based on their specific country experiences, which are a spill-over from the activities from the core. This externalism has led to political instability, predatory governance, unworkable economic approaches, gross income inequalities and extreme poverty.

Ronnie Lessem – a Jewish African born in Zimbabwe in 1944 during South Africa's apartheid era and a period of intensive colonialism in the rest of Africa –

became conscious of his environment aged 13 while at Prince Edward School in the British colony of Rhodesia, now Zimbabwe. He is a Visiting Professor at the DaVinci Institute in South Africa and Palacky University in the Czech Republic, as well as co-founder of the TRANS4M Institute with Alexander Schieffer. The TRANS4M Institute is a Four World Centre for Social Innovation, where Lessem places enormous emphasis on African culture, religion, the possibility of another world system, and moral economic principles as imperative to achieve a stable overall system in communal colonies, and in particular in Africa.

Makau Mutua, in his 'Returning to My Roots: Africa 'Religions' and the State' (1999), sees religion in Africa as a precondition for the construction of social reality since it incorporates the African traditional religion, Islam, and even Christianity, but with even greater recognition of the traditional African indigenous religions. He agrees that the physical de-colonization of African states is due to a crisis of identity. Sam Amadi was born in Nigeria, and gained a master's and doctorate in Law from Harvard Law School and another master's in Public Management from the Kennedy School of Government at Harvard University. He naturally perceives the African world system from the perspective of the rule of law, and the institutional designs and economic development as they relate to the peculiarities of the Nigerian state. Amadi (2009) asked the question: 'Which of the institutions of the rule of law work – the courts? The police? The Civil Service/administration? The legislator? The electoral system?' He argued that the rule of law promised by Nigeria's president at the time, the late Umaru Musa Yar'Adua, lacked content, knowing well that when institutions work on issues of poverty and equality, they will naturally fall into place. Oshodi (2009), Amadi (2009) and UNCTAD (2005) favour an African-designed 'state-led development' approach where institutions are allowed to be effective. Oshodi's Integral Hybrid Framework tends towards the African World System approach, where he developed relationships between good governance, good enough governance, neo-patrimonialism and some modernization and dependency theories within Lessem and Schieffer's Four World Model.

Lele et al. (1994) implied in the conclusion of their IMF working paper *Economics, Politics and Ethics of Primary Commodity Development: How Can Poor Countries Benefit the Most?* that this encompassing African World System required agricultural development via technology, institutional and human capital development, resource allocation systems, financial sector reforms, and location-specific determination of the sets of public and private goods. Acemoglu et al. (2001) examined Botswana's economic success and attributed it to 'good economics', further concluding that the reason why other African countries were unable to achieve such a degree of success was because 'good economics' is bad politics, since it does not allow predators to remain in power. They also observed that Botswana benefited from pre-colonial institutions that restricted political elites, the fact that extent of British colonialism was minimal and the institutions built by the colonialists had been well maintained (maintenance and strengthening of private property was successful because it also protected the economic interests of the elite), the fact that country was diamond-rich, which created adequate rent for the 'co-operative' elite, and because the effective and critical decisions of leaders like Presidents Khama and Masire had strengthened the country. However, the greatest weakness of Botswana is the rapid spread of HIV/AIDS, unlike North Africa, where the disease is hardly present. Zambian-born economist Dambisa Moyo, who holds an MBA from Harvard and a PhD from Oxford University, argued in her book, co-written with Niall Ferguson, *Dead Aid* (2010) that foreign aid creates dependency to the core and exposes corrupt African governments to more rent-seeking behaviours, so aid should be replaced with the kinds of direct investment the Chinese set up in Africa. She says that paternalism, racism and neo-colonialism are the root causes of foreign aid. On the other hand, Azam et al. (1999) argue that aid reduction will hurt Africa in the short term.

In Nigeria, ethno-linguistic diversity and ethnic clashes, lack of well-established institutions, institutionalized corruption in both the public and private sectors, poor government policies, and a combination of both market and state failures as a result of lack of co-ordination have led to chronic poverty and inequality (Nwaobi 2009b; Thomas and Canagarajah 2002; Amakom 2008; Amadi 2009; Balogun 2010; Somoye 2010). Thomas and Canagarajah propose the promotion of broad-based growth to promote better health, education and infrastructure as a central strategy in fighting poverty, while Amakom blames dependency policies such as the Structural Adjustment Programme (SAP), which was badly implemented and is still being misrepresented as the main cause of poverty.

Muhammed Tanko from Amadu Bello University in Zaria, in his study of effectiveness of monetary and fiscal policy instruments used to control inflationary challenges in Nigeria, found that other factors contributed immensely to the country's persistent increases in the prices of goods and services, maintaining that deliberate harmonization, co-ordination and integration of several variables was necessary. Simeon et al. (2009) from Cross River State University of Technology found in their quantitative research that public borrowing and/or expenditure were capable of influencing private sector investments as inflation reduces private investment. This quantitative result may conflict with reality in typical African states considering the corruption embedded in public sector contracts and poor corporate governance in the private sector, and it may also be largely divorced from Wallerstein's five major divisions of race, nation, class, ethnicity and gender; however, it may be influenced by the forces of the triple heritage. In general, urbanization brings economic growth, but this was not the case in Africa, as observed by Fay and Opal (2000). Abdul Adamu (2009) from Nasarawa State University agrees that a different economic model is imperative if Nigeria wants to minimize the impacts of global financial crises.

Drawing from Twenty-first-century Economic Theories

NEW EMPIRICAL DEVELOPMENT ECONOMICS

Development economics investigates the causes of poverty, while low-income economies seek to make progress in designing policies that could help individuals, regions and countries to achieve greater economic prosperity (Acemoglu 2010). Unlike political economy, which deals with political and economic elements that influence allocation of resources, development economics is concerned with the efficient allocation of existing scarce (or idle) productive resources and their sustained growth over time. It is also concerned with economic, social, political and institutional mechanisms, both public and private, that would bring about rapid and large-scale improvements in living standards for people living in Africa, Asia, Latin America and transition economies (Todaro and Smith 2009). Development economics is conceived as scientific policy to furnish governments of poor countries and international economic organizations with tools for economic transformation (Toye 2005). In this regard, Ghosh (2009) identified sustainable development as the most important notion linking ecological services and quality of life with economic growth.

Mookherjee (2005) asserted that this new development approach had been increasingly driven by empirical and policy issues. As he examined how far the pendulum has swung, the need to reappraise research methodologies became apparent. He referred to Haavelmo's fourfold classification of the main problems encountered in quantitative research. The first stage involves the construction of a tentative theoretical model, which is the empirical description leading to theories, without violation of empirical patterns. Stage two consists of the testing of theories, which is prone to falsifiable implications. Stage three deals with the problems of estimation, leading to the modification or replacement of previous theories. The final stage involves the problem of prediction, or rather, the use of the least unsuccessful theory from the standpoint of empirical verification. Mookherjee acknowledged Haavelmo's critiques of stages three and four. Based on this information, Mookherjee (2005) analysed the role of theory and empirical research in the field of development economics, which started to emerge during the 1940s and 1950s. Transformation took place gradually, moving from the principles of coordination failures, poverty traps and take-offs into self-sustained growth, critical minimum effort, pecuniary externalities, balanced and unbalanced growth, dualism, surplus labour and institutional failures – which were largely based on implicit assumptions of pervasive externalities, missing markets, economies of scale, imperfect competition and imperfect information. He concluded that the 1960s and 1970s saw the beginning of a focus on issues of cost–benefit analysis, migration and optimal growth. The economic thoughts largely fell into stages one and two of Haavelmo's analysis.

The 1970s gave rise to theories of imperfect competition and asymmetric information, which led to issues concerning co-ordination failures, endogenous growth theory, incomplete markets and efficiency wages – usually applicable to the agricultural sector. Mookherjee (2005) stated that the 1980s saw the emergence of issues of dynamic implications due to contractual imperfections, political economy, governance issues and tailored functioning of social norms. In the same way, game theory came to replace price theory, highlighting the strengths and weaknesses of this new institutional economics – thus, institutions really matter. For Mookherjee, development of stages three and four needed to concentrate on what policy prescriptions sought to achieve in terms of welfare effects. In his conclusion, he believed that the field of economic development would pursue a more balanced portfolio of research methodologies, with little emphasis on theory. Bardhan (2005) supported much of Mookherjee's work, and said that a rush to generalizations from these numerous experiments would lead to false results because 'they ignore macro or political-economy or general-equilibrium effects of a programme when they are extended to a larger scale, and the whole is usually more than a sum of the parts'. He went on to say that theoretical and experimental work in economics never took the time to consider the behavioural issues in poor countries. Hence, a need for fairness and reciprocity in individual economic behaviour focused in the direction of moral economy.

Acemoglu (2010) raised the question of how empirical research in economic development considers political economy. He proffered a solution, saying the first step would be to use empirical work in order to develop a good understanding of political economic factors in development. Acemoglu explained this by borrowing from the publication of Goldstein and Udry (2008, in Acemoglu 2010) on southern Ghana's agricultural production issues, noting the involvement of local chiefs' abuse of power in villages and the confiscation of the land of the politically weak. Acemoglu then wondered how one could analyse such political-economy issues using microdata. Acemoglu concluded his argument by saying: 'A key objective of empirical work in development economics is to discriminate between theories about the causes of economic growth and to conduct counterfactual analysis to build a systemic understanding of how an economy will respond to large changes in factor supplies, technology or policy.'

When analysing the new development economics and its challenge to theory, Banerjee et al. (2005) referred to the World Bank sourcebook which mapped 'right' strategies for poverty reduction, hence providing a list of recommended projects such as: computer kiosks in villages; cell phones for rent in rural areas; scholarships targeting girls attending secondary school; school voucher programmes for poor children; joint forest management programmes; water user groups; citizen's report cards for public services; participatory poverty assessments; Internet access for small firms; land reform; micro-credit based on group lending and so on. Banerjee then wondered how this would be achieved empirically, which is not addressed in the sourcebook because its authors know full well that randomized evaluations leading to generic theories will be used, noting that randomized evaluations typically only assess the short-term impact of any particular intervention (Bardhan 2005; Banerjee et al. 2005). The only way to build trust in experimental and quasi-experimental results is to replicate the research in several other locations, which then exposes one to the challenge of size, therefore researchers would want to use relatively small samples, partly due to practical and financial constraints, but also because the they want experimental results before enlarging the programme (Banerjee et al. 2005). Theory can help to solve the problem of scope in the conventional structural approach where models are fitted to smaller numbers of observable parameters of the observed programme effects, and the model can be used to make out-of-sample predictions (Mookherjee 2005; Banerjee et al. 2005).

On the bigger challenge to theory, Banerjee concluded:

> *the most important role of theory in development economics, and indeed in all the rest of economics as well, is to help us understand*

what are the right questions. The formulation of a testable hypothesis in only the final stage of this process, and one that is often left for the empirical researchers to do, since it often depends on exact nature of the data. What is prior to that, and in some ways, even more importunately, is the ability of theory to locate the empirical results within a broader intellectual context and make us see why we ought to care.

Kanbur (2005) agreed with Mookherjee, Banerjee, Bardhan and Ghosh on the need for empirical analysis to be used in development economics, even asserting that it was becoming more common compared to twenty years ago, when the concentration was on theory, while Basu (2005) admitted that development economics has witnessed an upsurge in innovative empirical research. He concentrated on the stage four problems of prediction, and to a smaller degree, partly on the stage three problem of estimation in Mookherjee's work. Rima (2012) referred to the work of Ormerod, stating that the mathematical inclinations of economics left it isolated and separated from social ontology and practical reality; it was also separated from the physical sciences which it attempted to use it as a foundation for the new 'dismal sciences'.

On predictions, Kanbur noted that statistical findings were not useless for prediction, but needed to be combined with what he termed 'unscientific' intuition in order to be useful. Toye (2005) examined challenging perspectives in developing economies, reviewing early Keynesian influences, the critics of the Lewis model, development planning and project appraisal, national and international trade regimes, neo-liberalism (less state, more markets), structural adjustment to poverty reduction, and the re-introduction of institutions. He recalled that international experts tasked with helping developing nations with project planning in the early days could not lay their hands on economic statistics, so they planned without facts using desktop theories developed for the West, knowing very well that they were not applicable to the political context in which they found themselves. Ghosh (2009) and Munasinghe and Reid (2005) were generally concerned about how developing countries could move from economic growth to sustainable development based on broad issues – economic, social and environmental, aimed at poverty reduction, equity in the system, sustainability and co-evolution. The economic matters included growth, efficiency, and stability; the social included empowerment, inclusion/consultation and governance, while the environment involved resilience/biodiversity, natural resources and pollution. Achieving this would require pooling knowledge, preferably from empirical research. Much of this knowledge is a mere illusion of knowledge, since we human beings actually do not know that much (Basu 2005). From empirical analysis, Stiglitz's modern economic theory surfaced.

MODERN DEVELOPMENT THEORY

Joseph E. Stiglitz was born in 1943 in Gary, Indiana – a city afflicted with huge inequality, poverty and discrimination. He helped his father in his insurance agency business, and later in college he studied economics, physics, history and mathematics. He obtained his PhD from the Massachusetts Institute of Technology (MIT) in 1967, and joined the MIT faculty in 1966. He served at the Institute for Development Studies at the University of Nairobi under a Rockefeller Foundation grant, and later moved to Yale, Oxford, Stanford and Princeton Universities, and finally back to Columbia University from 2000 to the present. He received the John Bates Clark Medal in 1979, was part of President Clinton's Council of Economic Advisors, was appointed Chief Economist of the World Bank in 1997, and won a Nobel Prize in Economics in 2001. His economic perceptions did not align with those of the World Bank, so he resigned and returned to academia in 1999. Stiglitz designed the economics of information, which analyses equilibrium in markets in which there are asymmetries of information among the market participants (Hoff and Stiglitz 2008). He looked at completely new phenomena in economics where the price system only imperfectly solved the information problem of scarcity due to several other challenges embedded in the economy (Hoff and Stiglitz 2008).

Stiglitz sought to establish two things through his paradigm shift: that many of the implications of the standard neo-classical model do not remain valid where perfect information no longer exists, and to provide a better understanding of the workings of the economic system as a whole. Stiglitz argued that market socialism failed because neo-classical models were not accurate characterizations of a market economy. Two main ideas emerged from his work: first, 'the control/information system of market economies embraces far more than the price system of the neoclassical model', and second, that competitive equilibrium in economies with imperfect information and missing markets is not, in general, Pareto efficient. Hence, government interventions such as taxes and subsidies can help to improve market outcomes (Hoff and Stiglitz 2008). Stiglitz's ideas help to address the sources of externalities such as information, group reputation effects, agglomeration effects, knowledge spill-overs and pecuniary externalities.

Stiglitz examined the economies of uncertainty, based on the principles that individuals use in evaluating random distribution of returns. On the economics of information, he observed that there were hidden characteristics (adverse selection) and incentive issues (moral hazard) as barriers to product/service design. Grossman and Stiglitz (1980) said that the 'efficient market theory' was incorrect. This theory states that the observation of prices in capital markets suffices to reveal all relevant private information. They argued that if information is costly and markets are competitive, there must be an equilibrium degree of disequilibrium – that is, persistent discrepancies between prices and fundamental values that provide incentives for individuals to obtain information. They went on to say that the capital market makes people invest in information which subsequently affects price – causing pure economic rent, but really, all information is publicly conveyed. Hence, the market equilibrium prices serve to discriminate (imperfectly) among individuals with different search costs.

Another great work of Stiglitz, Stephen Ross and James Mirrlees is the Principal-agent Theory, which has also contributed immensely to economics. Stiglitz's experience in Kenya and the inefficiency of the institution of sharecropping gave him a lead on the theory. He wondered why incentives were not given to an agent who has worked simply because the tenant has produced no yields. For him, sharecropping should help to save monitoring costs, increase output, and reduce the risk borne by tenants, as opposed to tenants paying fixed land rent without partaking in risk markets. He later related this to incentive contracts not being awarded because an individual's contribution to output is not well observed, as is common in many organizations today. He then analysed competitive equilibrium and labour rent and how they can increase the unemployment rate in an economy. Concerning market imperfections in the field of development economics, Hoff and Stiglitz (2008) noted that economics was unable to figure out the sources of imperfections in markets before the economics of information and that of game theory models of political economy:

> The Keynesian orientation of the IMF was replaced by the free market mantra of the 1980's, part of a new 'Washington Consensus' – a consensus between the IMF, the World Bank, and the U.S. Treasury about the 'right' policies for developing countries – that signaled a radically different approach to economic development and stabilization.
>
> (Stiglitz 2002, p. 30, in Hoff and Stiglitz 2008)

The effect of these Washington consensus policies on developing nations has been to benefit the few at the expense of the many, the rich at the expense of the poor (Stiglitz 2002). On another note, Stiglitz refers to the:

> breakdown of the Washington consensuses – a consequence of neoclassical model which predicts that growth is inevitable in capital-poor market economies; thus economists lay down policy prescriptions that set the preconditions for growth. They include maintenance of macroeconomic stability (since high inflation interferes with the workings of the price system), limited government ownership of enterprise, and deregulation (stabilize, privatize, and liberalize). These prescriptions are failing since the evolution of economic theory has moved away from the perfect markets paradigm.
>
> (Hoff and Stiglitz 2008)

According to him, the three central and closely related economic theories are the economies of information, game theory and institutional economics. This new paradigm is no longer primarily about the process of capital accumulation, but a process of organizational change.

Hoff and Stiglitz, in their book *Modern Economic Theory and Development* (2008), mentioned that the neo-classical approach attributed economic failure and the reasons why an economy is not functioning well strictly to government impediments to the market, hence going beyond the fundamentals of resources, technology and preferences. They identified government failures without explaining how or when certain recommended interventions would overcome the political forces that initially led to distortions. Hoff and Stiglitz (2008) acknowledged the importance of government failures, but this required an explanation with appropriate institutional design, which can be limited. Apart from government failures, Hoff and Stiglitz recognized market failures as persistent, especially in developing countries, hence identifying four areas of focus – institutions, the distribution of wealth, history and 'ecology' – which have spill-over effects. Hoff and Stiglitz also recognized information and enforcement as issues that would limit economic possibilities, similar to the limitations of technology. There is a need, however, to scrutinize the black boxes in institutions – that is, to explore institutional rigidity, taking note of complementarities in industrialization, rural credit, labour markets savings rates and political constraints. Under distribution of wealth, it is necessary to establish the extent to which wealth plays this role. Wealth distribution affects the market decisions of individuals, it affects macro-variables such as prices and wages, so the welfare of any single agent depends on the entire distribution of wealth. Finally, because wealth distribution affects contracts, incentives and outcomes in one period, it affects the distribution of wealth in the next. In the case of history, it influences a society's technology, skill base and institutions. Ecology in neo-classical economics draws not on the mechanical dynamics of the economy, but on biological and physical models under modern development economics.

In their analysis of stagnant development due to lack of co-ordination, Hoff and Stiglitz (2008) talked about gaps in knowledge between industrial and developing countries, and between more advanced firms within developing countries and less advanced ones. Another issue is under-investment in knowledge. Hoff and Stiglitz (2008) referred to theories of the ineffectiveness of government intervention of the Public Choice school, which maintain that a government's engagement in business will be ineffective, unnecessary or counterproductive. Hoff and Stiglitz (2008) put forward a variety of interventions that could affect those outcomes, including interventions to solve co-ordination problems, information as an intervention, interventions to change the dynamics of the political process, and interventions to change the distribution of wealth.

In this modern economic theory and development, Hoff and Stiglitz (2008) analysed rational expectations and political barriers to economic development. Another new emerging train of thought in this vein is Spiritual Capital Theory.

SPIRITUAL CAPITAL THEORY

Sam Rima, an American of the Spokane Indian tribe in Washington State in the Pacific Northwest corner of the United States, was born in 1958 and grew up being influenced by two heritages: his indigenous Native American heritage and exogenous Christian faith. He received a BA in Political Science from Eastern Washington University, a master's in Divinity from Talbot School of Theology at Biola University, a Doctor of Ministry in Leadership from Biola University and a PhD from the University of Buckingham in 2012, where he developed his Theory of Spiritual Capital. A co-founder of the Movement for the Advancement of Spiritual Capital, he is also a former Director of Heliopolis University's Social Innovation Centre in Cairo, Egypt. While serving as the director of a doctoral programme and a faculty member at the Centre for Transformational Leadership, Rima focused on some burning world issues. Through this, it became clear to him that the Church never bothered to address fundamental social and economic injustices. Rima shared that 'in the entire seminary curriculum, there was not a single class devoted to a theology of social and economic justice'. As it is clearly and repeatedly articulated throughout the Bible, this saddened him. Moreover, in accordance with the historical evangelical reaction to what have been considered the liberal leanings of the 'Social Gospel' and 'Liberation Theology', the seminary offered no dedicated courses regarding the Church's responsibility to address the social and economic needs of society.

In his unpublished thesis 'Spiritual Capital Theory: A Catalyst for Individual, Institutional and Societal Renewal', Rima wrote:

> the shift from the study of political economy as a social phenomenon in the seventeenth and eighteenth centuries, to the study of economics as a purely mechanistic, empirical, hard science in the nineteenth through twenty-first centuries has removed the 'human' element from economics. Today economics is totally disconnected from any meaningful social ontology and is practiced in the existential vacuum of economic laws that mimic scientific laws and the ostensible rationality of Homo economicus. In today's study of economics there is no longer room for the application of philosophical fields of study such as morality, ethics and metaphysics.

In developing his Spiritual Capital Theory, Rima addressed several issues which may be responsible for the global financial meltdown, such as: At what point does debt become immoral? Why would people take credit cards that they do not need or do not have means to pay off? Why should banks/organizations offer them such cards? When does government debt, intended to stimulate consumer spending (much of it fuelled by debt) without the future means to service or pay off that debt, become unethical or immoral?

Rima quoted Simon Johnson from MIT, who said: 'we now have a financial system that is completely based on moral hazard', based on the rules of 'capitalism which lacks ethical concepts such as fairness and equality' (Ertuna 2009, p. 53, in Rima 2012). Spiritual Capital Theory is based on Lessem and Schieffer's Integral Research approach, drawing on wisdom and indigenous knowledge of all four worlds. Rima refers to integral research, in this context, as holistic and relational economics – economics that promotes wholeness:

> We must begin to recognize that economics is about more than just money and capital, it is also profoundly about ecology, spirituality,

relationality, morality, and a measure of equality; for if our economic practice is not deeply informed by these impulses, which are the prevailing concerns of all people, then of what benefit can economics be to the majority of humanity?

Like Mookherjee, Banerjee, Kanbur, Toye, Ghosh, Bardhan, Basu, and Lessem and Schieffer, Rima prefers empirics to mathematical modelling and econometrics. They should indeed be:

servants to the people, the communities they live in, the planet that sustains them and the spirituality and morality that makes life distinctly human, becoming kings. This transformation will demand that economic practice be infused with a moral core that determines how the earth's resources are extracted, utilized, distributed and held in trust by people, communities and organizations.

The current modern mainstream of neo-liberal economics is unsustainable and in the opinion of economists such as the University of London's Paul Ormerod, Cambridge's Tony Lawson, Joseph Stiglitz and others, our current economy is completely detached from the world's social realities and, I would add, void of any metaphysical impulses (Rima 2012).

What, then, is spiritual capital? Rima first referred to the definition of Zohar and Marshall, who wrote:

Spiritual Capital is a new paradigm. It requires that we radically change our mind-set about philosophical foundations and the practice of business. It is neither anticapitalist nor noncapitalist, but it does require the addition of moral and social dimensions to capitalism. Spiritual capital itself is not monetary wealth, but it argues the possibility of making a profit – perhaps even more profit – by doing business in a wider context of meaning and value. It can generate profit that both draws on and adds to the wealth of the human spirit and to general well-being.
                                   (Zohar and Marshall 2004, p. 21, in Rima 2012)

Another interesting definition for Rima is that of Theodore Malloch in his paper 'Social, Human and Spiritual Capital in Economic Development', Malloch wrote:

Spiritual capital can become a useful concept and term for a vital feature of economic development that has been largely overlooked in

*modern theories of development. Indeed, the often used terms of social
capital and human capital themselves are based to a large extent on
the existence of good faith, trust, stewardship, a sense of purpose and
other moral characteristics which cannot persist in the absence of piety,
solidarity and hope that come from religion and spiritual sentiments.
When this is lost, societies and economies often decline rather than
grow. When this abounds, societies and economies prosper.*

                                                    (Malloch 2003, p. 8)

According to Rima, spiritual capital is focused primarily on the empowerment
of individuals, societies and institutions that have been marginalized by current
practices of neo-liberal capitalism as a way of mitigating its hegemonic effects,
with the goal of injecting a more life-generating impulse to economic practice
(see Figure 5.1). Spiritual capital indeed confers wealth and advantage, but its
focus is on empowerment of the marginalized 'other' rather than the self.

Spiritual Capital Theory is based on the integral Four Worlds Model –
South, East, North and West – and the fourfold GENE. Grounded in the
critical individual influence (South), it then emerges in organizational policy
and procedure (East), navigating to production/distribution practices (North)
effecting sustainable socio-economic outcomes (West). This effect on society leads
to socio-economic transformation, later directed towards integral dynamics.

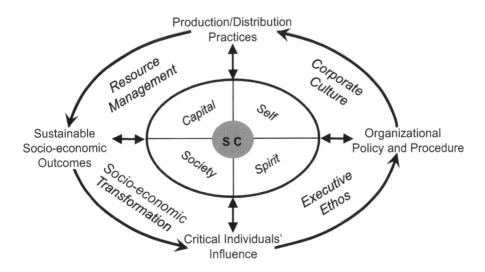

Figure 5.1   **How individual spiritual capital accrues to institutions**
Source: Rima (2012).

INTEGRAL DYNAMICS TOWARDS DEVELOPMENT

Ronnie Lessem is greatly influenced by and emotionally connected to his Zimbabwean birthplace, the Jewish zeal to upgrade creation, and the British capitalist system encompassing social welfare. From the London School of Economics he moved to Harvard Business School, and then to City University, where he obtained his PhD. He is a co-founder of the TRANS4M Institute, and now plays a leading role in the DaVinci Institute for Technology Management, South Africa – an opportunity to move closer to home. Alexander Schieffer studied economics, business administration, social sciences and law at the University of St. Gallen, Switzerland, where he also completed a doctorate on leadership. He lectures on Interdisciplinary Problem Solving and International Development at the same university, and is also a co-founder of the TRANS4M Institute. Lessem and Schieffer have been engaged in several publications, and some of their most prominent works include *Integral Research and Innovation* (2010b), *Transformation Management: Towards the Integral Enterprise* (2009) and *Integral Economics: Releasing the Economic Genius of Your Society* (2010a). A forthcoming book of theirs is *Integral Development*, which taps into moral philosophy, political economy and integral dynamics. Lessem and Schieffer seek to establish a whole new discipline of Integral Dynamics from the basis of Integral Studies and Cultural Dynamics.

Lessem and Schieffer (2013) analysed integral dynamics within the realm of political economy, drawing on the masterworks of Adam Smith and Karl Marx while moulding a whole new philosophy from trans-disciplinary and trans-cultural economy from where Smith and Marx left off. For Lessem and Schieffer, there should be a continuous flow or dynamism of these great works rather than their being static. Lessem and Schieffer argue that while Adam Smith's *Theory of Moral Sentiments* seeks to reach out integrally and inclusively, *The Wealth of Nations* searches for how to advance political economy. Karl Marx, on the other hand, had an innate feel for the dynamic flow of capital. Lessem and Schieffer asked why and how a new discipline is born – for example, why did political economy emerge from moral philosophy? They gave four reasons: because the world is forever changing and there is a need for mankind to understand the activities around them; there are always new issues that need solutions, which requires new thoughts as the world grows more complex; as our thinking evolves, the 'inner world' of the psyche and the spirit combine trans-personally with the 'outer world' of matter and energy, and vice versa, and finally, new trans-disciplinary and trans-cultural potential is opened up as diverse disciplines and diverse cultures combine.

Adam Smith was influenced by his Scottish and Protestant heritage, which spilled over into his moral philosophy, influenced by Hutcheson and Hume, and sought civil and religious liberty for the happiness of mankind 'in Europe', the only world he knew. For Hume, in his *Treatise of Human Nature* (1739–40), knowledge is rooted in passions, imagination, use of intellectual powers acquired through habit, custom, education and experience of common life – this underlines 'integral dynamics', grounded in passion, the emergence of imagination, navigation through intellect, and the transformational dynamics approach to individual nature. Adam Smith, his mentor, and his students were engaged in trans-personal learning, and communally creating and sharing knowledge, thus opening the way for communities of practice, or knowledge-creating enterprises as are evident today (Lessem and Schieffer 2012).

Marx came from a German Jewish heritage, bringing together divergent, trans-disciplinary and trans-cultural approaches within a European context (Lessem and Schieffer 2013) and creating knowledge from radically different conceptual blocs (Harvey 2010; Rima 2009). Marx hence talked about labour process and the process that exists only in motion. Lessem and Schieffer noted that Marx's overall methodology was derived from what had never been applied to economics before, drawing his dialectical ideas from Hegel, a totally different approach, and paving the way for change and transformation through his process of motion. Lessem and Schieffer felt that Smith and Marx converged to institute an Integral Dynamic platform which was Eurocentric. Therefore:

> both were inherently trans-disciplinary, trans-personal and trans-formational in orientation, though Marx was well to the fore in this dynamic, transformational respect. There Achilles heel, in both instances was their Eurocentricism, so that their trans-cultural orientation was limited to the integral constituencies of such. Indeed, in his later years, Marx became ever more conscious of his limitation and took a specific interest in indigenous peoples, including those in Russia.
>
> (Lessem and Schieffer 2013)

Adam Smith's root interest moved from natural theology, ethics, the quest for justice, law and government, and commercial expediency to his *Wealth of Nations*. In the same vein, political economics moved to classical economics, and then neo-classical economics in isolation, losing the integral and dynamic connection. For Lessem and Schieffer, Adam Smith's theology connects with 'nature and religion' in economic matters, and his moral core aligns with integral dynamics. However, Lessem and Schieffer's moral core spread over their new discipline of Integral Dynamics as it applies to cultures and societies in the South, East, North and West.

The 'Mainstem' of natural theology for Smith is the 'core' for Lessem and Schieffer, aligned with ethical doctrine, the 'bedrock' which articulates the theory of moral sentiments. More practically, Lessem and Schieffer complained that cultures and natures have not been explicitly linked to science and technology or economics and enterprise except in the North and the West.

Under 'branches', the power of markets controls law and government, but for Adam Smith, it is rooted in politics – justice, law and government – alongside economics. Lessem and Schieffer sought more anthropological studies of indigenous people in order to understand them better so that there would be no disconnect between the root (images) and main stem (ideologies) – hence the bridging role required of the new discipline of Integral Dynamics.

For Smith, the fruit of moral philosophy had enlightened Europe, while providing the fundamental moral core for various societies in this new discipline. 'Commercial expediency' for Smith translates to 'economics and enterprise' for Lessem and Schieffer. 'Political institution' for Smith refers to commerce, finance and the military, but is simply referred to in Integral Dynamics as the military-industrial complex through an economy built on prior law, justice and government, and prior ethics and natural theology, or morality.

The new discipline of Integral Dynamics, unlike Smith's political economy, draws on cultures and society from the Four Worlds – naturally and communally (natural theology), culturally and spiritually (ethics), in terms of social science and technology (justice, law and government) and economics and enterprise (commercial expediency). Dynamically, the main effects of economics and enterprise as they differ from commercial expediency are dispersed into societal, or macro, and enterprise, or micro, within the context of this new field of management or business administration (Lessem and Schieffer 2013).

When building an enterprise, Marx spelt out the kind of technology required, the relationship to nature, the social relations envisaged, the incorporation of systems of production, the daily life envisaged and the mental conceptions that would be involved. In Lessem and Schieffer's integral dynamics perspective, these issues are plugged with the Four World/GENE Model. Hence, social relations and relations to nature are 'grounded' in the South, reproduction of everyday life 'emerges' in the East, technology and mental conceptions 'navigate' in the North, while modes of production are 'effected' in the West, and the dynamism continues. The central core, which helps the model to keep its balance, is the 'dialectic of transformation'. In other words: 'all these elements co-evolve and are subject to perpetual renewal and transformation as dynamic moments within the totality – like an ecological totality' (Lessem and Schieffer 2013).

In Smith's *Theory of Moral Sentiments*, he talked about the nature of the civilizing process and how human beings should engage in ordinary business life in order to satisfy their moral needs while acquiring ethical beauty in order to aspire to a life of virtue. This is flawed, because he fell short by restricting his cultural horizons to the Scottish Enlightenment. This should also be applied to overall social and economic justice rather than just individuals (Lessem and Schieffer 2013). Marx shared with Smith an uncompromising commitment to social justice, protecting the interests of the poor and the oppressed at the expense of the affluent and great as laid down in biblical teachings, designed for Europeans, which became difficult when applied to Soviet-style communism.

Smith was concerned with how the exchange of goods and services could be circulated in society to different sectors of society in a relatively free market environment, laying emphasis on labour. Lessem and Schieffer incorporate passion and imagination as well as intellect and enterprise in their dynamic reinterpretation of labour theory. With regard to 'the labour theory of value', according to Marx, as captured in Lessem and Schieffer's Integral Dynamics, the capitalist ruthlessly forces the human race to produce for production's sake. In this way, he spurs on the development of society's productive forces and the creation of these material conditions of production, which alone can form the real basis of a higher form of society, a society in which the full and free development of every individual forms the ruling principle. This compels the capitalist to keep extending his capital to preserve it, and he can only extend it by means of progressive accumulation. Lessem and Schieffer's observation on Marx's narrative is that his approach was inflexible, since capital is not a thing, but a process – continually in motion, and dynamically in flow. This whole analysis raised new questions for Lessem and Schieffer. What happened in recent years to Smith's original moral and ethical law, governance and justice, ethics and theology? How about Marx's *Capital*? How did the contradictions evolve? Or rather, has practice fallen behind theory?

Becoming practical, Lessem and Schieffer referred to the Chinyika community in Zimbabwe as an integral dynamic economy. It started as a pathetic story. The Chinyika community had little or nothing to eat, especially in the period when Zimbabwe faced political and economic sanctions. Two angels arose from the tribe of Chinyika, selfless and passionate about their people, and they planted the seeds of sustenance – and hence, a self-sufficient economy. Chidara Muchineripi, son of a local chief, and Steve Kada, human resources director of a major food processing company, both completed their PhDs at the DaVinci Institute using the Chinyika case study. They revived an old seedstock, *rapoko*, with unique nutritional value, adaptable storage qualities and capable of being made into a variety of products. This magical seed provided 5,000 indigenous people with food security by 2006, and up to 100,000 by 2011. Then there was over-production, and Muchineripi and Kada persuaded the government to act as off-takers so that the people could have sustainable benefits from this exercise. The influential actors did not take the position of a capitalist by converting the indigenous workers to 'capital', or labour as it were, which was why Marx came out with his 'radical' approach against capitalism.

They also did not limit Smith's theory of moral sentiments to individuals, but to a whole community. The continuous, cyclical or dynamic evolution of this new enterprise (micro) led to societal (macro) transformation. Lessem and Schieffer equate this to the true spirit of Islamic economics – culturally and spiritually infused concepts of human well-being (*falah*) and communal good life (*haya al tayyibah*), attaching utmost importance to brotherhood and socio-economic justice based on the works of Umer Chapra. The Chinyika project has local grounding in human well-being and the good life, locally and globally emerging through Marxism and social justice, globally navigating through workerism, and effecting community building globally and locally (Lessem and Schieffer 2013), implementing Rima's Spiritual Capital Theory. Finally, the 'old' world on which Integral Dynamics draws, naturally and culturally, technologically and economically, is in fact the oldest one, that of 'indigenous' people around the globe (Lessem and Schieffer 2013).

Conclusion

The North and West were quick to promote Eurocentric economic models to developing nations, and it was not until the 1990s that the international community began to wonder why these policies were ineffective. They were designed using theories generated from micro-variables, which were never grounded in nature, never emerged with culture and spirituality, never navigated with politics and science, and thus were never effected in economics. Researchers and consultants from multilateral organizations and NGOs simply developed theories from Eurocentric precedents and made policy prescriptions to developing nations calling for such things as macroeconomic stabilization, good governance and deregulation while measuring economic growth, only to discover that growth and development are not synonymous. New economic development research methods and methodologies, and models grounded in the way of life of the people, are certainly making headway, using the Chinyika in Zimbabwe as a pilot case.

Chapter 6 will focus on Islamic economics and practical Islamic finance contracts. It will also showcase poverty reduction strategy models based on Islamic financial instruments.

6

Islamic Economics and Finance

Introduction

In the previous chapter, I traced a path through existing economic models, defining their specific characteristics, starting with the Physiocrats and their influence on Adam Smith and progressing to contemporary economic analysis. This chapter continues in that vein, first looking at the influence neo-classical economics have had on Islamic economics and finance. It will examine some other principles and practices of Islamic economics and finance, and review the works of the early writers in the 1980s, such as Anas Zarqa, Monzer Kahf, Muhammed Uzair, Mabid Ali Muhammed Mahmoud Al-Jarhi and Umer Chapra, within the context of Islamic economics. Hasanuzzaman's work on Islam and business ethics serves as an ethical bridge between Islamic economics and Islamic banking. Following this, it will analyse the most frequently used Islamic financial instruments or contracts, ranging from *mudarabah* (investment partnership) to *tawarruq* (Islamic overdraft), and from *qard* (interest-free loan) to *sukuk* (Islamic financial certificates). It will also assess the Islamic finance industry, encompassing global issues, the situation in Africa, and in particular the unfolding of the Nigerian regulatory framework, evaluating the general concept of the Islamic banking value proposition and using the Sterling Bank Islamic banking value proposition as a case study, looking at how it integrates with the primary purpose of the Islamic moral economic system while meeting the needs of the market. Finally, it will look at two aspects of Islamic finance that can be used to reduce poverty in Nigeria from a practical banking perspective: *sukuk* for infrastructural poverty reduction, and agro-commodity *murabahah* for consistent job-creation.

Neo-classical Islamic Economic Thoughts

As covered in Chapter 4, the foundation of the Islamic economic system is moral economics. The Islamic economic system is thus based on eliminating interest, uncertainty, gambling and unethical concerns while promoting justice and fairness in a trans-cultural and trans-disciplinary manner, in an integral dynamic (Lessem and Schieffer 2013) covering time and space. It seeks to promote a system founded on moral sentiment, love and sincerity; on production, labour and capital, and on the peaceful co-existence of all. A system that accommodates and aligns with any socio-economic and political variation established on man's happiness and God's pleasure. Based on this definition, perception and understanding, the early writers on Islamic economics in the 1950s, 1960s and 1970s aligned with neo-classical economic theories – the only real economic world they knew. As the economic analysis moved from a state-led development approach to world system theories, and from empirical research in development economics to integral dynamics, scholars tended to design alternatives based on Islamic commercial jurisprudence where applicable, covering macro (societal) and micro (enterprise) economics (Lessem and Schieffer 2013). Financial institutions have also sought alternatives, though at the risk of losing the primary foundations or tenets of this economic system, promoting Shariah compliance ahead of moral sentiment (Adam Smith), ethical or spiritual capital (Rima 2012) and Marx's *Capital* (Harvey 2010), and without taking into account the concepts of life-giving human well-being which is fundamental to brotherhood and socio-economic justice (Chapra 2008c).

Islamic scholars agree that the definition of *riba* (interest) in the late 1970s referred to any addition on capital which was clearly differentiated from credit sale. At this time, the next issue was how best to define 'Islamic economics'. From the approach of human welfare, Anas Zarqa (1980, pp. 13–15, in Khurshid et al. 1980) sought first to characterize neo-classical assumptions about consumer behaviour. Neo-classical economists assume that an individual consumer is strongly and primarily motivated by the desire for personal consumption and leisure. Zarqa mentioned that in Islam, God is the owner of everything, and all that man has is his 'will', which he disposes only by seeking God's pleasure. He referred to the work of Al-Ghazali, and later Al-Shatibi, saying that social utilities in Islam may be divided into a three-level hierarchy: necessities, conveniences and refinements. Necessities include things that are essential to the preservation of the five foundations of good individual and social life within the Islamic worldview: religion, life, mind, offspring and wealth. Conveniences are activities or things that are not vital to the preservation of the five foundations, but may be needed to relieve the impediments and difficulties of life. Refinements are activities or things that go beyond conveniences. Hence, Islam considers veering from refinement to prodigality as self-indulgent, and it is not allowed for individuals or society. Siddiqi (1997) added that Islam seeks moderation, and defined it with reference to the negative concept of extravagant (*israf*) spending on goods and services, meaning that it is prohibited (*tabdhir*). Indulgence in luxurious living and the desire to flaunt it is condemned in several verses of the Quran.

Monzer Kahf (1980, pp. 22–3, in Khurshid et al. 1980) examined the theory of consumer behaviour in both conventional and Islamic economics. In neo-classical economics, consumer behaviour is a function of economic rationalism and utilitarianism. Economic rationalism interprets human behaviour as founded on rigorous calculation and directed towards 'economic successes, or the making of money out of man'. This material acquisition is perceived as the ultimate goal of life and a measure of economic success. Kahf observed that Marxist economics did not deviate from the doctrine of '*Homo economicus*', but merely restated this doctrine in a historical perspective. He further noted that some trends in Marxist economics betray the increasing influence of early marginalist formulations of the utility theory as an expansion of consumer influence. In Islam, Kahf continued, economic principles are dominated by three factors: belief in the last day (the Day of Judgment), the Islamic concept of success (good actions and purification of human behaviour from evil) and the Islamic concept of riches (*mal* – 'treasury for all in your possession'). Kahf related these at length to the institution of *zakat*, which is an integral part of the socio-economic structure of the Islamic economic system, aimed at wealth redistribution.

Muhammed Uzair (1980, p. 38, in Khurshid et al. 1980) redefined the factors of production within the context of Islamic economics. He argued that capital does not exist as a separate factor of production, but is a part of enterprise. He redefined land to include natural resources, while holding that labour denotes all human beings. He said that technology is an important factor of production, and that production resulting from a combination of natural and human resources is determined by technology. He felt that the enterprise factor and the quality of the technology factor would lead to different outputs from productivity units in different countries. Concerning diminishing marginal utility or the law of diminishing marginal returns, he asserted that the qualifications regarding the quality of the commodities and the input remained unchanged. Uzair said this was impossible, except perhaps in primitive societies, and that the qualities of commodities or inputs would inevitably change over time, thereby agreeing with Stiglitz, Lessem and Schieffer.

Revisiting the issue of combining capital with enterprise, Uzair held that interest was distinct from profit is in two ways: 'A distinction has been made between the return on the capital and the risk premium to take care of the risk or uncertainties in recovery and other things. Conceptually, interest and profit have some resemblance – interest includes reward for risk while profit is reward for uncertainty.' Uzair referred to neo-classical economists' definition of interest, and asserted that their main considerations were based on time preference theory, abstinence theory and liquidity preference theory. Of the Austrian economist Eugen von Böhm-Bawerk, Uzair said that his rationale for interest was based on time preference – that is, the concept of technical superiority of the present over the future, while others maintained that the rate of interest was based on the basic interest rate risk premium and administrative cost. Uzair referred to the Keynesian concept of 'liquidity preference' as a justification or rationale for interest on the supply side being accompanied by marginal efficiency of capital on the demand side.

Mabid Al-Jarhi (1980, in Khurshid et al. 1980) defined the 'relative efficiency of interest-free monetary economies' within the neo-classical framework. He challenged this traditional arrangement of paying interest on money as an efficient monetary policy since it suffered from the logical ramifications of being based on perfect-market models. He stated that free-market economics saw interest as the price of money, and a price at which the producers of money sold their output, since that price depended on the quantities of money supplied, raising the question of the optimum supply of money. He argued that economies in which there were no interest payments on borrowing and no banks creating money were the most optimal of the different institutional arrangements, therefore it was most efficient if the government initially provided its own money free of charge, lent it free of charge and imposed a 100 per cent reserve ratio on banks. Faridi (in Khurshid et al. 1980), on the other hand, worked on *zakat*, and saw it as the irreducible minimum ingredient of the fiscal policy of an Islamic state, rejecting the idea that fiscal management in an Islamic state is coterminous with *zakat*. For him, this allowed the state additional resources for the production of 'social good', therefore *zakat* should be treated as an 'economic variable' even though it was founded in religion. He backed up his argument by saying that *zakat* was normative, in the sense that it defined the norms of economic activities and also of fiscal activities as a subsection thereof. The consistent flow and magnitude of *zakat* make it directional, since it moves in the direction in which the economy is desired to move.

UMER CHAPRA'S ISLAM AND THE ECONOMIC CHALLENGE

Muhammed Umer Chapra was born 1933. At the University of Karachi, he completed his B.Com. (BBA) in 1954 and his M.Com. (MBA) in 1956, and he gained a Ph.D from the University of Minnesota in 1961, majoring in Economics. He was Senior Economist and Associate Editor of the *Pakistan Development Review* published by the Pakistan Institute of Development, Associate Professor of Economics at the University of Wisconsin-Platteville, Associate Professor of Economics at the University of Kentucky, Economic Advisor and later Senior Economic Adviser to the Saudi Arabian Monetary Agency from 1965 to 1999, and from 1999 has served as Research Advisor to the Islamic Research and Training Institute of the Islamic Development Bank, Jeddah. In 1989, he received the IDB Award for his contributions to Islamic economics, and the King Faisal International Award. Among Chapra's books and articles, the most popular are *Towards a Just Monetary System* (1985), *Islam and the Economic Challenge* (1992), *The Future of Economics: An Islamic Perspective* (2000) and *Muslim Civilization: The Causes of Decline and the Need for Reform* (2008a).

Chapra began *Islam and the Economic Challenge* with the quotation from al-Ghazali on the objective of the Shariah which was cited in Chapter 4 of this volume, under 'The Foundation of the Islamic Moral Economic System'. The second quote he cited was from Ibn al-Qayyim:

> *The basis of the Shariah is wisdom and welfare of the people in this world as well as the Hereafter. The welfare lies in complete justice, mercy, well-being, and wisdom. Anything that departs from justice to oppression, from mercy to harshness, from welfare to misery and from wisdom to folly, has nothing to do with Shariah.*

Chapra raised questions about 'efficiency and equity', and wondered why countries around the world had been unable to realize the material elements of human well-being. He asked whether scarcity of resources could be responsible for failure. He argued that most economists would not agree that resources could be scarce in an absolute sense, but only scarce in relation to the claims on them. Hence, material goals could be realized in order to minimize instability and imbalances if available resources were used efficiently and equitably:

> *An economy may be said to have attained optimum efficiency if it has been able to employ the total potential of available human and material resources in such a way that maximum feasibility quantity of need-satisfying goods and service is produced with a reasonable degree of economic stability and a sustainable rate of future growth.*

The measure of efficiency thus became whether or not it created macroeconomic imbalances. On the other hand:

> *an economy may be said to have attained optimum equity if the goods and services produced are distributed in such a way that the needs of all individual are adequately satisfied and there is an equitable distribution of income and wealth, without adversely affecting the motivation for work, saving, investment and enterprise.*

How, then, can an overall economic system help achieve both efficiency and equity? This is the basis of Chapra's work. Chapra critiqued the challenges of capitalist, socialist and secularist welfare states in the light of *maqasid al-Shariah*. For Chapra, *maqasid al-Shariah* referred to everything required to achieve *falah* and *hayya al tayyibah* for the entire universe (Ghazali, in Chapra 1992 and 2008c). *Maqasid* is any thing or activity that is necessary to preserve and enrich faith, life, intellect, prosperity and wealth – indeed, the summary of development economics.

Chapra examined the limits of capitalism in its *laissez-faire* sense. He identified five dimensions of capitalism:

> *accelerated wealth expansion and maximum production; unhindered individual freedom to pursue pecuniary self-interest and manage private property; individual initiative to freely operate competitive markets in order to realize optimum efficiency in resource allocation; no recognition for government in allocative efficiency or distributive equity; and claims that serving of self-interest automatically serves the collective social interest.*

More emotionally, Chapra described the way capitalism leads everyone towards 'loss of the moral filter', maintaining that the loss of the religious sanction for values was a huge tragedy: 'Society became deprived of the socially-agreed filter mechanism. Self-interest, prices and profits replaced it as the primary criteria for allocating and distributing resources and for equating aggregate demand and supply.' The moral filter was now left to inner individual consciousness alone, which would not be sufficient to perform the function of a socially agreed upon filter mechanism essential to stem individual self-interest and social interest.

Moreover, Chapra observed five major flaws and effects in this Marxist strategy. It assumed that macro (societal) and micro (enterprise) actors would discharge their duties and work effectively for the social good of the state without pursuing self-interest. It assumed that people who did not have any ulterior motives for granting privileges to particular ethno-linguistic/ religious groups would run the state machinery. It assumed that the central planning bodies would have information about all the products, preferences, prices and costs entailed in taking decisions. It assumed that large general subsidies in the pricing system would benefit the poor. Finally, it assumed that large, monopolistic state enterprises would operate efficiently regardless of diseconomies of scale, lack of competition and the absence of market signals. Chapra argued that all these assumptions were very unrealistic.

The welfare state signals a move away from the social Darwinist principles of *laissez-faire* capitalism, seeking to give cognizance to the welfare of the people rather than leaving it in the hands of market forces, but is unable to break away from Enlightenment philosophy or general faith in the sanctity of the market system. The welfare state is expected to function in an environment of regulation of private property, nationalization of some key industries, a strong labour movement with a well-defined sense of economic security, fiscal policies relying on public expenditure, progressive taxation and borrowing, and a high rate of economic growth, and full employment. Chapra observed that this system lacked effective mechanisms to prevent the use of scarce resources for purposes that obstructed the realization of its egalitarian goals, since capitalism still operates undisturbed in this schema. In particular, the welfare state is faced with the challenge of scarcity of resources compared to other state structures. Increases in claims on welfare services will require the reduction of other claims on resources that may become a challenging task for the welfare state.

Neo-classical economics rooted in capitalism, and Keynesian (or rather, socialist) movements struggled for supremacy soon after the end of the Second World War, which shaped the formation of development economics, making it veer inconsistently, or as Chapra (1992) termed it, showing wavering allegiances from market to state and back to market, losing a sense of direction. Keynes's influence at the Bretton Woods Conference in 1944 broadened the path for government intervention in economies. The 'Big Push' was seen as an expression of the Stalinist 'road of socialist industrialization', calling for rapid growth and giving priority to the development of heavy industry. The main aim of the Big Push Model was industrialization, import-substitution and urban development (Chapra 1992). During this period, the state-led development approach ruled in Far Eastern countries, and some variations of it were apparent in Africa. During this same period, especially in the 1970s, when Keynes's influence began to wane, capitalists again promoted their policies to developing countries under the influence of their ethnocentric (Chapra 1992) or Eurocentric (Lessem and Schieffer) perception of development. They concluded that it would not be possible for developing countries to make progress unless they mimicked the social, economic, legal and political institutions of the Western capitalist economies. Chapra referred to the Eugene Staley, who studied some World Bank documents by Kindleberger and Spengler: 'The development of poor countries could be successful only if carried out in the image of the United States. They will have to adopt the social institutions and values of the West.' Overall, Chapra's argument is that there was largely a neglect of equity. In this regard, Chapra referred to the 1975 submission of Bauer and Yamey that 'redistribution of income in favour of the poor is not likely to promote economic growth in the sense of greater output per head'. Chapra (1992) mentioned that even the United Nations had ruled out distribution as a policy goal by stating that 'the most general objective of economic development is to maximize the national income or the rate of economic growth'. These documents never mentioned issues of poverty reduction, inequality and income distribution.

In a bid to actualize *maqasid al-Shariah*, there is a need to adopt a completely new economic system encompassing all the elements necessary for human well-being in accordance with the demands of brotherhood, fraternity and socio-economic justice (Chapra 1992). Chapra proclaimed that creating equilibrium between scarce resources and claims on them in order to achieve both efficiency and equity required that the focus be shifted from market and state to humans themselves: 'They are the ends as well as the means, and unless they are reformed and motivated to pursue their self-interest within the constraints of social well-being, nothing can succeed, neither the "invisible hand" of the market nor the "visible hand" of central planning, in actualizing socio-economic goals' (Chapra 1992). Worldview capitalism and socialism do not apply such human considerations to strategy development. This human variable thus needs to be expressed in brotherhood, socio-economic justice, and the trust nature of resources (Chapra 1992). It is also necessary to have this human element incorporated into research into development economics, making it more empirical.

From another perspective, the Islamic worldview is based on three fundamental principles – *tawhid* (unity), *khalifah* (vice-regency) and *adalah* (justice) – and they also constitute the fountainhead of *maqasid* and the strategy. The most important element in Islam is *tawhid*, or Oneness in the Unity of God. Humans have been endowed with spiritual and mental characteristics and material resources in order to act as God's *khalifah*, or vice-regent on Earth, the implications being: universal brotherhood across races, tribes, religions and ideologies; resources being held in trust (*amanah*) and being accountable for on the Day of Reckoning; a humble lifestyle not leading to extravagance and waste, and human freedom, or not subjecting others to any form of bondage. Justice is an indispensable ingredient of *maqasid al-Shariah* – eliminating all forms of inequity, injustice, exploitation, oppression and wrongdoing whereby a person deprives others of their rights or does not fulfil his or her obligations towards them (Chapra 1992). Chapra thus laid the foundation of 'the strategy' based on four indispensable and mutually reinforcing elements: a socially agreed-upon filter mechanism; a strong motivating system which would encourage individuals to give their best for personal and societal good; socio-economic and financial restructuring, with the aim of realizing *maqasid* regardless of scarce resources, and a positive and strong goal-oriented role for the government.

The defined structure of the overall Islamic economic concept will now be applied in the micro (enterprise) sense, leading to Islamic banking and finance innovation.

Islam and Business Ethics

Islamic banking and finance is only a subset of the Islamic economic system, which must be aligned with ethics and equity. The emergence of Islamic banking practices built on the platform of Islamic business ethics. Since our focus is now on man, it is necessary to examine human attitudes to business in the realm of *maqasid* before exploring actual practices and the risk of flaws. Hasanuzzaman elaborated on Islamic and business ethics, seeing human instinct and business as naturally dependent on love of wealth, maximization of earnings, growing rich overnight, ungratefulness to the Creator, and disregard for others' interests, which are embedded in man. This needs to be controlled and regulated to avoid it proving a curse to society. These evils reach unmanageable proportions when coupled with the doctrine of (unbridled) free enterprise and free-market mechanisms (Hasanuzzaman 2003). Hasanuzzaman then called for morality, a change in outlook and the philosophy of life, and consciousness of reward and punishment in this world and the next.

Hasanuzzaman wrote about the concept of wealth and affluence in Islam, arguing that Islam does not castigate wealth nor economic pursuits, which the Quran refers to as *khayr* (wealth virtue), *fadl* (honour) or *rahma* (blessing), all of which are all bounties of God. In this vein, Allah says in the Quran:

> *Beautiful for mankind is love of the joys (that come) from women and offspring, and stored-up heaps of gold and silver, and horses branded (with their mark) and cattle and land. This is the comfort of the life of this world. God! With Him is a more excellent abode. Say: Shall I inform you of something better than that? For those who keep from evil, with their Lord are Gardens …*
>
> *(Q3: 14, 15)*

Hasanuzzaman also quoted the Prophet Mohammed as saying: 'There is no harm in opulence (wealth, luxury, affluence) for the one who fears God. And for the God-fearing health is better than wealth. And happiness is also wealth.' Islam, then, is not opposed to free-market mechanisms, but focuses on the components of ethical values – of production, consumption, distribution, exchange, overall ethical norms, moral discipline, honesty and trust, and mutual consideration, all for the purpose of creating corporate ethics. Hasanuzzaman defined the market mechanism of Islamic finance and the need for regulation of supply, regulation of demand, and regulation of manipulations in price:

> *In Islam, buyers and sellers are, no doubt, motivated to maximize their personal utility or preference satisfaction. This maximisation is not marred by any unethical or unsocial act. A trader has complete freedom to maximise his profit through the optimum utilization of resources, planning, accurate anticipation and managerial efficiency, but not through the means that Islam treats as immoral or sinful. An Islamic government interferes in the market only as a referee to ensure that the game is being played with the best of skill, ability and fairness. It should not become harmful to the traders themselves, to the customers or to the community.*
>
> *(Hasanuzzaman 2003)*

This depiction will be the unfolding argument that emerges from this research, first looking at the Islamic financial contracts that are used for products and services offered in the market, then conducting a co-operative inquiry to paint a picture of the expectations of government – the financial regulators – to achieve *maqasid al Shariah* (the goal of Islam), poverty reduction and employment generation in an African setting: in Nigeria.

Islamic Financial Instruments and Contracts

MUDARABAH – PARTNERSHIP

Islamic banking and finance are generally based on the principles of equity-based banking, rooted in the *mudarabah* structure. The *rabb al-mal* (beneficial owner or sleeping partner) entrusts money to the *mudarib* (managing trustee or labour partner), who utilizes it in an agreed manner and returns principal and profit to the *rabb al-mal* while keeping the rest of the profit for himself. *Mudarabah* is a profit- and loss-sharing mode where one party provides capital while the other provides expertise, and the profit and loss are shared according to agreed terms where the owner of the capital bears any loss, and the client's loss is the time and effort invested in the project. The profit share for each party's contribution must be agreed upfront, and profits are distributed accordingly. Bashar and Dikko (2003) stressed that the entrepreneur manages the funds of an investor, and the former does not have the right to take executive decisions in the management of the funds invested. The Institute of Islam Banking and Insurance (IIBI 2006a) stressed that the proportionate share of profit is determined by mutual agreement at the start in a *mudarabah*. 1st Ethical (2009) defined *mudarabah* as equity finance with a sleeping partner, where one partner gives capital to another to invest in a commercial enterprise. In this Islamic mode of finance, 'an investor or group of investors entrust a pool of capital to an agent, manager, entrepreneur (*Mudarib*) to engage in a specific line of business' (Euromoney 2008).

In practice, the terms and conditions of a *mudarabah* must be well defined, while the contributions of the partners must also be precisely determined to avoid ambiguity and uncertainty. The relationship between capital and labour is measured in such a way that their influence on profit is crucial, thus a partner who contributes labour may have higher profits that one who provides capital. In a *mudarabah*, profit is not fixed, or is a predetermined amount, but shared according to pre-agreed ratio. Islamic financial institutions use this instrument for both asset and liability products. Islamic assets are based on the *shrikat* or *mudarabah*, which creates the equity-based 'loan' or contract, where the bank and the client enter into a deal and the profit or loss are shared as agreed beforehand. Islamic financial institutions (IFIs) raise liabilities from depositors using a Shariah-compliant mode, which is further invested in partnership contact with entrepreneurs who need assets.

This system creates a triple *mudarabah*, which involves the depositor of capital, the bank or IFI and the entrepreneur. In this case, the bank would agree certain terms and conditions with the depositors whereby the account holder authorizes the bank to invest its money in one of its projects using a particular mode of financing, then shares in the profits thereof after the expiration of a specific period; this is called 'investment with authorization'. Where the depositor 'chooses a particular project for investment plus mode of financing and may/may not specify the period of deposit, thus, the bank will share on agreed percentage of the profit of the chosen venture with the account holder' (Zafar 1999); this is termed 'investment without authorization'. Zafar further stated that in a triple *mudarabah*, the bank does not hedge against the risks to its investors (depositors) or by extracting an indemnity from the entrepreneur or by arranging insurance cover. IFIs are now generally guided by Basel II in managing risk under this system. Depositors are not liable for losses beyond the capital contributed, since central banks ensure this is enforced. The Central Bank of Nigeria (CBN) requires that the profit/loss attributed to depositors under this type of contract is evenly spread all through the year, while a percentage of excess profit is set aside for the future to absorb unforeseen losses. In a triple *mudarabah*, the entrepreneur does not guarantee the bank a profit, so is thus not liable for its losses except its time, efforts and reputation unless negligence or violation of contract terms are established. This mode of financing allows the IFI to extend profit to depositors where the entrepreneur makes a profit, but only the bank bears any financial loss. IFIs generally do not like to use this mode of financing because of its very high risks. It is also the mode with the highest risk in Islamic finance.

MUSHARAKAH – JOINT VENTURE

Musharakah is derived from the word *shirkat*, which 'signifies the conjunction of two or more estates, in such a manner that one of them is not distinguishable from the other' (Afzalua 1979). It also means 'sharing' (1st Ethical 2009; IFC 2012). In a *musharakah*, both parties pool their funds and expertise in a business transaction, and profit is shared according to an agreed ratio, while loss is shared in proportion to the capital invested. A *musharakah* is a 'profit and loss sharing partnership where: all parties provide capital; profits is shared according to a pre-agreed ratio and will not be a percentage of capital or fixed amount while losses are absorbed by all capital providers in proportion to the invested capital' (Euromoney 2008). *Musharakah* as it relates to banking operations is an agreement where liabilities are combined to provide assets to entrepreneurs in which all capital providers take part in managing. An IFI will usually appoint an agent to act on its behalf in the deal, profit is shared between the bank and the other parties in a pre-determined ratio, and loss is borne in proportion to the capital outlay of the parties (New Horizon 2009; Bashar and Dikko 2003). There is also a form of triple *musharakah*, where the client invest funds in the bank, and the bank enters into profit and loss transactions or projects with an entrepreneur, with any profit or loss attributed to the clients or depositors. Investment 'with or without authorization' is another option, where clients either choose from a list of investments or require the bank to invest in any of its projects or investments, which will vary in terms of profit and risk. Risk in a *musharakah* is quite balanced and more viable for the bank compared to a *mudarabah*, since equity is shared by both parties, but usually without collateral.

Another form of *musharakah* is 'diminishing *musharakah*', which is a combination of *musharakah* and *ijarah*. It allows equity participation and profit-sharing on a pro rata basis, where the bank's equity in the project or asset diminishes consistently until the asset is transferred to the entrepreneur or participants (New Horizon 2009; IFC 2012). This mode is usually used for home finance or mortgages. The bank buys the property for the client, while the client takes ownership, just like all other Islamic financial instruments. The house is occupied or used by the client, who pays periodic market rent to the bank while ownership of the asset increases steadily, after which ownership is transferred to the client. Three separate contracts are signed in this mode: 'contract of joint ownership of the asset with the provision or promise by the client to lease the property; contract to lease the property by the client; and contract that the client buy the Bank's share gradually at specific price over a specified period of time' (Euromoney 2008; IFC 2012). Diminishing *musharakah* is best for commercial property finance, and is also good for trade finance.

MURABAHAH – COST-PLUS FINANCING

Murabahah is an instalment credit sale with mark-up (Abbasi 2009b; IFC 2012), where the buyer takes delivery of the product at the time of the contract and pays for it on deferred basis over a specified period (Euromoney 2008). It is a particular type of sale rather than a mode of financing (1st Ethical 2008). In a *murabahah*, the bank buys an asset for the client at the latter's instruction, with a promise to buy same asset at a marked-up price which is paid in instalments. A rebate when purchasing the asset is shared or disclosed by both parties and considered in the general structure of the contract. The mark-up is not reviewed and does not increase. Where there is default on the part of the client, the bank may charge a penalty fee, but not usually at the first or even second default. The default may be a percentage of money owed for that month only, and may be waived where necessary. If such fees are not waived, then they do not constitute part of the bank's balance sheet or income, but go into an account which is only used for charitable purposes.

In a *murabahah*, the client may also choose to pay upfront or a lump sum (1st Ethical, 2008). Abu Umar narrated in the Hadith compilation of Sahih Al Bukhari that the Prophet Mohammed said: 'the buyer and the seller have the option to cancel or confirm the bargain before they separate from each other or if the sale is optional' (Sahih Bukhari, Chapter 43, Hadith no. 320). Thus, separation between bank officials and clients in a *murabahah* is very important. The deal is binding on both parties after they agree and sign the terms and conditions before separation. This singular rule also makes it impossible for the bank to increase the mark-up price regardless of market factors. *Murabahah* is the most common Islamic finance sale transaction because it is not as risky as the others and the bank may take collateral from the client in case of fraud or default.

TAWARRUQ – REVERSE MURABAHAH

Tawarruq is a kind of overdraft in Islamic banking, in practice a reversed *murabahah*. It 'has been used as a loan facility tool by Islamic bank. A bank buys commodity or listed shares or even receivables at spot price and sell it to a client on a deferred payment basis' (Euromoney 2008). The client sells an asset to the bank, agreeing to buy the same asset back in future at an agreed price, thus the bank provides cash for the asset, while the client uses the cash to meet his or her financial obligations. The client then pays back this money in instalments or as a lump sum at the end of an agreed period, after which the asset is returned to the client. Islamic jurists are of the opinion that this practice is not Shariah-compliant since both parties never share any risk by owing the underlying sum, and because the contract is merely a paper transaction without change in ownership of the underlying asset. Euromoney (2008) observed that commodity brokers generates hefty fees without lifting a finger in commodity-based transactions.

Tawarruq is commonly used in business and corporate banking divisions to provide working capital or short-term financing for clients, or as a bridging loan or credit card rollover, especially in the Middle East (Abbasi 2009b). Most Shariah scholars see *tawarruq* as a last resort in banking, while most countries do not practise it, especially those where the Hanafi School is adopted, such as Pakistan, Afghanistan, Turkey and Bangladesh.

IJARAH – ISLAMIC LEASE, OR SALE OF THE RIGHT TO USE AN ASSET

Ijarah literally means 'to give something on rent'. It is a sale of the right to use an asset (Euromoney 2008; IFC 2012) – a normal business transaction, and not a real mode of finance (1st Ethical 2008; Chapra 1985). The risks and rewards of ownership lie with the owner (the bank or IFI), any loss to the asset beyond the control of the lessee is borne by the lessor, and late payment cannot be charged to the income of the lessor (1st Ethical 2008). *Ijarah* payment cannot be linked to a floating cost of funds, while care must be taken to avoid the lease rentals being structured to build in an effective interest rate by increasing if the rental instalments are not paid on the due dates, since this means it will not be Shariah-compliant (Zafar 1999). *Ijarah* is the transfer of ownership of a legitimate and well-defined asset against a specific return for a specific period (Bashar and Dikko 2003), during which the ownership of the asset or equipment remains with the bank (New Horizon 2009).

There are various types of *ijarah*. In an operating lease, the asset is used by the client, who is liable for daily expenses of the asset, while the bank retains ownership. It is mainly used for very large assets or huge earth-moving machinery or aircraft, and the bank can lease the same asset to another client after the expiry of an agreement. A financial lease, hire purchase or lease purchase is where the client has the option to buy the asset at the end of the lease period at a pre-determined price set out in the lease agreement. *Ijarah wa iqtina* means 'lease with acquisition' and *ijarah muntahia bit tamleek* means 'leasing ending in ownership'. This kind of financial lease requires two contracts to be signed, which is less risky for the bank compared to operational leases. In Islam, two transactions are not allowed in one contract. Thus, in one contract the client agrees to lease the asset for a specified period at a given price, and in other the client agrees to purchase the same asset at the end of the first contract. In practice, this sale is usually at a token price or a pre-determined residual value. The Accounting and Auditing Organization for Islamic Financial Institutions (AAOIFI) and some Islamic jurists dislike future contracts, preferring that the asset be bought by the lessee at a token price at the expiration of the main lease contract or that the bank pass on the asset as a gift, with or without consideration, to the client or lessee. Shariah scholars generally dislike conventional financial leases, which also termed 'full payout leases' and 'operational leases', which are not meant to be the principal business of a bank that prefers Islamic financial leases – *ijarah wa iqtina* and *ijarah muntahia*.

Sale-and-lease-back *ijarah* is also accepted in Shariah, where a client in need of liquidity sells his or her asset to the bank to raise capital in one contract, and in another contract leases the same asset back while retaining possession of it. The bank may also wish to sell the asset back to the client at the end of the second contract.

ISTISNA AND PARALLEL ISTISNA – BUILD-TO-ORDER

Istisna is a contract for acquisition of goods by specification or order where price is fixed in advance, but assets are built or manufactured and delivered at a future date (New Horizon 2009; IFC 2012). This manufactured or constructed asset must conform to an agreed description within a pre-determined period and price (Euromoney 2008). It is a purchase order contract for an asset whereby a buyer places an order to purchase an asset to be delivered in the future, according to specifications in the sale and purchase contract (CBN 2009). *Istisna* allows cash payment in advance in return for future delivery (Abbasi 2009b). For instance, the bank or IFI may agree to build a factory for a client based on the client's design and specifications. At the end of the construction project, the bank will hand over the structure to the client, who will pay in instalments over a ore-agreed period. This mode can be used for plane, ship and heavy machinery construction, and for real estate projects.

Parallel *istisna* is where the bank that provides finance and is thus the owner of the project or manufactured item agrees to sell the project to the final consumer who instructs that the project be executed, which mitigates the bank's risk and provides a better option to execute the *istisna*. Abbasi (2009b) observed that 'the bank may maintain an "Asset Account" in which *Istisna* contracts cost is accumulated', and that 'when the percentage-of-completion method is used, a portion of *istisna* profit commensurate with the work completed during the financial period is also debited to this account', and that an *istisna* 'Cost Account' is maintained when a parallel *istisna* exists, and accumulates progress billings made by the subcontractor while a portion of the *istisna* profit commensurate with the work completed during a financial period is debited to this account.

SALAM – DEFERRED DELIVERY

Salam is a contract where advance payment is made for goods that are delivered later (New Horizon 2009; IFC 2012). This is very similar to *istisna*, except that *salam* is mainly used for agricultural produce. The original Islamic text in the Hadith generally forbade *salam* unless the conditions of specification of produce, price and delivery time were well defined. The Prophet said: 'Whoever pays money in advance for dates (to be delivered later) should pay for known specific weight and measure (of the dates)' (Sahih Bukhari, *The Book of Salam*, no. 441). Parallel *salam* is where there is an off-taker at inception of the contract, which reduces the risk for the bank.

QARD AND QARD-HASSAN

In Islam, money should not earn interest, and the same applies to loans. *Qard* is simply a loan from one person to the other: 'Narrated Jabir bin Abdullah, he went to meet the Prophet in the mosque who was owing him money and the latter repaid the debt he owed and also gave an additional extra amount' (Sahih Al-Bukhari, vol. 3, Hadith no. 579). The Prophet also said: 'there is no objection if the debtor gives more than he owes if the creditor has not stipulated it' (Sahih Al-Bukhari, vol. 3, Chapter 17). Islam is not opposed to a debtor paying a loan back and giving something extra willingly. However, this should not be part of the contract. In practical banking, the *qard* mode is used as a liability in current accounts, where clients or depositors lend money to the bank, and the bank keeps the money and gives it back to the client on demand. In a *qard*, the bank is allowed to use the money for other Shariah-compliant business transactions, but is not under any obligation to give anything back to the client. Abbasi (2009b) mentioned that *qard* cannot have any contractual compensation or gift attached to it, and that the bank can utilize the funds for its own liquidity or short-term investments, but any losses incurred must be borne by the bank, not the depositor.

Another form of *qard* is *qard-hassan* (good loan). Allah says in the Quran: 'Who is he that will lend Allah a *qard-hassan* so that he will multiply it for him (the lender) many times over?' (Q2, verse 245). This mode is not common among IFIs, but studies are being carried out to explore its relevance to micro-finance, where a very small amount is required to start a micro-business. Monies generated from the *zakat* fund can also be given out to very small-scale entrepreneurs or those in need based on *qard-hassan*.

WADIAH – SAFE-KEEPING

Wadiah means 'safe-keeping', and is very similar to *qard*. The main difference in banking is that *qard* allows the bank to utilize funds generated via current accounts, while *wadiah* also allows the utilization of funds, but the customer will also bear losses. *Wadiah* is just safe-keeping, and does not guarantee that the client will get his or her money back if it is stolen or lost through some unforeseen event, which is the main reason why banks prefer to use a *qard* for current accounts, but a *wadiah* may be used for some other liability products. If the bank loses the principal deposit in the process of doing business 'due to negligence, they will not be held liable in a *wadiah* which makes it very risky for the customers' (Abbasi 2009b). Bank Negara, the Central Bank of Malaysia, introduced a special form of *wadiah* with guarantee (*wadiah yad damanah*) which guarantees depositors' funds held in current accounts.

AMANAH – TRUST

Amanah literarily means 'trust' and is theoretically associated with current accounts: 'Amanah entails absence of liability for loss except in case of lack of due diligence while the bank has no authority to use the funds' (Abbasi 2009b). Abbasi also observed that an explicit authority can be sought from the client to use the fund, which transforms *amanah* into a *qard*.

WAKALA – AGENCY

Wakala refers to an agency agreement between contracting parties; thus, the bank may be an agent in a business transaction and earn commission and fees. On the other hand, a bank may appoint an agent to act on its behalf in a business transaction such as a *mudarabah*, *musharakah*, *murabahah*, *tawarruq* or *ijarah*, especially an *ijarah muntahia bit-tamleek*, where the bank makes the client the agent to take care of major maintenance as the representative of the bank (Abbasi 2009b). In summary, *wakala* is a contract of agency where one party appoints someone else to perform a certain task on his or her behalf for a fee

(New Horizon 2009), which reduces the bank's operational risk with reference to Basel II.

Wakala can also be used by the bank in the issuance of letters of credit to make payment for imported goods on a client's behalf, in which case the bank will receive fee income. Other forms of intermediate contracts include *takaful* (Islamic insurance), *kifala* (guarantee) and *ju'ualah* (service fee).

SUKUK – ISLAMIC FINANCIAL CERTIFICATES

Sukuk are asset-backed or asset-based financial certificates which represent proportionate beneficial ownership in the underlying asset (New Horizon 2009; IFC 2012). In a *sukuk*, investors have the right to 'participate in the income of an underlying asset or a pool of assets. The cash flow of the underlying assets, after deducting expenses etc. is passed on to the *sukuk* holders' (Euromoney 2008). *Sukuk* is designed as a form of a private equity where several parties buy a small part of a project or asset-backed investment and profit is shared among the participants at the end of the contract or project. Other Islamic financial instruments such as *murabahah*, *ijarah* and *mudarabah* can be used to develop a *sukuk*. The *sukuk* is best for long-term infrastructural and manufacturing projects. Information disclosure is very important in a *sukuk*, and speculation must be avoided since it is a form of gambling. In the same vein, proper Shariah-compliant regulation must be in place to guide the operations and trading in this financing mode. In summary, Islamic banking and finance is all about partnership, trading, leasing and fee-based transactions, as illustrated in Table 6.1.

A clear picture of the functionalities of Islamic banking and finance instruments and their application to financial products leads us now to an overall assessment of Islamic banking globally, within the African continent, and with specific reference to Nigeria's Jaiz Bank, Stanbic IBTC Bank and Sterling Bank. The main practicality of these contracts or Islamic financial instruments is directly related to how best the core banking system or Islamic banking solution can roll out innovative products. Detailed consideration of this aspect of applied Islamic finance would require a whole book of the same size as this one to explore the DaVinci Institute's TIPS – management of Technology, management of Innovation, management of People and Systemic thinking – in the realm of real-life organizational operations.

Table 6.1   Islamic banking financial modes and applications

Nature of Islamic Finance Contract	Mode of Financing/ Contracts	Generic Definition	Application to Banking and Finance
Partnership	*Musharakah* (joint venture)	Investment partners/ parties share equity and expertise	Project finance, trade finance, property finance, home finance
	Mudarabah (partnership)	One party brings capital, and another brings expertise	Project finance, trade finance, property finance
Trading	*Murabahah* (purchase and resale at mark-up)	Sale of an asset by the financial institution to a customer at cost plus a profit margin.	Commodity trading, trade finance, property finance, home finance, asset finance, investment account, equity investment
	Salam (deferred delivery)	Purchase contract with delivery (usually agricultural produce) at a later date while payment is made at the time of contract	Agro-commodity trading, general agricultural banking
	Istisna (build to order)	Manufacturing/ construction order contract which allows cash payment in advance and future delivery	Project finance, property finance, asset finance
Leasing	*Ijara* (Islamic lease agreement)	Lease agreement for the use of an asset with a definite rent	Asset finance, property finance
Fee-based agency contract	*Wakala* (agency)	Fee-based agency contract	Equity investment
	Qardh (loan)	Interest-free loan	Current account
			Savings account without profit *Personal loan*
Certificate	*Sukuk* (Islamic financial certificate)	Certificate of equal value representing undivided share in an underlying asset	Real estate bond, commodity bond, infrastructural bond

Islamic Banking Assessment

GLOBAL ISSUES

There are well over 500 financial institutions in more than 80 countries that offer Shariah-compliant financial services. These were worth over US$750 billion in 2008, which increased to over US$1.3 trillion in 2013, with an annual growth rate of 15–20 per cent. Many financial analysts believe that the industry will exceed US$5 trillion before 2020. The bulk of this market is in the Middle East, Asia and Europe. The Gulf States and Malaysia account for the largest Shariah-compliant investments, while the UK competes favourably in funds management. South Korea, Sweden, Russia, China, Indonesia, Kazakhstan, Bangladesh, Singapore, Australia, the US and Canada also offer Shariah-compliant financial products (New Horizon 2009). The performance of *sukuk* in the global market has been massive over the last five years, during which over US$85 billion has been issued (IIBI 2006a). The United Arab Emirates have taken the lead in this regard, while Japan, China and the UK are building up liquidity potentials to develop innovative *sukuk* instruments. The UK now has over six stand-alone Islamic financial institutions. In 2007, the UK Islamic real estate fund had sales of over US$116.5 million (New Horizon 2007), while Indonesia attracts Middle Eastern banks (New Horizon 2007).

The *World Islamic Banking Competitiveness Report 2007/2008* predicted that the value of Islamic banking assets and assets under management would reach US$1 trillion by 2010, and asserted that Islamic banks were growing more rapidly than the average banking sector in many countries (McKinsey, in New Horizon 2008b). The World Bank, on the other hand, developed Islamic banking financial stability standards using the comparison of average z-scores, which combine a bank's capitalization, profitability and measure of risk into one single index. The Institute of Islamic Banking and Insurance in London organizes annual workshops at the University of Cambridge that structure innovative Islamic financial products which serve as a standard for new and unique products for the Islamic banking market. The complexities of Islamic financial instruments also call for highly innovative companies such as InfrasoftTech, Path Solutions, Olympic Banking and Finacle to develop easy-to-use IT packages for Shariah-compliant products.

The UK's Muslim population is less that 2.5 million, but the country has been proactive compared to other European countries in creating a very conducive and competitive environment for the market. The nature of Islamic banking instruments such as diminishing *musharakah* (joint venture), *mudarabah* (investment partnership) and *sukuk* (Islamic financial certificates) calls for the Islamic financial institution to own the asset first and pay stamp duty, after which the client pays further stamp duty when the asset is transferred to him or her. The UK government has limited such taxes to only one imposition in the case of Shariah-compliant transactions. The Prime Minister also mentioned in 2008 that London wants to be the gateway for Islamic finance. The over 80 per cent excess liquidity of the Gulf Cooperation Council (GCC) is mainly invested in Europe and North America. In more recent times, the GCC has preferred to invest in Europe since its accounts are frozen in the US as a result of issues around the World Trade Centre bombing and terrorism allegations. The bulk of these funds need viable investments, and the GCC is looking at opportunities in developing economies in Asia and Africa, especially where they are willing and able to adopt Shariah-compliant financial modes. On the other hand, the Islamic economic system spells out a moral economic system, an ideology and a civilization that the Middle East wants to spread.

THE AFRICAN STORY

The impact of the triple heritage still haunts Africa. In particular, the perception that the Western economic system is the route to achieving economic development, as experienced by Europe, is still being imposed on Africa through international organizations. Economic influence from the Far East had been minimal over decades since they had their own houses to put in order and preferred to learn from the Japanese, South Korean, Taiwanese and Malaysian economic successes. Africa has only just begun to shift rapidly away from the neo-classical economic model. Islamic finance in the Sudan, for example, is a state-led programme that specifically designs products to alleviate poverty through the use of *musharakah* (joint venture), *mudarabah* (investment partnership) and *murabahah* (purchase at mark-up) as well as setting tailored guidelines and products to address productive families (Badr-El-Din 2003).

This is a rather new phenomenon in Nigeria, but large conventional commercial banks seeking to offer Islamic banking simply see it as an opportunity to offer another financial product on the market. The leading banks in Kenya and Nigeria argue that it will help provide financial services for the huge Muslim population who do not currently use banks, while increasing money flow in the formal economy. There is also evidence from Nigeria and Tanzania that some banks offering Shariah-compliant products only have liability products that do not give anything back to customers, on the basis that Shariah-compliant deposits need to be generated before asset products can be considered. In general, Islamic finance would benchmark profits to interest in order to remain competitive while mimicking virtually all the conventional banking products if Shariah-compliance could be established. Farooq (2009c), on the other hand, argued that Islamic economics does not identify poverty as its primary focus, but a counterpart to conventional economics.

Lessem and Schieffer (2010a) were in favour of moral economic core rather than just Shariah-compliance. The next phase for Islamic finance in Africa will involve aggressive competition, making a bid for market size and market leadership, while shareholders' primary motive will be excessive profits, except perhaps the stand-alone Islamic banks whose aim may be different at inception. In South Africa, a major bank preferred other jurisdictions to the saturated home market in order to capture virgin markets. Nevertheless, the Islamic finance industry in Africa will enjoy great success in the area of *sukuk*. South Africa, with its barely one million Muslims, is to launch the first sovereign *sukuk*-based investment fund outside the Muslim world, while Nigeria is making efforts to do the same. Nigeria currently has a relatively favourable regulatory regime and may have more *sukuk* in terms of value than the rest of African countries in the next ten years. While South Africa has sound infrastructure, Nigeria will need to use *sukuk* to address its infrastructural poverty challenge. Kenya patiently waits for *sukuk* to cover bonds and the T-bill market, while Gambia gives some priority to *takaful*. In Tunisia, AfDB is committed to using *istisna* contracts to improve the country's real estate, infrastructure and energy sectors while creating thousands of jobs and other benefits. IDB is also making its presence felt more in the continent and paying attention to large-scale agriculture, which will create employment and have a positive impact on most categories of poverty. Stanbic IBTC Bank in Nigeria is considering using agro-commodities *murabahah* as a liquidity management instrument, which will also touch the lives of the rural poor in many ways, while consideration of an agro-*sukuk* will benefit Africa as a whole. Sterling Bank prefers to base its short-term liquidity management instruments on oil and gas as the underlying assets. In the first quarter of 2013, AfDB set forth a unique proposition aimed at developing a department or unit within the bank to handle Islamic finance. The bank believes that infrastructural development in Africa can easily be achieved through the use of *sukuk*. It will, however, be more effective for the regional bank to consider other Islamic finance contracts across Africa, especially the use of *istisna* (build-to-order) for project finance, *salam* (deferred delivery) for agricultural finance and variations of *murabahah* (purchase and resale at mark-up) for trade finance. Thus, they may also consider other kinds of Shariah-compliant partnerships with multilateral institutions, development banks, infrastructural banks, government departments and Islamic financial institutions. A somewhat less preferred *sukuk* solution would be to set up a *sukuk* fund which would help to generate or attract needed capital from the Middle East, Malaysia and China.

In Africa, it is envisaged that there will generally be a shift from retail banking and micro-finance banking to investment banking; however, Sudan's integral Islamic finance micro-credit style should also be encouraged across Africa to support poor entrepreneurs. The primary purpose of Islamic finance is to achieve a moral economic system based on *maqasid al Shariah* which should increase wealth-creation while reducing poverty, income inequality and unemployment. In reality, Islamic finance on its own in today's neo-liberal world cannot reduce poverty, but will need to take its place in the context of the overall socio-economic and political framework in order to have a real impact. While Nigeria takes advantage of its oil wealth to create investment opportunities, Mali may not have as much potential for wealth-creation regardless of the size of its Muslim population. The rebirth of Egypt and Libya should witness new investments in unique Islamic banks offering Shariah-compliant products and services primarily aligned to customer value architecture or people-bias propositions. Islamic finance should be an investment not only to meet the conditions of Shariah-compliance, but also serve to reduce all forms of poverty associated with Africa. EFInA's *Access to Financial Services in Nigeria* survey in 2012 showed that Nigeria has 30.5 million adults who are likely or somewhat likely to use Islamic financial products, out of which 23.6 million are interested in savings, 15.3 million are interested in loans, 9.5 million are interested in trading and 7.9 million are interested in current accounts. This is indeed a huge market that no other country in Africa can match.

Islamic banks in Sudan and South Africa should invest in Mali, Niger and Chad based on customer overall socio-economic needs, while the continent should float *sukuk* funds for the region – a role IDB and AfDB can play jointly with other financial organizations. Africa should also set up an Islamic finance reserve institution primarily aimed at poverty reduction while fostering co-operation, peace and love in a moral economic environment. There is, however, a need to borrow aspects of Wallerstein's World Systems Theory, which stresses development issues and unequal opportunities across nations. It addresses both political and intellectual issues, where theory and practice are interwoven (Wallerstein 2000; Modelski 1995: Lessem and Schieffer 2010a), giving birth to the Islamic African World System, which may be described as the combination of a wide array of social, religious, cultural, behavioural, moral, economic, political, international, organizational, institutional and evolving circumstances that affect Africa's socio-economic transformation (Oshodi 2010). This is a new theoretical position founded on the Islamic economic system within the context of general economic development thinking.

We will now examine the Nigerian situation, starting with regulatory issues.

The Framework for Non-interest Banks in Nigeria

HISTORICAL BACKGROUND

Nigeria's first Banking Act was in 1952, and defined banking as 'the business of receiving from the public on current account money which is to be repayable on demand by cheque, and of making advances to customers'. Section 2 of the Banking Act 1958 defined banking as 'the business of receiving money on current account from the general public, of paying or collecting cheques drawn by or paid in by customers and making advances to customers'. The Banking Act 1968 and its amendments limited the activities of banks to receiving money as deposits, granting money as loans, accepting credits, purchasing bills and cheques and selling securities. It prohibited banks from undertaking any investment or acquiring or holding share capital of any financial, industrial or other undertaking. Section 66 of the Banks and Other Financial Institutions Act 1991 (BOFIA) recognizes profit- and loss-sharing banks with the approval of the Governor of the CBN. It states in Section 61 that 'profit- and loss-sharing bank' means 'a bank which transacts investment or commercial banking business and maintains profit and loss sharing accounts'. This was the only legal definition of a non-interest bank in the Nigerian statute books until 2009, when the *Draft Framework for the Regulation and Supervision of Non-interest Banks in Nigeria* was released by the CBN.

THE DRAFT FRAMEWORK

On 4 March 2009, the CBN issued its draft framework for the operation of the Islamic banking system to all stakeholders. Nigeria has never had Shariah-compliant Islamic banks apart from an asset management company, Lotus Capital, that began operations in 2004 and registered with the Nigerian Securities and Exchange Commission. Several banks and financial institutions in the country have offered a number of products to the Muslim market which are not Shariah-compliant because they lack Shariah governance. Funds and liabilities generated from the Muslim population are used to create assets for the interest-based population, so their processes were not end-to-end Shariah-compliant. This concern led the CBN to release the draft framework for the regulation and supervision of what is termed 'non-interest banking', which is used to represent Islamic or Shariah-compliant banking. The word 'non-interest' was adopted because of fears that the over 50 per cent of the population who are non-Muslim might react negatively to the use of 'Islamic' or 'Shariah'.

The CBN describes a non-interest bank as:

> a bank which transacts business, engages in trading, investments and commercial activities, as well as the provision of financial products and services in accordance with the principles and rules of Islamic commercial jurisprudence. Transactions and contracts under this type of banking are non-permissible if they involve: interest, uncertainty or ambiguity to the subject matter, term or conditions; gambling; speculation; unjust enrichment; or exploitation/unfair trade practices.

The CBN allows all licensed banks in the country or prospective banks wishing to offer Shariah-compliant products to operate either as fully fledged non-interest banks or subsidiaries, to have a non-interest banking branch if the bank is already offering conventional banking products, and to operate a non-interest banking window if the bank is already a conventional one.

The CBN allows non-interest banks to use a wide variety of Islamic banking financial instruments, such as *murabahah, mudarabah, musharakah, ijarah, salam* and parallel *salam, istisna, sukuk* and any other financing mode approved by the central bank. The CBN forbids cross-selling of products or services – that is, a conventional bank with a non-interest banking window or branch can offer both conventional and Islamic banking products in a conventional branch, but can only offer Shariah-compliant products in an Islamic banking branch. The CBN requires that conventional banks with Islamic banking windows be required to execute service level agreements in respect of shared services between the window and other department or units of the bank.

Account separation and Shariah governance

One of the most important requirements of this whole framework is that conventional banks offering Islamic banking products must maintain separate accounting books, thus separate balance sheets, audited in recognition of Shariah principles. This provision had always been absent in Nigeria's banking history, which was why conventional banks offering supposed Islamic banking products commingled these different funds, distorting the end-to-end Shariah process.

One major requirement in Islamic banking is Shariah governance. Non-interest banking without Shariah governance or a Shariah advisory or supervisory board is not Shariah-compliant. The CBN requires that banks offering Shariah-compliant services must have at least three Shariah Advisory Committee (SAC) members who understand *fiqh al-muamalat* (Islamic commercial jurisprudence) and an internal Shariah-compliance review mechanism as part of the bank's governance structure. The CBN also has its own governance structure called the CBN Shariah Council, which is outsourced. The Accounting and Auditing Organization for Islamic Financial Institutions (AAOFIF) is a Bahrain-based international Shariah governance standard-setting body, and its rulings on Islamic finance operational modes are globally accepted, and the CBN also requires Islamic banks to operate in accordance with AAOIFI standards.

Liquidity and risk management

The CBN requires that Islamic banks adopt proper strategies and procedures to maintain adequate liquidity ratios in their operations, and that they maintain a minimum of 30 per cent of deposit liabilities in liquid assets. Islamic banks cannot invest their monies in interest-based securities unless they are Shariah-compliant, and the CBN proposes that these monies could be invested in Commodity *Murabahah* Certificates issued by the London Metal Exchange, CBN Islamic Treasury Bills and Debt Management Office (DMO) Islamic Bonds. Islamic banking and finance is also termed profit/loss banking, where the bank and customers share both risks and rewards. The envisaged fluctuation of profit/loss calls for what the CBN refers to as the Profit Equalization Reserve (PER), which serves as an income-smoothing mechanism and risk mitigating tool to hedge against volatility of returns to investment account holders, especially under *mudarabah* contracts. The bank also requires that that the reserve be funded by setting aside a portion of gross income before deducting the bank's own share as agent, while details of transactions and profits must be sincerely disclosed.

Risk in Islamic banking is a lot more severe if not properly mitigated compared to conventional banking, which is why the CBN requires that Islamic banks put proper and adequate measures in place to control their exposure to risk. Some very common types of risk highlighted by the CBN include Shariah risk, reputational risk, mark-up risk, displaced commercial risk, fiduciary risk and transparency risk. It recommends applying international standards such as the Basel Committee Risk Management Guidelines, the Islamic Financial Services Board Standards for Risk Management, the Generic Risk Management Guidelines, the Guidelines for the Development of Risk Management Frameworks for Individual Risk Elements, and Prudential Guidelines.

CRITIQUE OF THE CBN NON-INTEREST BANKING FRAMEWORK

The CBN draft guidelines for Islamic banking have been criticized by both non-Muslims and financial service operators. The non-Muslims, especially the Christians in Nigeria who constitute over 40 per cent of the population, argue that the CBN wants to Islamicize the nation by introducing non-interest banking for Muslims. Ex-CBN governor Professor Chukuma Soludo, a non-Muslim, started this whole project as a feasible solution to economic growth and development and a means by which the country could achieve the 2020:20 target based on Goldman Sachs's *World Economic Report*, which projected that Nigeria could be the twentieth-largest economy in the world by 2020 based on its socio-economic and governance performance trends compared to other economies in the world. The new CBN governor, Lamido Sanusi, a Muslim from the north, took office in August 2009 and immediately set the ball rolling to release new guidelines for non-Interest banking.

Meanwhile, operators in the financial services industry criticized the draft guidelines on the following grounds:

- There is nothing like Shariah risk, since Shariah itself is not a risk, but rather a perfect law that guides Muslims. Thus, they proposed Shariah non-compliance risk, to ensure that transactions complied with Shariah governance.

- The whole concept of window operation was unclear, especially as it related to cross-selling of products on one hand and the separation of accounts on the other. If cross-selling meant that conventional products could not be sold in Shariah-compliant branches, then, account separation remained undefined. Separate general ledgers and separate annual reports might be created, but special software might also be required by IFIs to take account of the nature of credit and debit using Islamic financial instruments. The existing creation of general ledgers only required IT and finance departments to manually spool or extract the Shariah-compliant entries from the conventional ones, so there was greater scope for errors. Operational risks might render the Islamic banking concept Shariah non-compliant.

- The guidelines did not take account of very important Islamic financial instruments and modes such as *qardh* (loan), parallel *istisna* (build-to-order), *ijarah wa iqtina* and *ijarah muntahia* (Islamic lease with ownership), *tawarruq* (overdraft), *wakala* (agency), *kifala* (guarantee) and *ju'ualah* (service fee).

- The CBN had called for a Profit Equalization Reserve as an income-smoothing mechanism extracted from net profit, but also needed to consider the Investment Risk Return (IRR) approach, which appropriates the profit shared with investment account holders (IAH) after deducting the bank's *mudarib* shares. Some amount from IRR is released to curb the losses that arise from unrestricted investment account holders (UIAHs) and the same may be done for restricted investment account holders (RIAHs), leading to greater transparency. IRR is generally derived from part of the UIAH profit. In the same vein, the CBN would need to change the Profit Sharing Investment Account to an Un-restricted Profit Sharing Investment Account (UPSIA) and Restricted Profit Sharing Investment Account (RPSIA).

- The word 'Islamic' could not be part of the licensed name of a Nigerian bank, and compliance would be signified by a uniform logo to be designed and approved by the CBN. It might be quite challenging for an international bank operating in Nigeria to change its logo.

- Banks would be expected to comply with too many accounting standards, such as GAAP, NASB, IFRS, IAS and FAS, issued by the AAOFIF.

- The CBN had yet to develop the Treasury Bills and DMO Islamic Bonds in which non-interest banks were expected to invest their funds to comply with the prescribed minimum liquidity ratio.

THE FINAL AND REVIEWED NON-INTEREST BANKING FRAMEWORKS

On 13 January 2011, the CBN released the final *Framework for the Regulation and Supervision of Institutions Offering Non-interest Financial Services in Nigeria* (CBN 2011a), *Guidelines on Shariah Governance for Non-interest Financial Institutions in Nigeria* (CBN 2011b) and *Guidelines on Non-interest Window and Branch Operations of Conventional Banks and other Financial Institutions* (CBN 2011c). These guidelines took into account virtually all the critiques of the draft guidelines, except that the CBN insisted there would be a logo to differentiate conventional financial institutions from the Islamic banks. However, the release of this final version led to nationwide argument, which heated up the polity, the non-Muslims believing it was a plot to Islamicize the country. They insisted the word 'Shariah' should be completely removed from the guidelines. On 21 June 2011, the CBN released a reviewed guideline with the following amendments:

- The CBN accepted two types of Non-Interest Banking Model, one based on the Islamic Commercial Jurisprudence Model, the other based on any other finance model with established principles.

- The CBN acknowledged the name 'Institutions Offering Islamic Financial Services' rather than just 'Non-interest Financial Institution' as contained in the previous guidelines.

- The word 'Shariah' was completely removed from the guidelines.

- The registered licensed names of banks could not include the word 'Islamic' except with the consent of the CBN governor.

- The Shariah Advisory Committee was changed to the Advisory Committee of Experts (ACE).

- The CBN Shariah Council was also changed to the CBN Advisory Council of Experts.

Many pro-Islamic banking analysts have argued that the CBN is empowered under the law (Section 66 of BOFIA) to regulate specialized banks, including micro-finance banks, mortgage banks, development banks such as the Federal Mortgage Bank, and community banks (the NIFI is just one form of specialized bank). Section 33(1)(b) of the CBN Act allows the CBN to issue guidelines to any person or institution under its supervision. Some relevant provisions dealing with specialized banks under BOFIA are Section 61, which empowers the CBN to regulate the activities of financial institutions and specialized banks, and Section 66, which allows the CBN to label any bank as a specialized bank. By 21 July 2011, the House of Representative endorsed Islamic banking.

We will now turn to practical issues, looking at the Islamic value proposition and the degree to which it aligns with *maqasid al Shariah*.

UNDERSTANDING THE ISLAMIC BANKING VALUE PROPOSITION

A value proposition (VP) is a business or marketing statement that summarizes why a consumer should buy a product or use a service. This statement should convince a potential consumer that one particular product or service will add more value or solve a problem more effectively than other similar offerings. Laura Lake (n.d.) observes: 'It's important when developing your value proposition that it be clear and concise. It's best to start by brainstorming and forecasting on what members of your target demographics group have in common.' A strong VP is also expected to increase revenue, decrease costs through a faster time to market while increasing market share, and improve operational efficiency and customer retention levels (Konrath, in DiVanna 2006). For NetEdge the VP is a 360-degree value-driven approach that creates and distributes value via its people or staff, technology, methodology, products, solutions, alliances and quality of services (NetEdge, in DiVanna 2006). For KPMG, internal auditing, corporate governance, enterprise and risk, and internal control/compliance services make up its VP (KPMG, in DiVanna 2006). Protis Executive Innovators (in DiVanna 2006) prefers mutual accountability, transparency and metric-driven concepts as its VP. For 9ciphers, thought leadership and innovation, rapid delivery led by SMEs at each phase, engagement exceeding industry standards, return on investment with each engagement, customer delight, and efficient and secured enterprises constitute its VP.

In Islam, the VP is rooted in the values and beliefs of Shariah, as explained in *fiqh* (explanation of Shariah), and may adopt other conventional values that do not conflict with the principles of Islam. This VP also aligns its rules with the general concept of an Islamic economic system, which seeks to embody brotherhood, equality and justice in society. DiVanna (2006) mapped the Islamic economic system's VP in terms of three principles:

the quest for justice, avoidance of *riba* and acceptance of *halal* (permissible activities in Islam), and avoidance of *gharar* (risky sale). He based it on four philosophies: safe-keeping, risk-sharing, profit-sharing and promotion of economic and social development. DiVanna particularly emphasized *zakat* as a form of improvement of society, which belongs to the philosophical pillar of the Islamic VP. Tripp (2006) examined this *zakat* philosophy more closely, and asserted that 'the challenge of equating *riba* with interest lay not simply in escaping the theoretical contradictions which might arise from arguments pro and con, but in constructing a framework which would negate the principle, allowing social action under a moral order uncontaminated by *riba*'.

Egypt's first Islamic bank of the 1960s, Mit Ghamr Savings Bank, re-emerged in the 1970s as Cairo-based Nasser Social Bank, mainly providing services to assist economically disadvantaged students with funding for small projects and higher education. In early Malaysian banks, DiVanna identified the VP as focused on helping people save for *Hajj*, co-ordinate their *Hajj*, manage their accounts professionally, invest in *halal* deals that were Shariah-compliant, and providing the services and information demanded by their customers. With reference to Grameen Bank in Bangladesh, DiVanna observed: 'the biggest opportunity for Islamic banks in the development of their VP is to provide financial services to specific segments of a nation's population that are not currently served by banking products (the unbanked)'. He observed that Grameen Bank applied classical Islamic values, but used conventional lending practices to provide credit to the poorest of the poor in the rural parts of the country who lacked collateral. EFInA in Nigeria has borrowed from the Grameen concept by providing innovative funds to banks and financial institutions that are able and willing to serve the very poor in the country. Islamic financial institutions in Nigeria now enjoy research support from EFInA which is being applied to their VPs in a manner that promotes financial inclusion, yet is Shariah-compliant.

The Dow Jones Islamic Fund's VP is based on Shariah-compliance in terms of ethical concerns/products, diversification in terms of business sectors, low expenses/fees, accessibility and flexibility, active portfolio management based on Shariah values, a Shariah supervisory board from all four schools of thought, and a brand identity which signifies trust and goodwill towards the company. IHilal's VP maps out the best strategies to confirm that an investment or project is largely Shariah-compliant through qualitative screening to confirm that unethical concerns are dealt and that businesses it transacts with are not exploitative, and quantitative screening to measure the debt–asset ratio, interest-related income ratio and monetary assets held by the company. Trading practices is a third consideration, which mainly involves ensuring that transactions such as short-term speculation are prohibited, sound analysis is carried out, and the consideration and mitigation of risk are well defined. The Islamic Bank of Britain's VP is based on faith (Shariah banking practices and a code of ethics), value (service at a competitive rate), convenience (transparent transactions and services) and trust (building long-term relationships) (IBB, in DiVanna 2006). Innovation and customer focus are the two main focuses for AmBank, the sixth-largest bank in Malaysia (AmBank Group Malaysia, in DiVanna 2006), which provides financial services for both Muslims and non-Muslims.

These initiatives are very innovative, and specifically provide offerings that are not only Shariah-compliant, but also very different from their conventional services. DiVanna (2006, p. 92) listed a number of VP fundamentals that will also apply to Islamic banking, including: value added and how it complements the market being served, the creation of mechanisms for market sensing, product re-branding which reflects identity, efficiency in managing relationships and competencies in customer relationship management (CRM), innovative technology to support transactions while building good relationships with technology and service providers, and evolving the market with innovative offerings. The Bank of Beirut's VP is based on Shariah-compliance, sound banking practices, customer focus, investment strategy, integrity and service excellence (Bank of Beirut 2009). DiVanna (2006, p. 156) summarized the twenty-first-century Islamic VP as consisting of:

- perceived value (standardization/customization);

- value for money (price/cost);

- convenience (availability/time);

- adherence to principles (beliefs, morals and ethics).

Business and financial organizations often misplace the Islamic VP, either through lack of adequate knowledge of Shariah and *fiqh muamalat* in relation to conventional economics and finance, or simply because they are carried away with the conventional financial approaches. This has led many Islamic financial institutions to develop substitute products for their Muslim customers based on those that already exist in conventional banking, seeking profitability without taking into consideration the Islamic beliefs, values, real emotional needs, geography, demographics and perceptions of the market they wish to serve. In fact, the five pillars of Islam are not in any way controversial, nor are there tangible differences in the way these pillars are practised.

Zakat is one of them, a pillar of Islam that is hardly institutionalized or organized, but it is a means of national wealth redistribution and a poverty reduction measure rather than just an individual act where a Muslim goes and drops off his *zakat* in a local mosque for anyone to pick up. This institution alone can give birth to several financial products that comply with the real values of the Islamic faith. A variety of asset and liability products can be developed from *zakat*: specialized investment funds, mutual funds, pension funds and insurance; personal loans not for business purposes and *qard-hassan* for micro-finance for the lower segment of the unbanked population, charitable activities or a specialized *zakat* fund, *waqf* funds and charity funds, and fee income for the IFIs, since the Quran allows the administrator of *zakat* to benefit from it. Several other Islamic financial instruments can also be combined with the *zakat* methodology or within the *zakat* framework.

Another area critical to the Islamic faith is inheritance, which is based on the Islamic law of succession. Belief in the hereafter – life in the grave and on the final Day of Judgment or Reckoning – is one of the six articles of faith of Islam, and Muslims are expected to live their lives in compliance with the Shariah, including sharing their assets. The concept of a will (*wasiyya*) is very different in Islam, since Muslims can only bequeath a maximum of one third of their property to charity while the Quran clearly defines how a minimum of the remaining two thirds should be shared. IFIs can develop financial products to meet this emergent need for the Muslim market – a need that is very important to the purpose of creation, which will inevitably arise when death comes. The Prophet Mohammed said: 'It is the duty of a Muslim who has anything to bequeath not to let two nights pass without including it in his Will (wasiyya)' (Sahih al-Bukhari).

Core Islamic scholars and the general Muslim population have been unable to establish the effective and efficient allocation of willed property and assets to beneficiaries. IFIs can use their technology and financial skills to address this untapped opportunity and build a whole new VP around their financial offerings. 1st Ethical is a very innovative IFI in the UK that tailors its products to the real values and needs of Muslims. The company is regulated by the Financial Services Authority (FSA) in the UK, and has unique products like its *Musharakah* Fund, as well as a hand-full of *zakat*- and *wasiyya*-related services, in particular Islamic inheritance tax planning and will writing, which most IFIs avoid. Some believe that *musharakah* deals are too risky, but they accommodate all elements of value in *fiqh muamalat* such as risk/reward sharing, availability of assets and full Shariah-compliance, and are applicable to most projects and types of business financing. *Zakat* and inheritance are barely considered at IFI board meetings, as they tend to focus on profitability and the free flow of Middle East funding, which generally subdues the concept of VP in Islamic finance. How, then, have Nigeria's Jaiz Bank and Stanbic IBTC performed? What about the rapidly emerging Sterling Bank?

The Emerging Value Proposition for Islamic Financial Institutions in Nigeria

Generally, the value proposition is an integral part of Islamic financial institutions in Nigeria. Jaiz Bank, Stanbic IBTC Bank and Sterling Bank have set up units to develop detailed VP research on new products with the aim of developing accurate and precise information about the market and a good grasp of the banks' financial expenditure on these innovative products. The Islamic banking VP for these institutions continues to evolve, and it focuses on:

- end-to-end Shariah-compliant operational processes;

- Shariah governance;

- effective technology;

- innovative product development;

- human resource development.

END-TO-END SHARIAH-COMPLIANT OPERATIONAL PROCESSES

The banks that attempted Islamic banking in Nigeria prior to the 2011 CBN guidelines only developed very basic non-interest current and saving accounts. There were no restricted or un-restricted investment accounts with profit sharing, just liability products that took money from Muslims without complementary asset products. Thus, liabilities generated in a Shariah-compliant way were invested in interest-based assets or loans, while Shariah governance was absent to guide the day-to-day business processes. Human skills were scarce, there was no regulatory guidance, and many of these banks had a conventional balance sheet. This process gap led to huge market of customers and reputational risk for the bank. Post-guidelines Islamic financial institutions are now developing VPs that lay much emphasis on strict end-to-end Shariah-compliance in their operations and dealings even if they come at a cost to the bank (see Figure 6.1).

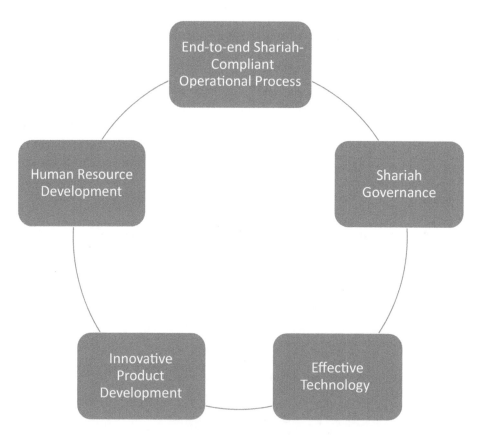

Figure 6.1   The unfolding value proposition among Islamic banks in Nigeria

SHARIAH GOVERNANCE

The Shariah Board or Shariah Supervisory Committee or Advisory Committee of Experts is a very important element in Islamic banking since it monitors the activities of bankers who may become carried away with enthusiasm for excessive profits and unethical financial dealings. Other than Lotus Capital and Al-Baraka Micro-Finance Bank, the banks and other quasi-Islamic financial institutions in Nigeria had never had a Shariah Board or any formal Shariah governance in place. IFIs now meet global best practice principles by setting up ACE members to guide them in ensuring the Shariah-compliance of their products and processes. ACE members are drawn from Muslim-dominated regions of the country and have a sound knowledge of Shariah, *fiqh al-muamalat* and the conventional socio-economic system, evincing a desire for constructive change and tolerance while also having sound formal educations. They are also referred to as External Shariah Advisers, since they are independent and only act as consultants to the bank. They have their own opinions, and have the right to challenge or leave the bank if internal processes prove non-Shariah-compliant.

EFFECTIVE TECHNOLOGY

Conventional banking has come a long way, and is generally well organized in terms of effective systems development. Islamic banks have only begun to develop IT systems over less than the past two decades, and they are a lot more complex than conventional ones. Islamic banks, conscious of their leadership position in the industry, see this IT development as critical to the successful implementation of Islamic banking in Nigeria. Stanbic IBTC Bank opted to change its core banking system to accommodate Islamic financial contracts. Sterling Bank prefers to use a robust stand-alone Islamic banking solution with several modules. Jaiz Bank, on the other hand, is a stand-alone Islamic bank with a fully fledged Islamic finance package. Nigerian Islamic banks seem to prefer IT solutions that accommodate all the existing Islamic banking financial instruments rather than having to reconfigure their existing systems to cater for Shariah-compliant products. The most innovative Islamic banks in this regard will be able to release a lot more innovative products onto the market in good time, apart from adopting other marketing strategies.

INNOVATIVE PRODUCT DEVELOPMENT

The Nigerian Islamic banking market has hardly ever featured investment accounts with profit-sharing or *mudarabah* and *musharakah* transactions in their true sense. A very strong aspect of the new VP will involve the development of very innovative Shariah-compliant products to meet the demands of the Nigerian Muslim population. Nigerian Islamic banks are particular in identifying the precise financial needs of Muslims and customers in different locations in the country, taking account of their demographics, rather than imposing their own products on the market. They place much emphasis on 'desk' research – qualitative and quantitative research methodologies to further fine-tune their understanding of the Nigerian Muslim market – and are well guided in what products to offer to the various Muslim socio-economic segments. This will lead to the development of more innovative and complex products in the country, with special recognition for the unbanked or never-banked Muslim segments. Sterling Bank in particular has based its entire business case on well-defined market surveys which allow them to understand specific market demands. Another gradually unfolding aspect of innovative product development is market competitiveness, which Islamic banks will be able to achieve in the near future, with Shariah-compliant products being competitive with both conventional products and those of competing Islamic financial institutions.

HUMAN RESOURCE DEVELOPMENT

Successful implementation of Islamic banking anywhere in the world is dependent on the strength of human capacity available to drive this unique economic model. Nigerian financial institutions that attempt Islamic banking and finance face the major challenge of a serious lack of human skills in the industry, which means that even the CBN and other regulators are unable to develop areas that concern them. Even research organizations and international agencies that show an interest simply lack the human resource strength that will effectively and efficiently drive Shariah-compliant products. Because there are so few Islamic banks, they have struggled to hire the best hands in the industry, but they have concentrated on building their capacity. EFInA has also played a huge role in this regard by periodically bringing facilitators from the UK Islamic Finance Council to help to develop capacity in this specialized area. However, there is still a requirement for more Shariah scholars, Shariah risk and compliance managers, Shariah credit risk officers, Shariah internal auditors, product developers and even entire sales teams.

A question that now arises is whether a VP stressing end-to-end Shariah-compliant operational processes, Shariah governance, effective technology, innovative product development, and human resource development meets the goals of *maqasid al Shariah*. This leads to streamlining the degree at which a conventional bank offering Islamic banking services can comply with certain aspects of *maqasid al Shariah* in order to achieve *falah* and *hayya al tayyibah*, stressing poverty reduction in a manner that means that jobs will consistently be created.

Solving the Poverty Challenge with Islamic Finance

Many have focused on micro-finance as a way to reduce poverty, and the Grameen Bank model has been perceived as one of the most effective in tackling poverty, since 97 per cent of its borrowers are women. Todaro and Smith (2009) quote the research of Pitt et al., who found that credit for women had a positive effect on children's health in Bangladesh, while credit for men had no comparable effect. Even though Grameen Bank is 'interest-based', it was able create employment among the lower segment of society. Sudan's state-led Islamic micro-finance methodology has also been effective, adopting a good mix of *murabahah*, *musharakah* and *mudarabah* with small enterprises, covering agriculture and the retail and wholesale sectors, including craftsmen and artisans (Ibrahim 2003). Ibrahim went further in his analysis to demonstrate that this Sudanese model was tailored to addressing the issues of relative poverty. He made an important distinction between absolute and relative poverty:

> Absolute poverty (the inability to meet the basic needs, subsistence needs, in these prevailing socio-economic circumstances) can be a result of sickness, old age, or a continuous increase of prices. Relative poverty, on the other hand, is related to income inequality or as a result of a malfunctioning supply and demand mechanism.

This book limits its consideration of poverty reduction issues to the context of commercial banking, while addressing both absolute and relative poverty and drawing Nigerian Islamic banks as case studies. In this regard, *sukuk* (Islamic certificates) and agricultural commodity trading (commodity *murabahah*) are given priority, with a strong belief that they will effectively address infrastructural and individual or household poverty, as demonstrated in Chapter 3.

SUKUK – A SOLUTION FOR INFRASTRUCTURAL POVERTY

Sukuk is an asset backed Shariah-compliant certificate whereby investors have proportionate ownership of the underlying asset, which means it does not represent interest-debt as a predominant part of the asset. It is mainly issued based on *shirkah* (partnership) and *ijarah* (lease), and can be traded in the secondary market. *Sukuk* is like other bonds or certificates that provide fixed returns and secondary market trading facilities, and can be either a variable-return *sukuk* (VRS) or a fixed-return *sukuk* (FRS); although returns are fixed in the FRS, there is third-party guarantor. *Sukuk* therefore represents a group of investors sharing ownership of an underlying asset, and the shareholders will accrue returns or losses proportionate to their share in the investment.

Common structures of *sukuk* transactions include: *musharakah, istisna, mudarabah, murabahah, ijarah* and *salam*. The various classifications of *sukuk* certificates include:

- pure *ijarah sukuk* issued on stand-alone assets identified on the balance sheet, while rental rates may be fixed or floating;

- hybrid/pooled *sukuk*, usually comprising *istisna, murabahah* receivables and *ijarah* in order to allow greater mobilization of funds, but 51 per cent must be *ijarah* assets, so returns can be pre-determined;

- zero-coupon non-tradable *sukuk*, where a tradable asset has yet to exist under an *istisna* arrangement;

- embedded *sukuk*, including pure *ijarah*, hybrid or zero-coupon, with an embedded option to convert into other asset forms.

This book concentrates on one *sukuk* structure as an example: pure *ijarah sukuk*, with real estate as the underlying asset. In practice, the bank sets up the securitization team.

The sukuk *issue/securitization team*

The originator of the *sukuk* sells its assets to a special purpose vehicle (SPV) with the aim of utilizing the funds raised from investors. Sterling Bank's Islamic Banking window or the state or federal government may act as the *sukuk* originator. The SPV is an entity specifically set up to purchase the asset from the originator, securitize it and manage the issue. The investment bank acts as the issuing agent for *sukuk* underwriting, lead managing and bookkeeping services for a fee. The IFI usually recognized by the Securities and Exchange Commission's handles this aspect of the project. The *sukuk* subscribers to the SPV may include individuals, corporate organizations or government agencies. Other parties to a *sukuk* include the obligor, who funds the securitized cash flow; the lead manager, who provides services for issue management; the servicer, who collects rentals and manages assets, and the cash administrator or banker, who manages the inflow/outflow of funds and invests interim funds. Other parties include: the *takaful*/insurance company, credit rating agency, legal counsel and auditor.

Real estate ijarah sukuk

A real estate *ijarah sukuk* allows investors to hold securities in a commercial property where periodic rent will provide their profit in proportion to their share in the asset (see Figure 6.2 and Table 6.2 for an example based on a partnership between two imaginary companies, AAA Capital and ZZZ Fund). However, the lessor may decide to sell the leased asset if in need of liquidity or to make a profit. Investment certificates in this project are called *ijarah* certificates, and represent ownership of pro rata undivided parts of the property with all related rights and obligations. This *sukuk* model helps to solve the challenges of liquidity management common in Islamic finance. Liabilities generated from the current/savings account and other investment (*mudarabah*) accounts can be conveniently invested in this type of real estate *sukuk*. Examples of real estate *ijarah sukuk* include the Emirates Airport Sukuk, Dubai; the Zam Zam Towers Sukuk in Mecca, and Chelsea Barracks, London (£2.5 billion).

The ratio of capital expenditure to recurrent expenditure in Nigeria's 2012 budget was 28:72, meaning that bulk of the oil revenue was simply used to service the bloated presidential system of government. If this continues, the country will remain in perpetual infrastructural poverty, which will continue to spill over into other varieties of poverty. Thus, there is a need for public-private partnerships with Islamic financial institutions to provide *sukuk* to cater for a wide range of infrastructural needs, such as the provision of roads, railway lines, water transportation, hospitals, housing estates, dams, schools, large-scale agricultural production in a manner that does not allow room for corruption and which is aimed at achieving human well-being and communal good life.

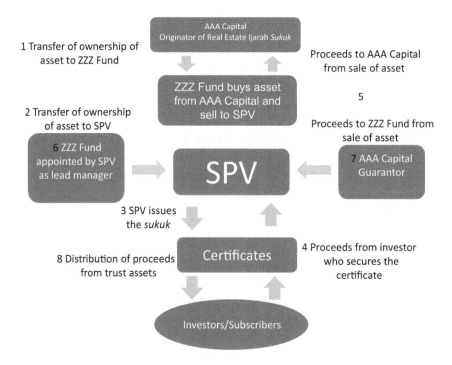

Figure 6.2   A real estate *ijarah sukuk*

Source: Derived from IDB: Sukuk Al Istitmar 2003 (US$400 million).

Table 6.2   Summary of a real estate *ijarah sukuk*

Sukuk Name	AAA Capital-ZZZ Fund *Ijarah* Real Estate *Sukuk*
Proposed *Sukuk* Value	NGN 5,000,000,000 (approximately US$ 7.5 million)
Nature of *Sukuk*	The fund aims to achieve long-term capital appreciation of its assets by investing specifically in a property that will be developed, leased and sold after five years
Investment Guidelines	If oversubscribed fund will be invested as appropriate by SPV
Transaction Structure	The SPV will manage the transaction and other parties to the Sukuk including maintenance of property and remittances to AAA Capital
	The SPV will pay certificate holders and sell the asset at maturity to fund the redemption of certificate holders
	Where there is lack of cash flow to fulfill the payment to certificate holders, AAA Capital account is used to meet the obligation.
	ZZZ Fund will set up the SPV
	Sukuk will be 100% *ijarah* arrangement
	Profit of *sukuk* will be used to give periodic returns to certificate holders
	Certificates will be redeemed at 100% of their principal value
	AAA Capital will retain the risk of default on the *sukuk* asset sold
Issuance Format	Privately placed *sukuk*
Offshore Investment	Applicable – this will also allow inflow of foreign funds

AGRO-COMMODITY MURABAHAH – A SOLUTION FOR UNEMPLOYMENT

In Nigeria, the agricultural sector employs over 70 per cent of the population, and there are 45 million peasant farmers in the country. Many farmers live below the poverty line. They are generally unable to secure credit from commercial banks or micro-finance banks in Nigeria because they usually do not meet the loan conditions. Intervention funds from the CBN specifically for banks to lend to farmers at single-digit interest rates never reach the peasant farmers. However, several off-takers' projects dealing with co-operative out-growers are showing some success. The Bank, off-takers and out-growers enter into a tripartite agreement on the loan amount, price and other modalities at inception. This resembles the parallel *salam* contract (deferred delivery with off-takers). An Islamic bank can engage in trading directly, unlike conventional banks. Thus, Islamic banks can directly embark on agricultural business using several forms of Islamic finance contract. Under *salam*, an Islamic bank can simply ask the farmers to produce so much of, say, cassava at the defined sales price. The bank releases funds/ inputs at inception, and waits for a year until the cassava is ready before buying/paying the farmers the difference, while the farmers enjoy a one-year moratorium.

Using the same example, it becomes a parallel *salam* if the bank, government, NGO, SPV or investor acts as the off-takers for the cassava when it is harvested. If the bank is the off-taker, it can buy the produce, store it, resell it at a future date, and make profit. It may also simply wish to finance an off-taker. This continuous process of agro-commodity trading can seek to achieve *falah* and *hayya al tayyibah* in the sense that the farmers can now cultivate much larger parcels of land knowing that non-interest funds are available for farm inputs and there are guaranteed buyers. More people can now be engaged in the agriculture sector across the whole value chain, leading to a massive and continuous reduction in unemployment. The bank, on the other hand, may be engaged in the agro-commodity stock exchange, where investors all over the world can buy these commodities. In lieu of *salam* and parallel *salam*, the bank may also adopt *mudarabah* and *musharakah*, especially with co-operatives and even large-scale farmers, on a roll-over basis. The commodity *murabahah* can also be used for import-export financing of agricultural produce, collateral financing and warehouse receipt finance, the bank using it as a short-term liquidity management instrument.

The characteristics of a typical agro-commodity *murabahah* product are as follows:

- The bank steps into the trade arrangement by allowing the client to maintain traditional procurement processes and relationships.

- The bank become the buyer of record by providing a 100 per cent funding model with no haircuts or required deposit.

- The bank forward sells to the client, creating a just-in-time inventory (complying with the rules of Shariah).

- The bank acts on the client's instructions about whether to hedge or not hedge forward the sale against commodity and FX exchanges.

- Forward sales are based on the finance curve, not the underlying commodity curve.

- Allocation of logistics, handling, storage and *takaful*, roles and responsibilities between client, bank and third parties is based on relative competence and cost, confirming maximum proficiency in the supply chain.

- It is accounted for as stock in the bank's balance sheet and a forward sale.

- It is accounted for as a forward purchase (*salam*) by the client.

This structure is derived from Standard Bank's commodity trading proposition, which fits somewhat into a commodity *murabahah* structure and is subject to Advisory Committee of Experts (Shariah Board) review before adoption.

Where more Islamic banks are licensed and engage in agro-commodity *murabahah*, the 45 million peasant farmers and more potential farmers will benefit from increased incomes and will be able to achieve *falah* and *hayya al tayyibah*. In another vein, commodity *murabahah* can also be applied to oil and gas and other metals. In Nigeria, another emerging Islamic financial institution is Kord Capital – a private equity company which devotes much effort to agro-commodity trading and other non-agro-commodity trading structures.

Conclusion

Early Islamic economics writers compared the Islamic economic system to various aspects of neo-classical economics. Chapra was more concerned with how *maqasid al Shariah*, which primarily translate into achieving *falah* and *hayya al tayyibah*, borrowed it from Al Ghazali, who died in 1111. Hence, there was a need to align Islamic economics and banking based on this unique foundation so that the system did not stray in the way that Adam Smith's *Theory of Moral Sentiments* and *Wealth of Nations* transformed into neo-liberalism, losing their original flavours.

Since the Islamic economic system eventually leads to Islamic finance, Hasanuzzaman was quick to map out the preconditions of business ethics in Islam. The Islamic financial instruments or contracts themselves are ethically motivated, but may be misused by banks while still being Shariah-compliant. A typical example of such misuse is *tawarruq* (Islamic overdraft), which is now practically shunned by popular scholarly opinion. Despite all the odds, Islamic finance has witnessed a consistent growth rate of over 15 per cent, and more countries are now becoming involved in it. The investment banking sector of the industry seems to be growing a lot faster, followed by retail banking, but micro-finance has been rather slow to take off, except in Sudan. In Nigeria, the conditions for operating Islamic banking and finance seem favourable, with the CBN issuing guidelines and other relevant regulators are doing the same. The value propositions of banks, in particular Islamic financial institutions, need to be more closely aligned with the needs of the people rather than the market. A helpful gesture in this respect in the operation of Islamic financial institutions is the commodity *murabahah* model, while the *sukuk* is a market yet untapped. These two concepts alone, in the absence of robust Islamic micro-finance, could drastically reduce poverty and unemployment in Nigeria.

The next chapter will deal with the development of economic models, from modernization theories to emerging twenty-first-century economic schools of thought.

7

New Integral Economic Models

Introduction

The previous chapter examined Islamic economics and finance in the light of neo-classical Islamic economic ideas, Islamic business ethics and financial contracts and an overall assessment of the industry. It also looked at the aspects of regulatory development and the way value propositions evolved among Nigerian IFIs. This final chapter will summarize the entire study, examining theories that emerged from the co-operative inquiry into Islamic finance, articulating African economic theory with its dynamic movements, and drawing on *Integral Dynamics* (Lessem et al. 2013).

African economic theory will then lead to the Integral African Development Economic Model, which crystallizes all the economic thinking covered in this study to set the course for Islamic finance in Nigeria, looking at very practical issues or the application of the model and the overall achievements of this research-to-action. These include: setting up Islamic finance in a local bank (an effective laboratory), influencing regulators through the co-operative inquiry (as part of a doctoral thesis undertaken for a navigational 'Mode-2' university), establishing a research centre (an emergent 'sanctuary' or reflective space for co-evolving science and society), and finally, building an integral financial institution (communal grounding). In other words, the practice of the theory was already established at inception, in effect evolving a knowledge- and value-production system, as is fitting for the Mode-2 University that is the DaVinci Institute (Nowotny, in Lessem and Schieffer 2010b).

Theory from the Co-operative Inquiry

In 2009, a co-operative inquiry group of 13 members who specialized in research, socio-economic development, financial regulation, and Islamic banking and finance was set up to influence policy. First, the inquiry group prioritized what it aimed to achieve within the framework of the burning issues in this book – primarily poverty reduction through higher employment in the Nigerian economy, which would also drag income inequality downwards. The imaginary traces of the African triple heritage are reflected in the co-operative inquiry group, which continuously seeks to humanize Islamic finance by meeting face-to-face and exploring members' inner experiences by satisfying the four knowings of co-operative inquiry – experiential knowing, imaginal knowing, propositional knowing and practical knowing – as the backdrop for moving from research to action.

By December 2012, the co-operative inquiry group had achieved the issuance of effective regulatory guidelines by the Central Bank of Nigeria covering supervision of non-interest banking, and other guidelines including those covering risk management, corporate governance, the Advisory Committee of Experts and Financial Regulation Advisory Council of Experts. Some of the guidelines released cover Islamic deposit insurance from the Nigerian Deposit Insurance Corporation (NDIC), and the Nigerian Securities and Exchange Commission has issued Islamic fund management and *sukuk* guidelines. Others include guidelines on investments of pension fund assets which accommodate Shariah-compliant classes of assets such as *sukuk*, Islamic treasury bills, Shariah-compliant money market instruments and variations of funds from the National Pension Commission (PENCOM), and guidelines for *takaful* operators from the National Insurance Commission (NAICOM). The Federal Inland Revenue Service (FIRS) also released draft guidelines and regulations on tax neutrality which will provide a level playing field for the Islamic finance industry.

The theory here draws on the importance of having effective regulation in place. Such regulations will embed the primary goals of an Islamic economic system in which operators will abide by these policies, which will lead to better lives for Nigerians and Africans.

Effective regulations are now in place where they are most urgently required that align with the values *maqasid al Shariah*, which primarily translates into achieving *falah* and *hayya al tayyibah*, meaning that Islamic finance can fulfil its primary purpose of maintaining socio-economic justice in society. In essence, Islamic finance can now begin to solve the challenges of poverty and unemployment if the moral core embedded in the overall Islamic economic system is embedded in effective regulation while borrowing, where necessary, from other ethical socio-economic and political models or theories grounded in African humanism.

The validity of this theory will be based on ongoing cyclical transformation or consistent review of regulations or policies over time, especially in terms of experiential exploration of human inquiry based on respect for people, organizations, societies and their rights or demands.

As a result, this theory can be said to achieve consensual validation, since the quality of critical awareness and discrimination in categorizing and evaluating the experiential effects of practical Islamic finance is referred to and linked to the achievement of well-being and the good life for fellow human beings, in accordance with the origin of an Islamic economic system.

Developing the African Economic Theory

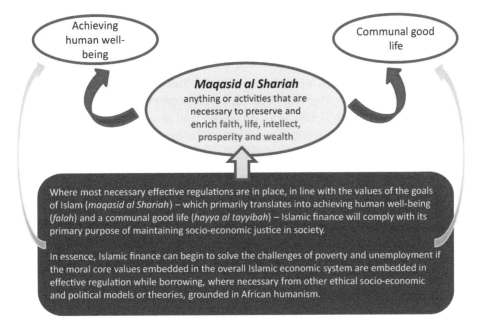

Figure 7.1   The Islamic finance model from the co-operative inquiry

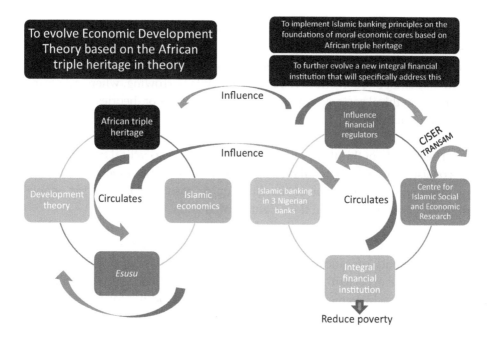

Figure 7.2   Movement of the research body
Source: Derived from the Integral Research Framework (Lessem and Schieffer 2010b).

This study, within the background of 'the story I am', released my GENE, being grounded in indigenous socio-economic practice (*esusu*), emerging through the spirituality of Islam, and in particular Islamic finance, navigating along the path of the African triple heritage of indigenous culture, Westernized Christianity and Islam, thereby effecting a new economic development model in response to burning issues around poverty and unemployment (see Figure 7.1). The 'why' of these questions gave birth to the three research sub-objectives. The first was to evolve an economic development theory based on the African triple heritage. These combined thoughts then influenced the more practical elements aimed at achieving the second and third objectives: to implement Islamic banking principles based on the moral underpinnings of the African triple heritage, and to create a new integral financial institution specifically addressing these. This was further influenced by the structure of Lessem's 'GENEalogy' (newly integral university) – feeling something is amiss.

Integral dynamics here is underlined by science and technology in a manner that has led to the attainment of Islamic finance by some Nigerian banks, leading to newly integral economics and enterprise. This has further influenced relevant financial regulators, using the co-operative inquiry, which relates to research-to-action, and then the establishment of value-oriented institutions within culture and spirituality – the unique Centre for Islamic Socio-Economic Research (CISER) and the Centre for *Integral* Socio-Economic Research (C*I*SER) in partnership with TRANS4M, Geneva. The essence of these cyclical movements, as applicable, is grounded in communality – setting up the integral financial institution as a symbol or instrument for poverty reduction, and the circles continue over time, renewing and refining the process and its outcomes, as illustrated in Figure 7.2. The major benefits Sterling Bank, Stanbic IBTC Bank, Jaiz Bank and other Islamic financial institutions will enjoy from these centres will be ease of operation of their businesses as a result of effective regulation that is being championed by the co-operative inquiry and other varieties of action research.

The Integral African Development Economic Model

The Integral African Development Economic Model rotates both clockwise and counter-clockwise. It is designed along the lines of the Integral Research Framework (Lessem and Schieffer 2010b), and incorporates the GENE. The model is grounded in the African socio-economic financial concept of *esusu* as practised originally by the forces of the African triple heritage – indigenous, Christian and Islamic – in the last century. This triple heritage clearly articulated the nature of labour, savings and loans that are acceptable to the African people based on which element of the triple heritage affects them most. What is essential here is that the people involved are happy with what they get – a major critical individual influence on society. This emerges in a new spiritual and psychological confession of personal character and values (Lessem and Schieffer 2013), found here in the original concept of Islamic banking based on the overall principles of *maqasid al Shariah*, achieving *falah* and *hayya al tayyibah* (Ghazali, in Chapra 1992).

It redefines money by paying attention to partnerships, trading, leasing and services. Navigation then takes place, to the North, and of 'self'. It examines the causes and nature of the African triple heritage, based on a different cultural setting within every tribe, language and religion of people from the same immediate geographic setting, within a state and within a country, but with different perceptions (Wallerstein 2000) which influence production and distribution practices. This is lodged in the final destination, or effected using various development theories, starting with modernization theories, linking up with dependency theories, the uniqueness of the world systems theories, and forms of the new twenty-first-century economic models, which encompasses the formation of these models.

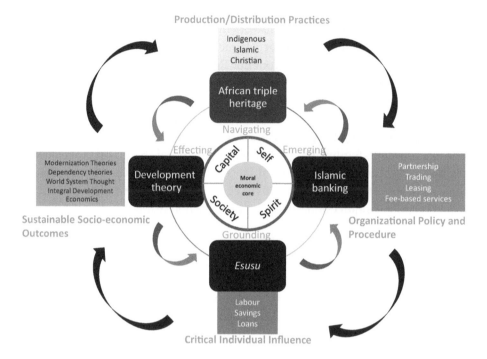

Figure 7.3   The Integral African Development Economic Model
Source: Derived from the Integral Research Framework (Lessem and Schieffer 2010b); Sekeim et al. (2012).

It is this formational process that guides policymakers in varying the theories' application to different economies. These development theories of capital lead to sustainable socio-economic outcomes. The cyclical process repeats itself several times, going back to 'grounding' issues, emerging new realities, navigating self, and back to effecting new changes for the betterment of man. This is the clockwise direction of the model. It is also designed to go counter-clockwise – from sustainable socio-economic outcomes putting forward the theories first, to production and distribution practices within the light of the African triple heritage, and to organizational policy and procedure, of the Islamic economic structure – its moral elements – thus piloting it in the direction of critical individual influence grounded in the traditional system of *esusu*.

On the other hand, while some parts of the model move counter-clockwise at a point in time, other parts may move clockwise, maybe following different timings – like a production process. A very important element of the model is the central 'moral core', which does not move. It supplies its light, ethics and wisdom to reflect into all corners of the Four Worlds. This model has specifically been applied in the establishment of effective Islamic banking and finance in Nigeria, hence it represents theory-to-action, as illustrated in Figure 7.3.

Theory-to-action

Starting clockwise, Figure 7.3 represents the model, which first looks at capital and the establishment of Islamic banking by an existing commercial bank in Nigeria, making entry into the market easy while enjoying economies of scale – a privilege the stand-alone Islamic bank would not enjoy. The author realized the importance of achieving action research through other players. In this case, Sterling Bank required scarce expertise to effect 'morally' based Islamic banking under its retail and investment arm designed to achieve sustainable socio-economic outcomes. 'The story I am' played an important role in actualizing my burning desires. First, I joined Stanbic IBTC Bank in June 2009, when the global financial meltdown was at its peak. In Nigeria, too, many local banks had started to fail, share prices fell or evaporated completely, and artificial property prices dropped – creating a historic situation in Nigeria. In addition, a universal banking system was not yet in existence, and there were only draft guidelines for non-interest banking or Islamic banking – a framework in which no bank could earn an operating licence. At this time, the Central Bank of Nigeria changed from being led by a Christian to being led by a Muslim – an important factor in ethno-religiously diversified Nigeria. Professor Chukuma Soludo, a Christian from south-east Nigeria introduced universal banking to the country in 2005, getting rid of small banks by introducing a much higher minimum capital requirement for banks in Nigeria, leading to a reduction from more than 90 banks to only 24 by 2006–7.

In what was described as a politicized policy, Soludo released the draft guidelines for non-interest Islamic banking because he wanted a second term of five years as the CBN governor. Early in 2005, he was replaced by Mallam Lamido Sanusi, a Muslim from northern Nigeria, who reviewed and dismantled the universal banking system on the grounds that smaller banks should be allowed to exist in the country. He categorized them as regional banks, national banks and international banks. The non-Muslim south saw this policy as a tactic for bringing in regional stand-alone Islamic banks with smaller capital requirements. A further argument was that Soludo's model robbed the north of its ownership of banks, reducing it to only one bank. It is in this socio-political and religio-economic environment that this model emerged.

For Stanbic IBTC Bank to proceed with Islamic banking operations, it needed the final guidelines to get a licence, which was not an urgent priority for the new CBN governor since it was seen as another way to Islamicize Nigeria. In July 2009, the co-operative inquiry group was set up as the Nigerian Islamic Finance Working Group, aiming to ensure that policies were grounded in the socio-economic needs of certain segments of the population. This was done in order to enable financial inclusion, which should translate to poverty reduction. The co-operative inquiry, as described briefly above, led to the development of a theory that is embedded in the model depicted in Figure 7.1. In other words, the overall knowledge- and value-creating network of 'production and distribution practice', by means of navigation, sought to continuously influence financial regulators and consistently develop theories that aligned with the conditions of co-operative inquiry described by Heron, Reason, Lessem and Schieffer.

Figure 7.4   Integral dynamic GENEalogy
Source: Extract from Lessem et al. (2013).

This research-to-action borrowed from Integral Dynamic GENEalogy (Lessem et al. 2013), grounded in community (in Nigeria), emerging via a sanctuary (the research institute), navigating via a university (the DaVinci Institute), and culminated in an 'effective laboratory' – 'doing' by setting up an Islamic banking window in Stanbic IBTC Bank and Sterling Bank. Figure 7.4 shows the GENEalogy path.

Support for Islamic banking and effective policy development in Nigeria is the 'becoming' of an 'emergent sanctuary' of spiritual purpose, culture and values (Lessem et al. 2013). It is this spiritual support that culminates in self-realization, in wholeness or in holiness. As a result, the new Centre for Islamic Socio-Economic Research (CISER) has the following aims and objectives:

- to propagate the spirit of true Islamic finance for the purpose of economic growth and development in Nigeria and the rest of the world;

- to promote research using integral methodologies, and to develop capacity in Islamic economics and finance throughout the country;

- to intensify and promote Islamic finance activities through lectures, seminars and symposiums;

- to publish professional and academic Islamic economics and finance materials, such as book series and journal series, as well as making documentaries;

- to establish an Islamic Finance Institute (IFI) in the country that has a presence in institutions of learning, the private sector and government in order to propagate qualitative Islamic finance to everyone;

- to sponsor local students in the realization of their educational desires in Islamic economics and finance;

- to establish a resourceful Islamic economic/finance library or centre for research on any Islamic economics/finance issue;

- to develop Islamic finance products for IFIs, including regulators and operators;

- to develop an integral *takaful* model for the Nigerian Muslim population;

- to institutionalize *zakat* in the country;

- to develop the *Waqf* Institute and implement *waqf* in Nigeria, embedded in the Islamic economic system;

- to develop and implement the Islamic will or estate plan or succession plan within the context of the Islamic economic structure of the country;

- to develop several *sukuk* structures and special purpose vehicles for regulators, governments, operators, Islamic organizations, academic institutions and any other institutions that call for them;

- to develop regulatory policies for Islamic finance in the country;

- to partner with international and multilateral organizations and any other organization or institutions in promoting Islamic finance in Nigeria and the entire world;

- to provide guidance in the setting up of Islamic financial institutions in the county and the entire world.

In other words, there is a need for the Nigerian people of various socio-economic classes to appreciate the beauty of a morally based Islamic socio-economic system, which seeks firstly to promote human well-being and good communal living for everyone, secondly to evolve a solution to the continuous issues that affect economic development in the country, and indeed Africa as a whole, through Integral Research, and thirdly to source its primary principles from the moral elements of an Islamic economic system fit to weather the storm of neo-liberalism. This research 'sanctuary' was fully registered in December 2011, and is already engaging members in co-operative inquiry that will propel its learning activities from politics, economics and African social humanism to the unfolding national and international circumstances. Hence, it is a socially relevant centre for knowledge-production – a republic of letters (Lessem et al. 2012) that has the potential to move back and forth between the territory of knowing (navigational university) and that of being (communal grounds).

The development of renewed organizational policy and procedure, as applied in this research-to-action, is the creation of a unique kind of financial institution that is based on critical individual influence and grounded in societal needs, rather than in what markets think are the needs of society. This integral financial institution is designed to address and influence structures that will help with poverty reduction in Nigeria. Chapter 6 explained that the use of *sukuk* and agro-commodity *murabahah* would help to dispel infrastructural poverty and provide employment opportunities, mainly in the informal sectors. A division of the integral financial institution will, however, look at other areas of micro-finance not captured in the *sukuk* and commodity *murabahah* structure. In terms of micro-finance, though somewhat outside the scope of this book, the integral financial institution would develop a customer value architecture or customer needs proposition with the hope of using its special funds, *zakat* fund, *waqf* funds, impermissible income and financial aid from international organization for micro-finance and social support activities based on *qard-hassan*, while complying with overall banking and risk ethics.

Actualizing this integral financial institution may now be reflected in the overall Sterling Bank, Stanbic IBTC Bank and Jaiz Bank Islamic banking value propositions. This means these financial institutions will extend beyond this research-to-action, or rather this book, as the purpose of the research will continue to have a positive impact on society – also influenced by humanistic discourse (Lessem et al. 2013). Once the integral financial institution grounded in African humanism (Serequeberhan 1999, Serequeberhan 2000) is established, the model will thus need to be validated by allowing a counter-clockwise movement to take place on the line of the GENE – from grounding, to emerging, navigating and effecting – which will help to ensure that the integral financial institution will truly achieve its primary objective of poverty reduction rather than being carried away by the neo-liberalized patterns common to many Islamic financial institutions. The Integral African Development Economic Model: Establishing Islamic Finance in Nigeria (see Figure 7.5) is the second version of the economic development model. The third version of the model is a Generic Integral Economic Development Model that can be applicable to other research-to-action programmes in other jurisdictions.

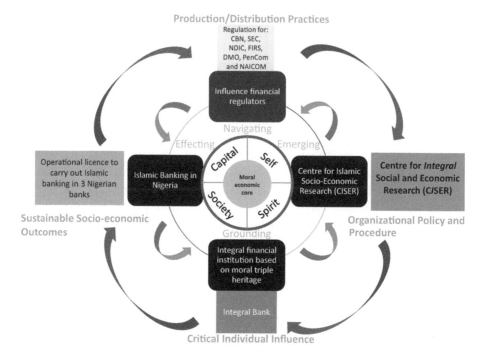

Figure 7.5   The Integral African Development Economic Model: Establishing Islamic Finance in Nigeria

Source: Derived from the Integral Research Framework (Lessem and Schieffer 2010b); Sekeim, Cairo, and Rima (2012).

The Integral Economic Development Model as Applied

The Generic Integral Development Economics Model shown in Figure 7.6 can be applied to various economic fields of study, research-to-action, and even the development of business strategies. This model identifies four major co-ordinations that are essential for achieving economic development: *falah* and *hayya al tayyibah*. After the faltering of Keynesian economics from the 1960s, economists assumed that the inability of developing countries to develop was due to market co-ordination failures. Todaro and Smith (2009) observed that many newer theories of the 1990s emphasized the presence of complementarities. Hoff and Stiglitz (2000) identified spill-over effects of institutions, the distribution of wealth, history, and 'ecology' and an emphasis on information enforcement. Acemoglu and Robinson (2012) placed more stress on extractive institutions – a spill-over from the extractive colonial institutions inherited by independent elites.

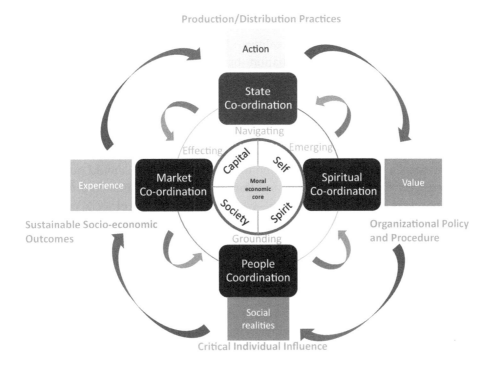

Production/Distribution Practices

Figure 7.6   Generic Integral Development Economics Model

Source: Oshodi (2012a, 2012b). Derived from the Integral Research Framework (Lessem and Schieffer 2010b); Sekeim et al. (2012).

International organizations are today concerned with the effects of state failures, which affect these economies the most, thereby dwelling more on good governance issues. As a result, aid donors now see the best form of financial assistance to developing economies as paying experts to help overcome the overall co-ordination failures, linking markets and state effectively, building upon the notion of embedded autonomy (Evans 1995; Kohli 2004), as exemplified by Japan, South Korea and Taiwan. Chapra's concern when reviewing Islamic economic theories to benefit people, and that of Lessem et al (2013) placed emphasis on indigenous people, while Serequeberhan (1999, 2000) paid attention to African humanism, and Mazrui (1986) emphasized the forces of the African triple heritage that greatly influence Africans' needs and perceptions. Rima (2012) also focused on spiritual capital, which builds on ethical foundations. In this model, all thoughts are linked together, whereby there is a need for the presence of complementarities co-ordinating the market, state, spirit and people – none of these can be left if we are to avoid systemic failure. Going counter-clockwise and following the mechanism of the GENE, people co-ordination is grounded in the needs of the people or social realities – indeed, critical individual influence, which emerges in the co-ordination of spirituality or value orientation, which serves as a driving force for organizational policy and procedure. This then navigates to state co-ordination, giving opportunities for action to exist while allowing production and distribution practices. This is further effected through market co-ordination based on experience of the actors, manipulating capital justly in order to achieve sustainable socio-economic outcomes. Going clockwise means existing attention on market co-ordination should quickly be merged with state co-ordination, and then to essential spiritual co-ordination, culminating in people co-ordination – which requires studies of social ontology, humanism and fulfilling other conditions of this relational path.

The *Muqqddimah* ('Introduction to History') of Ibn Khaldun no doubt covered these co-ordination gaps, consciously or unconsciously, relying particularly heavily on moral issues or the ethics required of states, markets, people and spirit – self-value. Lessem and Schieffer's centre point, in this case the moral core, shines its light on all paths evenly while maintaining dynamic balance and spreading information. This model is thus truly integral, emerging from the ground of Africa, but applicable to all fields, of economics, science, research, business strategy, value proposition, engineering and philosophy, among others. On the other hand, it can be used by each of the four worlds effectively. International institutions, donor institutions, governments and business organizations are now exposed to a revolving model, subject to review and amendments, but continuously cyclical, rotating like a machine used for industrial production.

The Centre for *Integral* Social and Economic Research

The ultimate end of this entire research-to-action project is generally larger than the Islamic finance research institute or the Centre for Islamic Socio-Economic Research and reflective sanctuary, covering various aspects of development economics as it relates to individual country cultures and socio-political structures – the Centre for *Integral* Social and Economic Research (C*I*SER) (see Figure 7.7). This new centre is truly fundamental, spanning the Four Worlds or the entire universe and specifically drawing resources from the enlarged Generic Integral Development Economics Model, and hence applicable across the board. C*I*SER is designed to be a global institution with a head office in Geneva, yet bringing together all the similar people and institutions that originally emerged via the TRANS4M ideology and working in association with them, partnering with the Centre for Islamic Socio-Economic Research in Lagos, the Movement for the Advancement of Spiritual Capital (MASC) in Vancouver, Sekem in Egypt, Business Training and Development (BTD), a management education institute in Harare, Zimbabwe, the African Institute for Cultural Economy (AICE) in South Africa, the DaVinci Institute in Johannesburg, while setting up new bases in London and Luxembourg.

CISER will also accommodate institutions formed by all those who pass through the TRANS4M/DaVinci doctoral programme or others that may be defined in the future. The big picture for CISER is not just to fit into the Generic Integral Development Economics Model, but also to seek to realize the well-being of humanity within an ethno-religiously and socio-politically diverse global environment. Moreover, TRANS4M in Geneva would co-evolve together with the individual country CISER, with the doctoral programme of fundamental research to transformative action serving as a key vehicle for this. In this regard, we seek to set up an annual gathering in Geneva/Hotonnes to bring all the transformational agents and institutions – doctoral and post-doctoral – together from around the world to pursue an integral course of cultural and economic research and innovation together, where each local is a centre or nucleus and the 'global' is a collectivity of peripheries orbiting it.

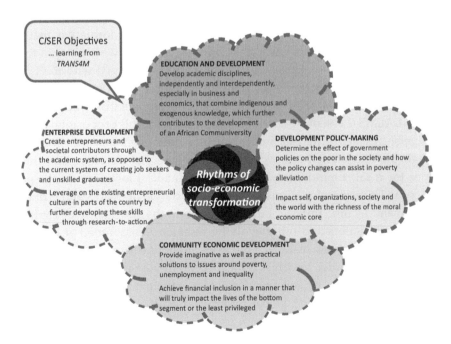

Figure 7.7   CISER's objectives

For Nigeria, specifically and practically, the success of C*I*SER hinges on the development of a Nigerian cohort that seeks to achieve social-economic transformation via social innovation. This requires that prospective social-innovators be constantly brought together to design and implement programmes that will help in the development of the country. This cohort will include people from various socio-economic and political interests who will set forth research-to-action agendas for the betterment of their immediate community, the country and the world at large, while it will have much positive influence in their own personal lives. This partnership may apply rather radical approaches, outside the norm of existing educational institutions, to achieve its desired results. This will be related to an overall moral economic structure, borrowing specifically from the Islamic economic system, as well as other moral structures, because of its integral moral attributes.

The Path to Socio-economic Transformation in Nigeria and Africa

This final topic focuses on two principal concepts – EUREKA and C*I*SER – as they relate to the four areas comprising the research interests of doctoral and post-doctoral researchers whose nucleus is TRANS4M, or rather the emergence of the African University for Humankind, South Africa. Overall, EUREKA (Energized, Understanding, Research, Education, Know-how and Application) draws on the distinctive nature of the four layers – formative method, normative methodology, emancipation and integration – which is akin to the C*I*SER RHYTHM (Lessem et al. 2013). This is further merged with the C*I*SER proposition, which is centred on community economic development, education and development, enterprise development and development of policy-making – C*I*SER REALMS (Lessem et al. 2013). More specifically, this proposition is based on diverse research interests which include socio-economic transformation through the educational sector, youth entrepreneurial development, micro-finance for rural communities, the impact of financial inclusion on the poor, the African University for Humankind, transportation networks and economic development, Islamic finance, Integral Research, the spirituality of capital in development matters and other evolving research topics aimed at achieving socio-economic transformation. This book therefore draws together these research areas in order to achieve socio-economic dynamic balance, leading to a gradual process of self-transformation, organizational transformation, societal transformation and global reforms – C*I*SER ROUNDS (Lessem et al. 2013) (see Figure 7.8).

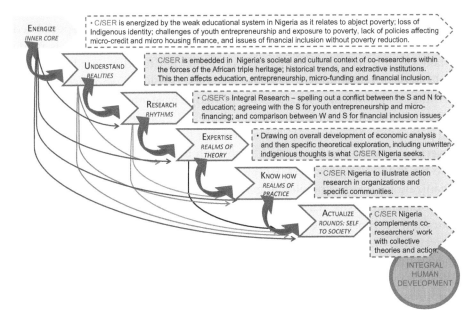

Figure 7.8   Integrating EUREKA with C*I*SER Nigeria

Source: Structure from Lessem and Schieffer (2013); Oshodi et al. (2012).

ENERGIZED

This book seeks to set out the foundations of a whole new socio-economic school of thought leveraged by a unique driver of this proposition. It is energized by the evolution of C*I*SER, which finds its root in the Integral Development Model (Lessem and Schieffer 2010b; Oshodi 2012a) and can be applied to various socio-economic fields of study, to the process of research-to-action, and even the development of business strategies. A very important aspect of the C*I*SER proposition is the recognition of how Nigeria's weak educational system relates to abject poverty and general loss of indigenous identity, leaning too much towards the neo-classical North and West – C*I*SER REALITIES (Lessem et al. 2013) – as opposed to the Eastern and Southern gap between opportunities and realities as well as spiritual poverty as a result of conflicts arising out of extreme foreign affiliation. This has a growing negative impact on the country's socio-economic fabric. Education can thus be reconceived in the transformative light on knowledge-creation, borrowing from the works of Nonaka and Takeuchi. This can be aligning for project team players, promoting and creating knowledge with a clear organizational vision by forming networks. In the case of C*I*SER, the network is part of a global ecosystem in which research actors constitute an integral yet specialized NGO, or rather a 'one-stop' research centre where transformation is made to take place. This transformative system embodies the dynamic knowledge circle which continuously creates, exploits, explores and accumulates institutional knowledge. It creates a knowledge base embedded in corporate vision, organizational or institutional culture, religion, technology, databases and perception. Nonaka and his team further link this knowledge base to the project team layer via the market, with high accessibility to the knowledge base for individual members. C*I*SER thus implements Nonaka's 'hypertext organization', where knowledge generated in the group is used to achieve developmental goals. C*I*SER, among other programmes, is focused on education as transmutive light, also borrowing from Nonaka and Takeuchi. Education is the key to creating, adapting and spreading knowledge; however, uneven distribution of access to education, especially to the poor, is evident (World Bank, 1998–9, in Todaro and Smith 2009). Furthermore, there is a lack of appropriate academic content to address Nigeria's societal ills. For Todaro and Smith, education and health are the basic objectives of development. C*I*SER thus places much emphasis on how an educational system with the appropriate and applicable content can reach the poor on one hand and impart knowledge that will aid development in a typical African country. Practically, by 2012 C*I*SER's Nigerian chapter had embarked on five main research areas that aligned with socio-economic needs and fitted within the Integral Research Framework as illustrated in Figure 7.9. A typical example of this is 'education', which is analysed with in the Northern path of Reason and the Southern Relational path.

In this way, C*I*SER is energized to develop academic disciplines, independently and inter-dependently, especially in business and economics, that combine indigenous and exogenous knowledge, contributing to the development of an African Communiversity. It is concerned with the enhancement and establishment of indigenous identity based on environmental contexts aimed at developing solutions to the society's developmental needs. Very importantly, C*I*SER, through the work of co-researchers in Nigeria and South Africa, seeks to achieve a paradigm shift of education/academics in order to bridge the gap between indigenous identity, indigenous history and current and future realities within the context of a contemporary African society and an increasingly complex world. This will require greater attention to school education.

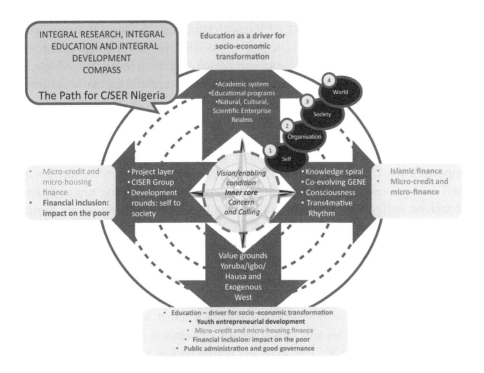

Figure 7.9   The Integral Research, Integral Education and Integral
Development Compass

Source: Structure from Lessem et al. (2013); Oshodi et al. (2012).

On the other note, C*I*SER is concerned about the high level of poverty and unemployment in Nigeria, and seeks to set in motion wealth-creation mechanisms – specifically, vehicles that will help people to change the way they regard entrepreneurship, thereby reduce overall poverty. African communism has been associated with the extended family structure which supports individuals socially and economically. The impact of the African triple heritage (Mazrui 1984) has now shrunk family sizes, and led to the nuclear family structure, following the path of Westernized Christianity. For C*I*SER, the burning issue is to see how entrepreneurship among young people can be achieved in the absence of family support, considering that white-collar jobs are mostly neither available nor permanent. Such entrepreneurship among young people is also, of course, interconnected with 'education'. Co-researchers from Nigeria, Egypt, Namibia, Zambia and Zimbabwe are jointly and individually working on this. Hence, this global 'one-stop' consultancy is equally energized by these issues, and will be driving the global C*I*SER objectives in this cyclical and pan-African manner.

Access to finance – another C*I*SER research interest – is a focus that generally drives financial inclusion strategies, especially in developing countries. Practically, access to finance is scarce in Africa, and even more unavailable to the poor, especially in rural areas, to the real sector – agriculture, manufacturing and infrastructure – and to new business startups. C*I*SER is energized by these issues, and seeks to have an impact on the country in a systemic manner by enabling financial access to these channels. Financial inclusion in this regard may also encompass the development of complementary currencies. It is important for C*I*SER that education, entrepreneurship and micro-finance as well as other emerging thoughts are all interconnected, leading to a uniquely conceived indigenous–exogenous approach that takes up from where Yunus and Grameen have left off in Bangladesh.

A Nigerian C*I*SER co-researcher laid much emphasis on objectives which would specifically address issues around financing the real sector while working to provide finance to a small community of entrepreneurs and small start-up businesses. A developing research interest here is 'evolving real sector financing policies and structures for sustainable economic growth and development in Nigeria'. This aims to change polices regarding micro-credit and micro-housing finance. C*I*SER is thus concerned about how best financial inclusion can work for the poor, or rather how it can have a positive impact on their socio-economic lives beyond merely having an account in a formal financial institution. Practically, a computer repairer in the suburb of Lagos who only opened a savings account in 2011 increases the number of those who now have accounts compared to the 2008 figures. Thus, the amount of money in the formal sector is expected to increase so that more people can have access to these funds. In reality, the technician's income would not have increased in any way, he would most likely not be eligible for a bank facility, his family size might have increased, and hence he might be gradually drowning in poverty – yet he has now been financially included simply because he opened a bank account. Via research, C*I*SER seeks research to uncover these realities, rather than just accepting improved financial inclusion figures from international agencies and local project drivers.

C*I*SER, with its sister bodies and local co-researchers worldwide, and especially in Africa, expects to venture into other areas, such as how financial inclusion benefits the entire educational system, in order to make them more effective. This requires capturing how access to finance has a positive impact on the lives of young entrepreneurs. Another burning issue is the real effect of EFInA's 2008, 2010 and 2012 surveys on how access to finance may drive the poor out of poverty in reasonable time and in a sustainable manner. Alternative money systems also need to be addressed. CISER is set to examine these perspectives within the light of the CISER objectives.

The synergy of a transformed academic system, a rejuvenated entrepreneurial spirit, financial inclusion, financial enablement and empowerment will create a powerful force for sustainable societal transformation, with power in the hands of every capable individual. Another concern for CISER is driving effective institutions rather than extractive ones in developing countries, by emphasizing issues of good governance and public administration. Governments in Africa, especially Nigeria, are gradually becoming profit-making business organizations and have forgotten that their primary obligation is to provide social good for the benefit of their citizens.

UNDERSTANDING

Understanding CISER's objectives underpinned by the research interests of the co-researchers requires us to define historical trends and the factors that have shaped Africa's socio-economic structures.

Overall, Nigeria, Benin, South Africa, Zimbabwe, Zambia, Egypt, and indeed the African socio-economic world as a whole, are split into three models: one is based on the Islamic socio-economic structure, the second is traditional, while the third is the Christian socio-economic model (Mazrui 1986; Serequeberhan 2000, p. 10; Richard 2004, p. 15; Lessem and Schieffer 2010a; Oshodi 2012a). Mazrui (1986) suggested a split in the African and Nigerian cultures – what he refers to as a triple heritage. On the other hand, Hoff and Stiglitz (2008) identified spill-over effects of institutions, the distribution of wealth, history, 'ecology' and an emphasis on information-promotion. CISER and the co-researchers have a good understanding of the forces of the triple heritage, historical trends and extractive institutions (Acemoglu and Robinson 2012). These three major factors specifically affect each of the researchers' interests.

The triple heritage influences the way we approach our education in general: the curriculum we adopt, the theories we use, the books and articles we prefer, and our learning styles as they all relate to our ethno-linguistic diversity (Easterly and Levine 1997). The triple heritage affects the attitude of young people seeking, without compromise, white-collar jobs rather than developing their entrepreneurial skills. Before colonialism, there were no records of formal employment. People either worked on communal land or family land or were tenants. Even the soldiers working for the royal families had personal farms, while guards and servants still had to rent land and pay royalties or tributes to landlords. Hence, the culture of seeking formal employment emerged alongside colonialism. What is termed as the real sector today did not exist in that form, since agriculture, local manufacturing and industries, and housing were communal and family efforts. In a search for a better word, *esusu*, or rotational labour, savings and loans also evolved along the path of the triple heritage. It is this *esusu* structure that provided the lower segment with easy access to finance through varieties of co-operatives. This structure also ensured that poverty and unemployment never existed. All these developments were before the colonial masters invaded African cities.

The influence of Islam in the African continent in recent years does not seem to properly reflect the true spirit of the Islam Mohammed (Peace and Blessings of Allah be on Him) envisaged. The peace and beauty of Islam are now gradually being suppressed by the behaviour of many Islamic groups whose perception of upholding the tenets of Islam is largely associated with violence and destruction rather than knowledge, diplomacy and tolerance. The nature of the Islamic creed (*aqidah*) is gradually being misplaced within the context of socio-economic development. In other words, the somewhat negative effect of certain interpretations of the primary sources of Shariah – the Quran and Hadith (the practice of Islam by Mohammed) – is that Muslims do not see much benefit in formal educational structures; they do not want to influence policies through constitutional means; they show less interest in the organized private sector, and they avoid financial institutions because they deal in interest, uncertainty, gambling and unethical concerns. Going by the teachings of Mohammed, the focus is to change the system and make it better than it was, rather than shying away from the renewal process required. For CISER, co-researchers across the continent are focused on setting the stage for positive and socio-economic transformational change to take shape in a manner that does not go against the Islamic creed.

Christianity in Africa certainly has its own level of impact on socio-economic development. Africans are quick to accept ideas from the North and the West, focusing on individual self-realization. While a Muslim from northern Nigeria might gladly go on the streets to beg for money every day without saving, a Christian from the east of the country would rather work free of charge for his master, who may later set him up in business so that he can sustain himself thereafter. The Westernized Christian heritage allows personal development, but also accepts every belief held by the colonial masters, the Western-imposed economic prescriptions, the uncompromising right of the Zionist movement, the interest-based financial system; and even the choice of clothing. For these people, the West developed and became civilized on the basis of these ideologies, so why shouldn't they copy them? CISER is concerned with how to decolonize the hearts of Africans through the power of knowledge-sharing in such a way that choice of socio-economic theories should not just be based on sentiment, but on variables that are well analysed and make collective sense.

The other major issue of which CISER requires a sound understanding is the subject of history or historical trends and how they have shaped today's socio-economic situation. Pre-colonial history, post-colonial history, economic history, religious history, educational history, entrepreneurial history, political history and overall development history require applicable understanding so that they serve as good leads for co-researchers towards action research. In the same vein, 'good economics is seen as bad politics' (Acemoglu et al. 2001) in Africa, leading to contagious extractive institutions (Acemoglu and Robinson 2012) and predatory governance (Oshodi 2009), which lead to ineffective educational systems, an ineffective entrepreneurial environment, a lack of real sector funding, scarce micro-finance for the lower segment and financial inclusion strategies that do not align with the needs of the people, especially the poor.

RESEARCH

Contributing to the body of knowledge in Africa, in particular Nigeria, Namibia, South Africa, Zimbabwe and Egypt, requires the use of the Integral Research Framework (Lessem and Schieffer 2010b). For CISER to develop a truly integral approach to solving socio-economic issues, it will have to track virtually the four layers and the four parts. Co-researchers seek to cross-fertilize or cross-pollinate knowledge covering various aspects of socio-economic research on the platform of the Integral Research Framework. For instance, some studies simply pursue the Southern Relational path, displaying the richness of descriptive method, phenomenology, feminism and participatory action research. They are immersed in the socio-economic storyline, acting as broad foundation for a future focus on specific issues in relation to education and youth entrepreneurship. Co-researchers live or stay with their research communities to understand their needs and aspirations while gaining access to firsthand information about the reforms required. From a feminist perspective, they understand the lack of privilege and seek a better life for them. This they will achieve through action research with their new friends, their society.

It is this gradual transformational process that CISER seeks to achieve. Others may also consider exploring at least one layer in the East and the West as this research-to-innovation unfolds.

Another example is to examine the works of organizations dealing with aspects of financial inclusion across the world that conduct periodic national surveys, usually conducting in-depth interviews and focus groups to obtain fresh information before developing the survey questionnaire. CISER's approach to Integral Research means there is a need to at least compare these micro-data choices of survey/experimental methods to more integral conditions. More specifically, financial inclusion may be further screened by subjecting the Southern Relational path to Western pragmatism, layer by layer, pitting descriptive methods against survey/experimental methods, phenomenology against empiricism, feminism against critical realism, and participatory action research against action research. For CISER, the aim is to identify the relationship between method and methodology, critique and integration, seeking to effect social change in a manner acceptable to the masses.

There is evidence in Nigeria that NGOs and projects funded by donor organizations have high staff turnover, which means that these organizations have to rely heavily on international consultants for high-quality research reports. Consultants are usually chosen from donor countries, which means that the bulk of the financial aid returns to where it came from while local competencies are never developed. The role of CISER is to fill this gap perpetually. CISER seeks to have local experts in every aspect of development issues that affects the African continent. This is easily achieved, since almost every CISER member is expected to have completed doctoral or post-doctoral studies under the guidance of Geneva-based TRANS4M and the Johannesburg-based DaVinci Institute as well as other globally recognized educational institutions. CISER serves as a global, yet African, integral socio-economic consultancy group – a 'one-stop specialist organization'. CISER will certainly demonstrate not only research competencies, but also professional managerial-leadership competencies, since every member is a specialist in areas such as banking, finance, politics, governance, academics, philosophy and other social sciences.

EDUCATION

Further educational themes are drawn upon through the analysis of a broad range of philosophies, theories, concepts and wisdom. An understanding of the development of economic analysis is a given for all CISER co-researchers. Hence, it becomes imperative for all to scrutinize the ingredients of modernization theories, dependency theories, world systems ideas, and emerging twenty-first-century economic theories. Co-researchers now go the extra mile by aligning their work with more theories, philosophies and practices on, say, education and its processes, seeking to gain a better grasp of global, African and Nigerian trends. Lessem et al. (2013) observed that diverse approaches to education can be aligned with modernization (research university), growth (university of life), self-sufficiency (communiversity) and a developmental economy (developmental university).

Another area of work C*I*SER is developing is the examination of entrepreneurial ideas, borrowing heavily from experts in both the theoretical and practical world, and focusing on strategic management tools, globalization trends and international business perspectives on the global economic meltdown. Another emerging area for study reflects the desire to break through the barriers of the constituents of the real sector and funding styles across the world, Africa and Nigeria. Achieving the C*I*SER dream will require exploring the jewels of local community research material, seeking indigenous 'theories', as it were, written or unwritten. The post-doctoral work of some members will involve deep exploration of global financial inclusion as envisaged by donors and in relation to communal needs by building up financial strategies in the light of the African development triple heritage-laden approach, more akin to innovation than to conventional research.

The World Bank, the UN, DFID, GIZ, IDB, ADB, USAID and the Bill & Melinda Gates Foundation are naturally concerned about building inclusive financial systems, promoting women's financial inclusion and local financial infrastructure – linking local governments and financial markets, micro-finance and micro-insurance markets, financial literacy, financing agricultural value chains in Africa, Islamic finance, SME development, co-operatives and economic development and employment. For C*I*SER, it is not just about conducting another research project, but positively transforming societies via research.

KNOW-HOW

Know-how is designed on the platform of the DaVinci Institute's concept of TIPS (Technology, Innovation, People and Systems) in order to develop not only knowledge, but also know-how in order to respond to both societal and work-based practical challenges. C*I*SER members usually leverage the TIPS concept together with C*ISER*'s approach to implement research objectives. This will be achieved by injecting new research-to-action ideas into our proposed African University for Humankind.

Hence, a member's work will serve as the 'white paper' for TRANS4M and C*ISER*'s proposed integral African university. This study is being developed by TRANS4M, Nigeria and South Africa. C*ISER* intends to use TIPS to create new entrepreneurs among African rural and urban communities, thereby helping businesses by providing them with expertise, and linking them with finance and markets or off-takers. In this regard, recognition will be given to technological perspectives, the role of information and communication technology, mobile technology, and open sourcing in Kenya's emerging 'silicon valley'.

C*ISER* will focus on practical real sector funding issues by concentrating on one or two sectors – such as agriculture in particular rural communities where expertise, funding and markets can be provided or created. C*ISER* will be concerned with changing the overall perception of international donor organizations on how to tailor financial inclusion strategies to households that live in a single room even though they now have a savings account. The ability to see these practical processes though to fruition is what C*ISER* seeks to achieve over time while searching for real co-ordination between state, market, spirit and people (Lessem and Schieffer 2013; Oshodi 2012a; Rima 2012; Lessem et al. 2012). In other words, C*ISER* is paying attention to the exploration of true African humanism (Serequeberhan 1999, Serequeberhan 2000).

C*ISER* at this juncture is promoting what public administration or good governance can achieve in developing African societies. This study is expected to form part of the post-doctoral studies of a renowned political figure in Nigeria. There will then be knowledge- and experience-sharing among the partners and members in Africa. It is this unique knowledge-sharing that gives C*ISER* the strength of a truly integral socio-economic consultancy – a one-stop shop that is capable of addressing Africa's issues effectively.

APPLICATION

The application of the Integral Research Framework in line with GENE (Grounding, Emerging, Navigating and Effecting) through individual research interests will evolve new theories that will stand the test of time, and develop the partnership between C*ISER* and TRANS4M. In clearer terms, co-researchers will come up with new educational theories to suit the Nigerian African environment. Other co-researchers will propound new ideas about entrepreneurship in line with African humanism, culture and needs. Some will collectively evolve a whole new form of real sector funding that is effectively in their chosen communities. This will then become a new theory. The continental group will then reposition theories or shift the paradigm from neo-classical models associated with financial inclusion strategies in Africa to people-oriented ones. In particular, some experts in Islamic economics and finance will seek to embed the ethical capital concept into African societies, while others will address issues of governance and public policies. CISER members representing several countries will then become core drivers of the University for Humankind. A new book that will share the journey and successes of this integral group and university is envisaged in the coming years.

Conclusion

The development of suitable socio-economic or development economic theories has over the years been very chequered, especially in the field of African development. Researchers from the North and West such as Wallerstein, Stiglitz and Lessem, with some African orientation, were quick to align their thoughts with behavioural and cultural economics, making them the roots of their writings. African writers now show more affiliation with their origins. Since the 1960s, Wole Soyinka's works have been rooted in the African heritage, Serequeberhan and Mutiso examined the socio-political elements, but many writers still lean towards the neo-classical, forgetting their roots, the ground that grew their ideas. This research-to-action, though familiar with most relevant Western socio-economic writing from Smith to Mkandawire, hence chose to adopt a truly integral concept based on the influence of the African or Nigerian triple heritage and 'the story I am'. From among these grounded thoughts emerged three socio-economic models, bearing resemblances and rich in scope and content, navigating the North and its systems, and most importantly effected through action – a unique kind of research – the path to poverty reduction in Africa. Finally, this new model led to the formation of a global institution, the Centre for *Integral* Social and Economic Research, designed to effect socio-economic transformation worldwide. It is engaged in transformative action, seeking to develop transformative concepts born and bred in Africa, albeit informed by theories and practices from abroad.

*CI*SER was born out of consciousness of the need for a better self, organization, community, Africa, and indeed a better world. The primary output is to see socio-economic transformational processes take place through action research. This book, characterized by research-to-innovation, demonstrates the research interests of co-founders and co-researchers. This integral template for innovation is also expected to earn doctorate and post-doctorate degrees for members, thus also benefiting them. It is also intended to benefit the organizations co-researchers are associated with, in line with the DaVinci Mode-2 university philosophy. Most importantly, the aspiration of TRANS4M and *CI*SER is to see noticeable achievements in the socio-economic transformation of the African world, and indeed the entire world, starting with immediate communities. The ideas emerging from the integral African University for Humankind are expected to cast their light on the world – like the sun reflects into every corner of the solar system. This is the expectation of this new movement – *CI*SER.

Glossary of Islamic and African Banking Terms

adalah	justice
amanah	trust
aqidah	Islamic creed
asabiya	social solidarity
esusu	rotational savings/labour
fadl	honour
falah	human well-being
fiqh	explanation of Shariah
fiqh al-muamalat	Islamic commercial jurisprudence
gharar	risky sale
halal	permissible activities in Islam
hayya al tayyibah	communal good life
ijarah	Islamic lease agreement
istisna	build to order
ju'ualah	service fee
khalifah	vice-regency
khayr	wealth virtue
kifala	guarantee
maqasid al Shariah	the goal of Islam
miysir	gambling
mudarabah	partnership
mudarib	managing trustee or labour partner
murabahah	purchase and resale at mark-up
musharakah	joint venture
qardh	loan
qardh-hassan	non-interest loan
qiyas	estimating and measuring
rabb al-mal	beneficial owner or sleeping partner

rahma	blessing
riba	financial interest
salam	deferred delivery
shirkah	partnership
sukuk	Islamic financial certificate
takaful	Islamic insurance
tawarruq	overdraft
tawhid	unity
wadiah	safe-keeping
wakala	agency
waqf	endowment
wasiyya	Islamic will
zakat	alms-giving

Bibliography

Abbasi, J. 2009a. *Comments and Suggestions on CBN Draft Framework for the Regulation and Supervision of Non-interest Banks in Nigeria*. Lagos, Nigeria: GISBA Consulting and D-vaR Consulting.

Abbasi, J. 2009b. *Risk Management in Islamic Finance and Banking Course Pack*. Lagos, Nigeria: GISBA Consulting and D-vaR Consulting.

Abdul-Gafar, A.L.M. 1999. 'Islamic Banking and Finance: Another Approach'. Paper presented at the Islamic Hinterland Conference on Critical Debates Among Canadian Muslims, Toronto, Canada, 1999.

Acemoglu, D. 2010. 'Why is Africa Poor?', *Economic History of Developing Regions* 25(1), 21–50.

Acemoglu, D. and Robinson, J.A. 2012. *Why Nations Fail: The Origins of Power, Prosperity and Poverty*. London: Profile Books.

Acemoglu, D., Johnson, S. and Robinson, J.A. 2001. *An African Success Story: Botswana*. Cambridge, MA: Massachusetts Institute of Technology.

Adam, N. and Thomas, A. 2004. *Islamic Bonds: Your Guide to Issuing, Structuring and Investing in Sukuk*. London: Euromoney Books.

Adamu, A. 2009. The *Effect of Global Financial Crisis on Nigerian Economy*. Keffi, Nigeria: Nasarawa State University, Social Science Research Network.

Adebayo, R.I. 2010. 'The Motivating Factors for the Viability of Islamic Banking in Nigeria'. Paper presented at the International Conference on Islamic Banking and Finance held at Crescent University: Islamic Finance in Nigeria. Abeokuta, Nigeria. 20–22 March, 2010.

Ades, A. and Tella, R.D. 1999. 'Rents, Competition, and Corruption', *American Economic Review* 9(4), 982–93.

Adesina-Uthman, G.A. et al. 2011. 'Islamic Financial Culture: Alternative Economic System for Rapid and Sustainable Economic Growth in West African Countries', *Australian Journal of Basic and Applied Sciences* 5(7), 286–94.

AFRCE. 2006. *Recent Economic Performance in Sub-Saharan Africa*. Washington, DC: AFRCE.

Afzalua, R. 1979. *Economic Doctrine of Islamic Banking and Insurance*, vol. 4. London: The Muslim Trust.

Ahmed, K. 1976. *Studies in Islamic Economics*. Hayling Island, Hampshire: Redwood Burn.

Ake, C. 1996. *Democracy and Development in Africa*. Washington, DC: Brookings Institution.

Ali, Y. 1983. *Text, Translation and Commentary of The Holy Quran*. Brentwood, MD: Amana.

Amadi, S. 2009. *The Rule of Law and Economic Development: Fundamental Insight and Institutional Designs for Economic Development in Nigeria*. Lagos, Nigeria: Nigerian Bar Association Policy Paper.

Amakom, U. 2008. *Post Independent Nigeria and Industrialization Strategies: Four and Half Erratic Decades*. Awka, Nigeria: Department of Economics, Nnamdi Azikiwe University.

Anagwonye, B. 2009. *Greatest Speeches of Historic Black Leaders*. Lagos, Nigeria: Mindex Publishing.

Anderson, E., Renzio, P. and Levy, S. 2006. *The Role of Public Investment in Poverty Reduction: Theories, Evidence and Methods*. London: ODI Working Paper 263.

Anghel, F. and Glavan, B. 2005. *New and Old Trends in Development Economics*. Bucharest: Universitatea Romano-Americana.

Arora, R. 2002. 'Implementing Knowledge Management: A Balance Scorecard Approach', *Journal of Knowledge Management* 6(2), 204–49.

Asad, M. 1980. *The Message of the Quran: Translated and Explained*. Dublin: Cahil Printers.

Azam, J., Devarajan, S. and O'Connell, S.A. 1999. *Aid Dependency Reconsidered*. Washington, DC: World Bank.

Balogun, S.U. 2010. 'The Essence of Islamic Banking'. Paper presented at the International Conference on Islamic Banking and Finance held at Crescent University: Islamic Finance in Nigeria. Abeokuta, Nigeria, 20–22 March 2010.

Badr-El-Din, A. 2003. *Poverty Alleviation via Islamic Banking and Finance to Micro-Enterprise (MEs) in Sudan: Some Lessons for Poor Countries*. Bremen: University of Bremen, Institute for World Economics and International Management (IWIM), Sudan Economic Research Group Discussion Papers.

Bakar, M.D. 2002. *Islamic Finance: Innovation and Growth*. London: Euromoney Books and AAOIFI.

Banerjee, A.V. et al. 2005. *New Development Economics and the Challenge to Theory*. Cambridge, MA: Department of Economics, Massachusetts Institute of Technology.

Bardhan, P. 1997. 'Corruption and Development: A Review of Issues', *Journal of Economic Literature* 35(3), 1,320–46.

Bardhan, P. 2005. 'Institutions Matter, but Which Ones?', *Economics of Transition* 13(3), 499–532.

Barro, R.J. 1990. 'Government Spending in a Simple Model of Endogenous Growth', *Journal of Political Economy* 98(5), 103–26.

Bashar, M.L.A. and Dikko, H. 2003. *Economics of Zakat: Investors' Liability to Zakat*. Sokoto, Nigeria: Futures Business Equipment.

Basu, K. 2005. *The New Empirical Development Economics: Remarks on its Philosophical Foundations*. Cambridge, MA: Department of Economics, Massachusetts Institute of Technology.

Beckman, T. 1999. 'The Current State of Knowledge Management', in J. Liebowitz (ed.), *Knowledge Management Handbook* 1(1). Boca Raton, FL: CRC Press, pp. 1–22.

Beddington, F. 2009. 'Nigeria, a BRIC in the Making', *Global Investor*, 26 October.

Beeson, M. 2004. 'The Rise and Fall(?) of the Developmental State: The Vicissitudes and Implications of East Asia Interventionism', in L. Low (ed.), *Developmental States: Relevancy, Redundancy or Reconfiguration?* New York: Nova Science Publishers.

Bello, A. 2007. *Interest-free Banking? Yes!* Kaduna, Nigeria: Ahmed Bello Publications.

Bennett, D. and Vaidya, K. 2001. *Meeting Technology Needs of Enterprises for National Competitiveness*. Birmingham: Aston Business School.

Black, R.D.C. 1971. *Readings in the Development of Economic Analysis*. Plymouth: Latimer Trend.

Bornschier, V. and Chase-Dunn, C. 1985. *Transnational Corporations and Underdevelopment,* New York: Praeger.

Brooking, A. 1997. 'The Management of Intellectual Capital', *Long Range Planning* 30(3), 365–6.

Budd, C.H. 1986. *Islamic Economics and Capitalism: Islam's Challenge to Western Economics*. Canterbury: Centre for Associative Economics.

Budd, C.H. 2011. *Finance at the Threshold: Rethinking the Real and Financial Economics*. Farnham: Gower Publishing.

Callaghy, T. 1987. 'The State as Lame Leviathan: The Patrimonial Administrative State in Africa', in E. Zaki (ed.), *The African State in Transition*. London: Macmillan.

Cardoso, F.H. and Faletto, E. 1979. *Dependency and Development in Latin America*. Berkeley, CA: University of California Press.

Carkovic, M.V. and Levine, R. 2002. *Does Foreign Direct Investment Accelerate Economic Growth?* Minneapolis, MN: University of Minnesota Department of Finance Working Paper.

CBN. 1999. *CBN Briefs*. Abuja, Nigeria: Central Bank of Nigeria.

CBN. 2009. *Draft Framework for the Regulation and Supervision of Non-Interest Banks in Nigeria*. Abuja, Nigeria: Central Bank of Nigeria.

CBN. 2011a. *Framework for the Regulation and Supervision of Institutions offering Non-interest Financial Services in Nigeria*. Abuja, Nigeria: Central Bank of Nigeria.

CBN. 2011b. *Guidelines on Non-interest Window and Branch Operations of Conventional Banks and other Financial Institutions*. Abuja, Nigeria: Central Bank of Nigeria.

CBN. 2011c. *Guidelines on Shariah Governance for Non-interest Financial Institutions in Nigeria*. Abuja, Nigeria: Central Bank of Nigeria.

CBN. 2011. *Re: Framework for the Regulation and Supervision of Institutions offering Non-interest Financial Services in Nigeria*. Abuja, Nigeria: Central Bank of Nigeria.

Chapra, M.U. 1985. *Towards a Just Monetary System*. Leicester: The Islamic Foundation.

Chapra, M.U. 1992. *Islam and the Economic Challenge*. Leicester: The Islamic Foundation and the International Institute of Islamic Thought.

Chapra, M.U. 2000. *The Future of Economics: An Islamic Perspective*. Leicester: The Islamic Foundation.

Chapra, M.U. 2008a. *Muslim Civilization: The Causes of Decline and the Need for Reform*. Leicester: The Islamic Foundation.

Chapra, M.U. 2008b. 'The Global Financial Crisis: Can Islamic Finance Help?' Lecture delivered at the Pinners Hall, British Bankers Association, London, organized by the Institute of Islamic Banking and Insurance, London and supported by Fajr Capital Limited (UAE).

Chapra, M.U. 2008c. *The Islamic Vision of Development in the Light of Maqasid Al Shari'ah*. London: International Institute of Islamic Thought, Occasional Papers Series 15.

Chirot, D. and Hall, T.D. 1982. 'World System Theory', *Annual Review of Sociology* 8, 81–106.

Choudhury, M.A. and Malik, U.A. 1992. *The Foundations of Islamic Political Economy*. London: Macmillan.

Clark, C. and Chan, S. 2004. 'What Can One Learn from the Asian Flu? Implications for the Developmental State', in L. Low (ed.), *Developmental States: Relevancy, Redundancy or Reconfiguration?* New York: Nova Science Publishers.

Clawson, J.G. 2001. *A Leader's Guide to Why People Behave the Way They Do*. Charlottesville, VA: University of Virginia Darden School Foundation.

Collier, P. and Gunning, J.W. 1999. 'Why Has African Grown Slowly?', in G.M. Meier and J.E. Rauch, *Leading Issues in Economic Development*. Oxford: Oxford University Press.

Court, J. and Hyden, G. 2001. *Towards a World Governance Assessment: Preliminary Findings from the Pilot Phase*. Helsinki: United Nations University World Governance Assessment Working Paper 3.

Cypher, J.M. and Dietz, J.L. 2009. *The Process of Economic Development*, 3rd edn. London: Routledge.

DaVinci Institute. 2011. *The Management of Technology: Introduction to the World of the Management of Technology*. Modderfontein, South Africa: DaVinci Institute for Technology Management.

Davarajan, S., Rajkumar, A.S. and Swaroop, V. 1999. *What Does Aid to Africa Finance?*, Washington, DC: World Bank.

Davis, W. 1991. *Japanese Religion and Society: Paradigms of Structure and Change*. New York: New York University Press.

De Capua, J. 2005. 'World Bank Indicators Measure Good Governance', Washington, DC: Voice of America, http://www.voanews.com/content/a-13-2005-05-09-voa18/391477.html (accessed 9 August 2013).

DiVanna, J. 2006. *Understanding Islamic Banking: The Value Proposition that Transcends Cultures*. Cambridge: Leonardo and Francis Press.

Doi, A.I. 1983. *Shariah: The Islamic Law*. Ibadan, Nigeria: Iksan Publishers.

Easterly, W. and Levine, R. 1997. 'Africa's Growth Tragedy: Policies and Ethnic Divisions', *Journal of Economics* 112, 1,203–41.

Eboh, E.C. 2009. *Fiscal Federalism, Subnational Governance and MDGs in Nigeria*. Enugu, Nigeria: African Institute for Applied Economics.

Eboh, E.C. and Lemchi, J.I. 2009. *Measurement and Explanation of Informal Sector of the Nigerian Economy*. Enugu, Nigeria: African Institute for Applied Economics.

Eboh, E.C. and Lemchi, J.I. 2010. *Business Environment in Nigerian States 2010: Tackling the Security Challenge*. Enugu, Nigeria: African Institute for Applied Economics.

EFInA. 2008. *Access to Financial Services in Nigeria: Key Findings – National Survey*. Lagos, Nigeria: Enhancing Financial Innovation and Access.

EFInA. 2010. *Access to Financial Services in Nigeria: Key Findings – National Survey*. Lagos, Nigeria: Enhancing Financial Innovation and Access.

EFInA. 2011. *Understanding the Low Income Population in Nigeria*. Lagos, Nigeria: Enhancing Financial Innovation and Access.

EFInA. 2012. *Access to Financial Services in Nigeria: Key Findings – National Survey*. Lagos, Nigeria: Enhancing Financial Innovation and Access.

El Diwany, T. 1997. *The Problem with Interest*. London: De-Luxe Printers.

El-Gamal, M. 2006. *Islamic Finance*. New York: Cambridge University Press.

Enyi, E.P. 2009. *Banks Consolidation in Nigeria: A Synergistic Harvest*. Abakaliki, Nigeria: Ebonyi State University.

Escobar, A. 2008. *Territories of Difference: Place, Movements, Life, Redes*. Durham, NC: Duke University.

Euromoney. 2008. *Euromoney Training EMEA*. Harrow: Liwa Capital Management.

Evans, P. 1995. *Embedded Autonomy: States and Industrial Transformation*. Princeton, NJ: Princeton University Press.

Evans, P. 2004. *Government's Role in Development: The Case of Brazil under the Workers Party*. Los Angeles, CA: UCLA International Institute.

Farooq, M.O. 2007. *Partnership, Equity-financing and Islamic Finance: Whither Profit-loss Sharing?* Bahrain: Royal University for Women.

Farooq, M.O. 2009a. *Global Financial Crisis and the Link between the Monetary and Real Sector: Moving Beyond the Asset-backed Islamic Finance*. Bahrain: Royal University for Women.

Farooq, M.O. 2009b. *On Overstretched Critique and Mathematization of Islamic Economics: Comments on Masudul Alam Choudhury's 'Islamic Critique and Alternative to Financial Engineering Issues'*. Bahrain: Royal University for Women.

Farooq, M.O. 2009c. *The Challenge of Poverty and the Poverty of Islamic Economics*. Bahrain: Royal University for Women.

Fay, M. and Opal, C. 2000. *Urbanization without Growth: A Not So Uncommon Phenomenon*. Washington, DC: World Bank.

Firebaugh, G. 1992. 'Growth Effects of Foreign and Domestic Investment', *American Journal of Sociology* 98(1), 105–30.

1st Ethical. 2008. *Why Islam Has Prohibited Interest and Islamic Alternatives for Financing*. Bolton: 1st Ethical.

1st Ethical. 2009. *Understanding and Calculating Zakah*. Bolton: 1st Ethical.

Forrester, J.W. (1992), *System Dynamics, Systems Thinking, and Soft OR, Sloan*. Cambridge, MA: School of Management, Massachusetts Institute of Technology.

Forster, M.N. 2005. 'Hermeneutics'. Chicago, IL: Department of Philosophy, University of Chicago, http://philosophy.uchicago.edu/faculty/files/forster/HERM.pdf (accessed 9 August 2013).

Francis, D. et al. 2006. *An Experiment in Co-operative Inquiry: Final Report from Equinex Project*. Newport, South Wales: Centre for Community and Lifelong Learning.

Fritz, V. and Menocal, A.R. 2006. *(Re)building Developmental States: From Theory to Practice*. London: ODI Working Paper 274.

Fritz, V. and Menocal, A.R. 2007. 'Developmental States in the New Millennium: Concepts and Challenges for a New Aid Agenda', *Development Policy Review* 25(1), 531–52.

Gadamer, H. 1989. *Truth and Method*. New York: Continuum International Publishing Group.

Geleta, E.B. 2005. *Development as a Background*. Cork: University College Cork.

Gerald, M.M. and Rauch, J.E. 2005. *Leading Issues in Economic Development*. Oxford: Oxford University Press.

Ghosh, N. 2009. *The Road from Economic Growth to Sustainable Development: How Was it Traversed?* Chakala, India: MCX Academia of Economic Research.

Gold, T. 1986. *State and Society in the Taiwan Miracle*. Armonk, NY: M.E. Sharpe.

Goldman Sachs. 2005. *Global Economics Paper No: 134*. New York: Goldman Sachs.

Gourlay, S. 2003. *The SECI Model of Knowledge Creation: Some Empirical Shortcomings*. Kingston upon Thames: Kingston Business School, Kingston University.

Gray, P.H. 2001. 'A Problem-solving Perspective on Knowledge Management Practices', *Decision Support System* 31, 87–102.

Grindle, M.S. 2002. *Good Enough Governance: Poverty Reduction and Reform in Developing Countries*. Cambridge, MA: Kennedy School of Government, Harvard University.

Grindle, M.S. 2005. *Good Enough Governance Revisited: A Report for DFID with Reference to the Governance Target Strategy Paper, 2001*. Cambridge, MA: Harvard University Press.

Grossman, S. and Stiglitz, J. 1980. 'On the Impossibility of Informally Efficient Markets', *American Economic Review* 70(3), 393–408.

Gueye, S.P. 1999. *African Renaissance as an Historical Challenge, in African Renaissance*. Cape Town, South Africa: Mafube Publishing (Proprietary) and Tafelberg Publishers.

Guidat, C. and Morel, L. 2001. *The Design and Management of an Engineering School as a Permanent Process of Development and Adjustment to Industrial Needs*. Nancy, France: Innovation in Education and Coordination for Regional Development.

HaKohen, Y. 2009. *Judaism: Behar – a Holy Economic System*. Berkeley, CA: Zionist Freedom Alliance.

Hans, D.S. 2001. 'Mainstreaming Informal Financial Institutions', *Journal of Developmental Entrepreneurship* 6(1), 83–95.

Hanson, J.L. 1973. *Economics for Students*. Bungay, Suffolk: Richard Clay.

Harrod, R.F. 1939. 'An *Essay in Dynamic Theory*', *The Economic Journal* 49(193), 14–33.

Harvey, D. 2010. *A Companion to Marx's Capital*. London: Verso.

Hasanuzzaman, S.M. 2003. *Islamic and Business Ethics*. London: Institute of Islamic Banking and Insurance.

Haykal, M.H. 1976. *The Life of Muhammed*. Lagos, Nigeria: Academy Press.

Hayter, R. 1990. *Industrial Transformation and Challenge in Australia and Canada*. Montreal: McGill-Queen's University Press.

Hellman, J., Jones, G. and Kaufmann, D. 2000. *Seize the State, Seize the Day: State Capture, Corruption and Influence in Transition*. Washington, DC: World Bank Policy Research Working Paper 2444.

Heron, J. 1971. *Experience and Method: An Inquiry into the Concept of Experiential Research*. Guildford: Human Potential Research Project, University of Surrey.

Heron, J. 1996. *Co-operative Inquiry*. London: Sage.

Heron, J. and Reason, P. 2001. 'The Practice of Co-operative Inquiry: Research With Rather than On People', in P. Reason and H. Bradbury (eds), *Handbook of Action Research: Participative Inquiry and Practice*. London: Sage Publications.

Heron, J. and Reason, P. 2008. 'Extending Epistemology within a Co-operative Inquiry', in P. Reason and H. Bradbury (eds), *Handbook of Action Research*. London, Sage Publications.

Hettne, B. 1995. *Development Theory and the Three Worlds*. Harlow: Longman Group.

Hoff, K. 2008. *Joseph E. Stiglitz*. Washington, DC: World Bank, Development Research Group – Macroeconomics and Growth Groups Policy Research Working Paper.

Hoff, K. and Stiglitz, J. 2008. *Modern Economic Theory and Development*. Washington, DC: World Bank, Development Research Group – Macroeconomics and Growth Groups, Policy Research Working Paper.

Hozien, M. 2009. 'Ibn Khaldun: His Life and Work', http://www.muslimphilosophy.com/ik/klf.htm (accessed 9 August 2013).

Iarossi, G., Mousley, P. and Radwan, I. 2009. *An Assessment of the Investment Climate in Nigeria*. Washington, DC: World Bank.

Ibrahim, A.R. 2003. 'The Motivating Factors for the Viability of Islamic Banking in Nigeria'. Paper presented at the International Conference on Islamic Banking and Finance held at Crescent University. Abeokuta, Nigeria, 20–22 March 2010.

Ichijo, K., Krogh, G. and Nonaka, I. 1998. 'Knowledge Enables', in G. Krogh, J. Roos and D. Kleine (eds), *Knowing in Companies*. Thousand Oaks, CA: Sage, pp. 173–203.

IFC. 2012. *Islamic Fund Management Training Pack*. London: Islamic Finance Council.

IIBI. 2006a. *Diploma Course Pack*. London: Institute of Islamic Banking and Insurance.

IIBI. 2006b. *Encyclopaedia of Islamic Banking and Insurance*. London: Institute of Islamic Banking and Insurance.

Initiaz, M. 1980. *Riba (Usury or Interest): Its Condemnation by the Shariah (Islamic Law) and a Proposed Alternative*. Riyadh: International Islamic Publishing House.

Jagersma, P.K. 2003. 'Innovate or Die', *Journal of Business Strategy* 24(1), 25–9.

Jensen, N.M. 2003. 'Democratic Governance and Multinational Corporations: Political Regimes and Inflow of Foreign Direct Investment', *Journal of International Organization* 57(3), 587–616.

Jobst, A.A. 2007. *The Economics of Islamic Finance and Securitization*. Washington, DC: IMF Working Paper.

Johnson, C. 1982. *MITI and the Japanese Miracle: The Growth of Industrial Policy*. Stanford, CA: Stanford University Press.

Johnson, C. and Start, D. 2001. *Rights, Claims and Capture: Understanding the Politics of Pro-poor Policy*. London: ODI Working Paper 145.

Jomo, K.S. 2004. 'Southeast Asian Developmental States in Comparative East Asian Perspective', in L. Low (ed.), *Developmental States: Relevancy, Redundancy or Reconfiguration?* New York: Nova Science Publishers.

Joseph, R. 1983. 'Class, State and Prebendal Politics in Nigeria', *Journal of Commonwealth and Comparative Politics* 21(3), 21–38.

Karatas, S.C. 1993. *Economic Theory of Ibn Khaldun and Rise and Fall of Nations*, http://www.bilgesam.org/en/index.php?option=com_content&view=article&id=182:economic-th. (accessed 9 August 2013).

Kaufmann, D. 2004. 'Corruption, Governance and Security: Challenges for the Rich Countries and the World', in World Economic Forum, *Global Competitiveness Report 2004/2005*. New York: World Economic Forum

Kaufmann, D., Kraay, A and Mastruzzi, M. 2006. *Governance Matters V: Aggregate and Individual Governance Indicators 1996–2005*. Washington, DC: World Bank.

Kaufmann, D., Kraay, A and Mastruzzi, M. 2007. *Governance Matters VI: Aggregate and Individual Governance Indicators, 1996–2006*. Washington, DC: World Bank.

Kaufmann, D., Kraay, A. and Mastruzzi, M. 2008. *Governance Indicators: Where are We, Where Should We be Going?* Washington, DC: World Bank.

Khalil, T.M. and Ezzat, H.A. 2001. 'Emerging New Economy: Responsive Policies'. Paper presented at the Global Forum on Management of Technology, Vienna International Centre, Austria, 29–30 May 2001.

Khan, M.M. 1977a. *Sahih Al-Bukhari*, vol. 3. Chicago, IL: Kaxi Publications.

Khan, M.M. 1977b. *Sahih Al-Bukhari*, vol. 8. Chicago, IL: Kaxi Publications.

Khan, M.M. 2005. 'Review of DFID's Governance Target Strategy Paper'. Brighton: mimeographed paper prepared for DFID.

Khurshid, A. et al. 1980. *Studies in Islamic Economics*. London: Redwood Burn.

Killick, T. 1990. *Problems and Limitations of Adjustment Policies*. London: ODI Working Paper 36.

Kim, D.H. 1992. 'Guidelines for Drawing Causal Loop Diagrams', *The Systems Thinker*™ 3(1).

Kirkwood C. 1996. 'Integrated Business Process Analysis'. Unpublished monograph.

Knierim, T. 2002. *Introduction to Buddhism*, http://www.thebigview.com/download/buddhism.pdf (accessed 9 August 2013).

Kohli, A. 2004. *State-directed Development: Political Power and Industrialization in the Global Periphery*. Cambridge: Cambridge University Press.

Kolb, D, Boystzis, R.E. and Mainemelis, C. 1999. *Experiential Learning Theory: Previous Research and New Directions*. Cleveland, OH: Department of Organizational Behavior, Weatherhead School of Management, Case Western Reserve University.

Kondo, M. 2001. *Networking for Technology Acquisition and Transfer*. Yokohama: Yokohama National University.

Krogh, G. 1998. 'Care in Knowledge Creation', *California Management Review* 40(3), 133–53.

Krogh, G. and Roos, J. 1995. 'A Perspective on Knowledge, Competence and Strategy', *Personnel Review* 24(3), 56–76.

Krogh, G., Nonaka, I. and Aben, M. 2001. 'Making the Most of Your Companies' Knowledge: A Strategic Framework', *Long Range Planning* 34, 421–39.

Krogh G., Nonaka, I. and Nishiguchi, T. 2000 *Knowledge Creation: A Source of Value*. New York: Palgrave Macmillan.

Krogh, G., Roos, J. and Slocum, K. 1994. 'An Essay on Corporate Epistemology', *Strategic Management Journal* 15, 53–7.

Kurtz, C.F. and Snowden, D.J. 2003. 'The New Dynamics of Strategy: Sense-making in a Complex and Complicated World', *IBM Systems Journal* 42(3).

Lake, L. n.d. 'Develop Your Value Proposition', About.com Money Marketing, http://marketing.about.com/od/marketingplanandstrategy/a/valueprop.htm (accessed 9 September 2013).

Lambo, T. 1987. *Nigerian Economy*. Ibadan, Nigeria: Evans Brothers (Nigeria Publishers).

Lee, Y. and Lee, S. 2007. 'Capabilities, Processes, and Performance of Knowledge Management: A Structural Approach', *Human Factors and Ergonomics in Manufacturing* 17(1), 21–41.

LeFauve, R.G. and Hax, A.C. 1992. 'Managerial and Technological Innovations at Saturn Corporation', *MIT Management* (Spring), 8–19.

Lele, U., Gockowski, J. and Adu-Nyako, K. 1994. *Economics, Politics and Ethics of Primary Commodity Development: How Can Poor Countries Benefit the Most?* Washington, DC: IMF Working Paper.

Lessem, R. and Schieffer, A. 2009. *Transformation Management: Towards the Integral Enterprise*. Farnham: Gower Publishing.

Lessem, R. and Schieffer, A. 2010a. *Integral Economics: Releasing the Economic Genius of Your Society*. Farnham: Gower Publishing.

Lessem, R. and Schieffer, A. 2010b. *Integral Research and Innovation: Transforming Enterprise and Society*. Farnham: Gower Publishing.

Lessem, R., Chidara, P. and Kada, S. 2012. *Integral Community: Political Economy to Social Commons*. Farnham: Gower Publishing.

Lessem. R. et al. 2013. *Integral Dynamics: Cultural Dynamics, Political Economy and Business Enterprise*. Farnham: Gower Publishing.

Lews, W.A. 1965. 'A Review of Economic Development', *American Economic Review* 55(2), 1–16.

Low, L. et al. (eds). 2004. *Developmental States: Relevancy, Redundancy or Reconfiguration?* New York: Nova Science Publishers.

Lynch, R. 2006. *Corporate Strategy*. Upper Saddle River, NJ: Pearson Education.

Magnuson, J. 2008. *Mindful Economics*. New York. Seven Stories.

Malloch, T.R. 'Social, Human and Spiritual Capital in Economic Development'. Cambridge, MA: Templeton Foundation, Working Group of the Spiritual Capital Project, Harvard University: http://www.metanexus.net/archive/spiritualcapitalresearchprogram/pdf/malloch.pdf (accessed 22 August 2013).

Manor, J. 2000. 'Local Government in South Africa: Potential Disaster Despite Genuine Promise'. Brighton: mimeographed paper prepared for DFID.

Martinez-Vela, C. 2001. *World Systems Theory*. Cambridge, MA: MIT ESD.83 Doctoral Seminar in Engineering Systems, Fall, http://web.mit.edu/esd.83/www/notebook/WorldSystem.pdf (accessed 9 September 2013).

Marx, K. and Engels, F. (1968 [1888]), *The Communist Manifesto*. New York: Penguin.

Masudul, A.C. and Uzir, A. 1992. *The Foundations of Islamic Political Economy*. London: Macmillan.

Maxwell, N. 2007. *From Knowledge to Wisdom: A Revolution for Science and the Humanities*, 2nd edn. London. Pentire Press.

Mazrui, A. 1986. *The Africans: A Triple Heritage*. London: Guild Publishing.

Microfinance Nigeria. 2010. *Esusu: Expanding Nigeria's Financial Services*. Lagos, Nigeria: AB Microfinance Nigeria.

Mkandawire, T. 1998. 'Thinking about Developmental States in Africa'. Paper presented at UNU-AERC Workshop on Institutions and Development in Africa, Tokyo.

Modelski, G. 1995. *World System Evolution*. Washington, DC: Department of Political Science, University of Washington.

Momoh, S.Y. 2000. *The Birth of a New Beginning in Nigeria*. Lagos, Nigeria: Rendezvous Communications.

Mookherjee, D. 2005. *Is There Too Little Theory in Development Economics Today?* Cambridge, MA: Department of Economics, Massachusetts Institute of Technology.

Moyo, D. and Ferguson, N. 2010. *Dead Aid: Why Aid is Not Working and How There is a Better Way for Africa.* New York: Farrar, Straus and Giroux.

Mudimbe, V.Y. 1994. *The Idea of Africa.* Bloomington, IN: Indiana University Press.

Muhammed, Z. 2010a. 'Establishing a Case for Islamic Microfinance Institutions (IMFI): A Review of Profitability, Barriers to Entry and IMFI Instruments'. Paper presented at the International Conference on Islamic Banking and Finance held at Crescent University, Abeokuta, Nigeria, 20–22 March 2010.

Muhammed, Z. 2010b. *Islamic Economics and Management Sciences Course.* Johannesburg, South Africa: Islamic Finance Institute of Southern Africa.

Munasinghe, M. and Reid, W. 2005. 'The Role of Ecosystems in Sustainable Development', in N. Sengupta and J. Bandyopadhyay (eds), *Biodiversity and Quality of Life.* New Delhi: Macmillan.

Muslehuddin, M. 2007. *Banking and Islamic Law.* New Delhi, India: Adam Publishers and Distributors.

Mutiso, G.C.M. 1974. *Socio-political Thought in African Literature.* London. Macmillan.

Mutua, M. 1999. 'Returning to My Roots: African "Religions" and the State', in *Proselytization and Communal Self-determination in Africa.* New York: Orbis Books.

Myrdal, G. 1986. *Asian Drama: An Enquiry into the Poverty of Nations.* New York: Twentieth Century Fund.

New Horizon. 2007. 'Institute of Islamic Banking and Insurance', *New Horizon* 164.

New Horizon. 2008a. 'Institute of Islamic Banking and Insurance', *New Horizon* 167.

New Horizon. 2008b. 'Institute of Islamic Banking and Insurance', *New Horizon* 169.

New Horizon. 2009. 'Institute of Islamic Banking and Insurance'. *New Horizon* 173.

Nnodim, O. 2012. 'Nigeria's Misery Index, Unemployment Will Rise in 2012 – Experts', *Punch Nigeria,* 25 January, http://www.punchng.com/business/appointments-management/nigerias-misery-index-unemployment-will-rise-in-2012-experts/ (accessed 9 September 2013).

Nonaka, I. 1991. 'The Knowledge-creating Company', *Harvard Business Review,* November–December, 96–104.

Nonaka, I. 1994. 'A Dynamic Theory of Organizational Knowledge Creation', *Organization Science* 5(1) 14–37.

Nonaka, I. and Takeuchi, H. 1995. *The Knowledge-Creating Company: How Japanese Companies Create the Dynamics of Innovation*. New York: Oxford University Press.

Nonaka, I. and Toyama, R. 2003. 'The Knowledge-creating Theory Revisited: Knowledge Creation as a Synthesizing Process', *Knowledge Management Research and Practice* 1, 2–10.

Nonaka, I., Toyama, R. and Konno, N. 2000. 'SECI, Ba, and Leadership: A Unified Model of Dynamic Knowledge Creation', *Long Range Planning* 33, 5–34.

Nwaobi, G.C. 2009a. *Corruption and Bribery in the Nigerian Economy*. Abia State, Nigeria: Quantitative Economic Research Bureau.

Nwaobi, G.C. 2009b. *Inflation, Unemployment and Nigerian Families: An Empirical Investigation*. Abia State, Nigeria: Quantitative Economic Research Bureau.

Nwaobi, G.C. 2009c. *The Nigerian Wars, Regional Crises and Ethnic Disturbances: Policy Responses and Democratic Implications*. Abia State, Nigeria: Quantitative Economic Research Bureau.

Nwafor, M. et al. 2011. *Cost-effective Agriculture Growth Options for Poverty Reduction in Nigeria: Evidence and Policy Implications*. Enugu, Nigeria: African Institute for Applied Economics.

Nyazee, I.A.K. 2000. *Islamic Jurisprudence*. Islamabad, Pakistan: IRI Press.

Ó Riain, S. and O'Connell, P.J. 2000. 'The Role of the State in Growth and Welfare', in B. Nolan, P.J. O'Connell and C.T. Whelam (eds), *Bust to Boom? The Irish Experience of Growth and Inequality*. Dublin: Institute of Public Administration, pp. 310–39.

Oates, B.J. 2002. *Co-operative Inquiry: Reflections on Practice*. Middlesbrough: University of Teesside.

Obadan, M.I. and Odusola, A.F. 2000. *Productivity and Unemployment in Nigeria*. Ibadan, Nigeria: National Centre for Economic Management and Administration (NCEMA).

O'Dell, C. and Grayson, J. 1999. 'Knowledge Transfer: Discover Your Value Proposition', *Strategy and Leadership* 27(2), 10–15.

Oduh, M. et al. 2008. *Measurement and Explanation of Informal Sector of the Nigerian Economy*. Enugu, Nigeria: African Institute for Applied Economics.

Orok-Duke, O.E., Edu, B.E.E. and Ekot, G.A. 2002. *Critical Review of Financial Sector Reforms and Financial Liberalization in Developing Countries: A Practical Discussion in Nigeria Context*. Calabar, Nigeria: Cross River State University of Technology.

Oshodi, A.R. 2010. *The Legitimacy of Non-interest Banking in Nigeria*. Lagos, Nigeria: Strachan Partners (Solicitors and Advocates).

Oshodi, B.A. 2008a. 'Appraising the Good Enough Governance Agenda and State-led Development: Towards Achieving Private Sector Development in Sub-Saharan Africa'. Rochester, NY: Social Science Research Network, 1 September: http://dx.doi.org/10.2139/ssrn.1145664 (accessed 19 August 2013).

Oshodi, B.A. 2008b. 'Good Governance and State-led Development in Nigeria: Comparative Analysis with India'. Rochester, NY: Social Science Research Network, 28 August: http://dx.doi.org/10.2139/ssrn.1145648 (accessed 19 August 2013).

Oshodi, B.A. 2009. 'Developing Integral Governance and Economic Framework for Sub-Saharan Africa'. Rochester, NY: Social Science Research Network, 9 June: http://dx.doi.org/10.2139/ssrn.1416851 (accessed 19 August 2013).

Oshodi, B.A. 2012a. 'Islamic Economics and Finance within the Context of Development Economics in Nigeria'. Rochester, NY: Social Science Research Network, 9 May: http://dx.doi.org/10.2139/ssrn.2055093 (accessed 19 August 2013).

Oshodi, B.A. 2012b. Islamic Finance Revisited: Towards and Integral Approach to Development Economics for Nigeria and Africa. PhD thesis, Modderfontein, South Africa: DaVinci Institute for Technology Management.

Oshodi, B.A. 2012c. 'Reducing Poverty: The Prospects of Islamic Finance in Africa'. Rochester, NY: Social Science Research Network, 9 May: http://dx.doi.org/10.2139/ssrn.2055126 (accessed 19 August 2013).

Oshodi, B.A. et al. 2012. 'Concept Paper: Centre for Integral Social and Economic Research (CISER), Nigeria'. Unpublished paper developed for CISER Nigeria, September.

Patzer, M. and Voegtlin, C. 2010. *Leadership Ethics and Organizational Change: Sketching the Field*, Zurich: University of Zurich Institute of Organization and Administration Science Working Paper Series.

Paulin, D. 2006. 'The Effects on Knowledge Creation and Transfer in Production Processes Verification Due to Virtual Prototypes', *Electronic Journal of Knowledge Management* 4(2), 181–8.

Pryor, F.L. 1991. 'A Buddhist Economic System: In Practice', *American Journal of Economics and Sociology* 50(1), 17–33.

Randall, W.L 1995. *The Stories We Are: An Essay on Self-Creation*. Toronto: University of Toronto Press.

Reason, P. (ed.). 2002. *Special Issue: The Practice of Co-operative Inquiry, Systemic Practice and Action Research* 15(3).

Reason P. 2003. 'Keynote Address: Choice and Quality in Action Research Practice'. Paper presented at the Action Learning Action Research and Process Management 6th World Congress and Participatory Action Research 10th World Congress, Pretoria.

Richard, A. 2004. *The Languages and Literatures of Africa*, transl. N. Morgan. Cape Town, South Africa: David Philip Publishers.

Richardson, G.P. (1986), 'Problems with Causal-loop Diagrams', *System Dynamics Review* 2(2).

Rima, I. 2009. *Development of Economic Analysis*. London: Routledge.

Rima, S.D. 2012. *Spiritual Capital Theory and Economic Transformation: A US Perspective*. Farnham: Gower Publishing.

Roberts, J.T. and Hite, A. 2000. *From Modernization to Globalisation: Perspectives on Development and Social Change*. Oxford: Blackwell.

Rodrik, D. 2004. *Getting Institutions Right*. Munich: CESifo DICE Report 2/2004.

Santos, B.S. 2006. *The Rise and Fall of the Global Left: The World Social Forum and Beyond*. London: Zed Books.

Sauer, C. and Sauer, R. 2011. 'Jewish Theology and Economic Theory', *Action Institute* 17(1).

Sawani, M. and Patterson, S. 2001. 'Informal Saving Practices in Developing Countries', *Journal of International Business and Cultural Studies*, February.

Scandizzo, P.L. 2001. 'Financing Technology: An Assessment of Theory and Practice'. Paper presented at the Global Forum on Management of Technology, Vienna International Centre, Austria, 29–30 May 2001.

Schumacher, E.F. 2001. *Buddhist Economics*. Great Barrington, MA: E.F. Schumacher Society.

Seibel, H.D. 2001a. 'Mainstreaming Informal Financial Institutions', *Journal of Development Entrepreneurship* 6(1), 83–95.

Seibel, H.D. 2001b. *Microfinance in Nigeria: Origins, Options and Opportunities*. Germany. University of Cologne.

Sekuriti, S. 2009. *The Islamic Securities (Sukuk) Market*. Kuala Lumpur: Securities Commission Malaysia.

Serequeberhan, T. 1999. *African Philosophy*. New York: Paragon House.

Serequeberhan, T. 2000. *Our Heritage: The Past in the Present of African-American and African Existence*. Lanham, MD: Rowman & Littlefield.

Siddiqi, N. 1997. *Banking without Interest*. Citli Qbar, Delhi: Markazi Maktaba Islami.

Simeon, E.J., Inyang, E.J. and Akpan, P.L. 2009. *Determinants of Exchange Rate Instability in a Developing Economy: Conceptual Issues and Further Evidence for Nigeria (1970–2005)*. Rochester, NY: Social Science Research Network.

Singer, H.W. 1965. 'Social Development: Key Growth Sector', *International Development Review* 7(1), 3–8.

Sklair, L. 1991. *Sociology of the Global System*. Hemel Hempstead: Harvester Wheatsheaf.

Skocpol, T. 1977. The Tocqueville Problem: Civic Engagement in American Democracy', *Social Science History* 4(4), 455–77.

So, A.Y. 1990. *Social Change and Development: Modernization, Dependency, and World System Theories*. Thousand Oaks, CA: Sage Publications.

Somoye, R.O.C. 2010. *The Roles of Islamic Banking and Finance for Sustainable Entrepreneurship and Innovation in Nigeria: A Faith Finance Hypothesis*. Abeokuta, Nigeria: Crescent University.

Standard Bank. 2009. *Training Pack for Shariah Banking*. Lagos, Nigeria: Stanbic IBTC Bank.

Stern, N. 1991. 'The Determinants of Growth', *Economic Journal* 101(404), 122–33.

Than, T.M.M. 2004. 'Mimicking a Developmental State: Myanmar's Development Experience since 1948', in L. Low (ed.), *Developmental States: Relevance, Redundancy or Reconfiguration?* New York: Nova Science Publishers.

Thomas, S. and Canagarajah, S. 2002. *Poverty in a Wealthy Economy: Case of Nigeria*. Washington, DC: IMF Working Paper.

Todaro, M.P. and Smith, S.C. 2009. *Economic Development*. Upper Saddle River, NJ: Pearson Education.

Toye, J. 2005. *Changing Perspectives in Development Economics*. Cambridge, MA: Department of Economics, Massachusetts Institute of Technology.

Tripp, C. 2006. *Islam and the Moral Economy: The Challenge of Capitalism*. Cambridge: Cambridge University Press.

UNCTAD. 2002. *Economic Development in Africa: From Adjustment to Poverty Reduction – What is New?* Geneva: United Nations.

UNCTAD. 2005. *Economic Development in Africa: Rethinking the Role of Foreign Direct Investment*. Geneva: United Nations.

UNCTAD. 2006. *Foreign Direct Investment Inflow to Africa Hit History High*. Geneva: United Nations.

Usmani. M.T. 2007. *Sukuk and their Contemporary Applications*. Bahrain: AAOIFI.

Vu Le, M. and Suruga, T. 2005. *The Effects of FDI and Public Expenditure on Economic Growth: From Theoretical Model to Empirical Evidence*. Kobe, Japan: Graduate School of International Cooperation Studies, Kobe University.

Wade, R. 1990. *Governing the Market: Economic Theory and the Role of Government in East Asian Industrialisation*. Princeton, NJ, Princeton University Press.

Wallerstein, I. 2000. *The Essential Wallerstein*. New York: The New Press.

Weber, M. 1973. *From Max Weber: Essays in Sociology*. Oxford: Oxford University Press.

Wicks, P.G. and Reason, P. 2010. *Initiating Action Research: Challenges and Paradoxes of Opening Communication Space*. London: Sage.

Williams, J.N. 2007. *Propositional Knowledge and Know-how*. Singapore: School of Social Science, Singapore Management University.

World Bank and IMF. 2006. *Global Monitoring Report: Strengthening Mutual Accountability – Aid, Trade and Governance*. Washington, DC: World Bank and IMF.

You, J. and Khagram, S. 2005. 'A Comparative Study of Inequality and Corruption', *American Sociological Review* 70, 136–57.

Yunus, M. 2010. *Building Social Business: The New Kind of Capitalism that Serves Humanity's Most Pressing Needs*. New York: Public Affairs.

Yusuf, A. 1983. *Text, Translation and Commentary of The Holy Quran*. Brentwood, MD: Amana.

Zafar, S. 1999. *Muslim World League Journal* 26(11).

Index

Page numbers in **bold** refer to figures and tables.

Takeuchi, H. 211
Tanko, Muhammed 130
tawarruq (reverse *mudarabah*) 149,
    162–3, 193, 224
tawhid (unity) 157, 224
Than, T.M.M. 126
The Theory of Moral Sentiments (Smith)
    111–12, 142, 145
Things Fall Apart (Achebe) 68
Thomas, S. 130
Thunen, Johann Heinrich von 114
TIPS (Technology, Innovation, People
    and Systems) 4, 5, 167, 219–20
Todaro, M.P. and Smith, S.C. 33
    complementarities 206
    credit for women 187
    dependency theories 121
    education and health 212
    GNI 44
    industrialization 49
    ineffective government 34
    PPP 50
    Rostow's model 119
Torah 82, 83, 84–5
Towards a Just Monetary System
    (Chapra) 153
Toye, J. 134
TRANS4M Institute 5, 129, 142, 199,
    209, 210, 220
Transformation Management (Lessem
    and Schieffer) 142
Treatise of Human Nature (Hume) 143
Triffin, Robert 117
Tripp, C. 96, 103, 180
Tunisia 171
twenty-first-century economic theories
    empirical development economics
        131–5
    integral dynamics 142–6
    modern development theory
        135–8

spiritual capital theory 138–41,
    141
tzedakah 84

UNCTAD (United Nations
    Conference on Trade and
    Development) 73, 76, 126, 129
unemployment 52–4, 118
UNIDO 49
United Kingdom (UK) 169–70, 183
unrighteous wealth 93
Urban III, Pope 94
usury 85, 91, 93, 94–5, 99, 107;
    see also interest
Uzair, Muhammed 151–2

Value and Capital (Hicks) 117
value propositions 149, 179–87, **184**,
    205
Vayikra 25:35 84
voice 36–7

wadiah (safe-keeping) 166, 224
wakala (agency) 166–7, **168**, 224
Wallerstein, Immanuel 109, 127–8
Walras, Leon 114
waqf (endowment) 103, 182, 204, 224
Washington Consensus 136–7
wasiyya (will) 182, 224
wealth accumulation 83–4, 90–91
wealth distribution 137–8
Wealth of Nations (Smith) 111–12, 142
Weber, M. 120
welfare state 97, 155
World Bank
    governance indicators 35, 36–42
    income measurement 49
    poverty measurement 50, 73
    poverty reduction strategies 133
    reports on Nigeria 2, 3, 15
    z-scores 169